Norm Efficacy and Justification in International Criminal Law

Gunnar M. Ekeløve-Slydal

2025
Torkel Opsahl Academic EPublisher
Brussels

Gunnar M. Ekeløve-Slydal is Director of the Coalition for International Criminal Justice (CICJ) and Deputy Secretary General of the Norwegian Helsinki Committee. He studied philosophy at the University of Oslo and worked for many years for the Norwegian Centre for Human Rights at the University of Oslo and as Editor-in-Chief of the Nordic Journal of Human Rights. He has written extensively on human rights, international institutions and philosophical themes, including textbooks, reports and articles.

Front cover: *A photograph of Roberto Caruso's portrait of Gunnar M. Ekeløve-Slydal. Photograph: By the painter.*

Back cover: *Above Vikten hamlet, Flakstad Island (Lofoten), not far from where the author spent childhood years in some of Europe's most beautiful and pristine nature. Photograph: CILRAP 2025.*

ISBNs: 978-82-8348-288-1 (print) and 978-82-8348-289-8 (e-book).

To my wife Beate and my son Viktor

PREFACE

This collection of essays examines the efficacy and justification of international criminal law norms. This discipline of international law requires solid foundations and support by actors on all continents. It can only succeed in reducing excessive use of force in conflicts – and the book focuses on war crimes, crimes against humanity, crimes of aggression and genocide – if its norms and the courts that enforce them are viewed as credible and legitimate. To gain worldwide support, leaders of international criminal jurisdictions must demonstrate high standards of integrity and professionalism, and avoid feeding perceptions of double standards.

Many actors can contribute to improved norm efficacy, including military leaders, prosecutors and judges, the community of legal scholars, and civil society groups that document crimes and advocate for justice. State officials must respect the norms and support enforcement. Religious and life stance leaders can play important roles in reducing crimes.

I explore these issues in essays that pose very different questions. But some assumptions run through all of them.

First, the effectiveness of norms depends on how well they are justified. I therefore examine various philosophical schools and religions and their perspectives on the values that international criminal law protects. The first essay examines how doctrines related to the defense of superior order can be interpreted through Western philosophies. Specifically, I analyse whether the prevailing 'Conditional Liability Doctrine' can withstand scrutiny from an existentialist perspective. The second essay investigates how religious leaders can combat religious intolerance, hate speech and violence by applying ethical norms rooted in religion. In the third essay, I explore British philosopher Jeremy Bentham's (1748–1832) ideas about how well-structured international laws based on the 'utility principle' could help to reduce inter-state conflicts and war. Several of the essays emphasize humanism, as redefined by Renaissance thinkers and developed over the centuries to the present day. The fourth essay on Thomas More (1478–1535) discusses his ideas about using reason and integrity to fight against tyranny and his personal example of integrity.

Secondly, I assume the necessity of those supporting or working in international justice doing so with 'integrity' and 'professionalism'. The fourth essay concerns integrity issues in international organizations and the International Criminal Court, while the fifth deals with the credibility of Norway as a supporter of international justice in light of its past wrongdoing against Romani and

Sámi populations and how it deals with that past. The sixth essay criticizes a sudden shift in the case law of the International Criminal Tribunal for the Former Yugoslavia, which disoriented victims and put the credibility of the Tribunal in question. I criticize a named judge for his role in this episode. As an 'informed observer', I felt morally obliged to address the ensuing risk of the institution losing public trust.

Thirdly, all chapters reflect my conviction that law matters. Its norms can lead to less excessive violence, less suffering and better lives. In the first essay, I refer to evidence of the violence-reducing role of humanitarian and human rights norms. International criminal law is, in the end, most important for all those it purports to protect, including those who need justice after being victimized.

I could not have written these essays without many years of experience working on the documentation of human rights violations and international crimes. I have done so for the Norwegian Helsinki Committee. I am grateful for the opportunities I have been given to work together with engaged and skilled colleagues. I also benefited from years at the Norwegian Centre for Human Rights, learning from pioneers in the field of human rights, such as Torkel Opsahl, Asbjørn Eide and Jan Helgesen.

I also wish to mention my collaboration with the Centre for International Law Research and Policy ('CILRAP'), which invited me to contribute to numerous research projects, events and publications, leading to several essays included in this book. In particular, its Director, Morten Bergsmo, and team members such as Ilia Utmelidze, Antonio Angotti, Rohit Gupta and Devasheesh Bais have been truly inspiring collaborators. I am proud that my organization, CILRAP and other prominent civil society groups established the Coalition for International Criminal Justice (CICJ), which issues clear policy statements to help advance law and practice. I should also mention Professor Terje Einarsen, with whom I worked on several cases and situations. Many others undoubtedly contributed to enhancing my understanding.

Last but not least, I am grateful to my wife, Beate Ekeløve-Slydal, a colleague and an expert in promoting respect for and protection of human rights from her position in Amnesty International Norway. There are hardly any questions in this book that I have not discussed with her.

Gunnar M. Ekeløve-Slydal
Oslo, 9 October 2025

TABLE OF CONTENTS

1

Subordinates' Responsibility in International Criminal Law in Light of Western Philosophies of Freedom and Responsibility

1.1. Introduction

A complex and challenging issue in international criminal law is defining the boundaries of criminal liability. Although concepts from domestic legal systems can assist in clarifying liability in some instances, others are specific to international criminal law because of the peculiarities of military organizations compared to other societal institutions. The rigorous training, legal obligations and informal pressure on subordinates to obey orders from superiors may place them in moral dilemmas and test their courage to disobey when such orders breach their moral conscience or international law. Should they always remain loyal to their superiors or refuse orders if they believe them morally wrong or illegal? In what circumstances should they be exempted from criminal liability if they commit international crimes under orders from superiors?

The only genuine international legal theories of criminal responsibility relate to 'command responsibility' and 'the defence of superior orders'. These theories, or at least their application, have no national origin. Other frequently applied concepts, such as 'aiding and abetting', 'common purpose' and 'joint criminal enterprise' ('JCE') liability, have been internationalized from their national pedigrees.[1] This chapter will focus on theories on the defence of superior orders and explore their philosophical assumptions.

Making questions about individual responsibility even more complicated, some combat situations are so urgent and chaotic that soldiers have little time to consider the legality of orders. Deciding in such situations is difficult from an individual moral standpoint and presents a complex challenge for international criminal courts.

Issues related to soldier recruitment can also complicate matters. If national laws or policies do not recognize conscientious objections to becoming a soldier, an individual's questioning of the moral standards of the armed forces or principled reluctance to participate in war may influence judgments about the

---

[1] Elies van Sliedregt, *Individual Criminal Responsibility in International Law*, Oxford University Press, 2012, p. vii.

soldier's responsibilities. One could argue that the younger soldiers were at the time of recruitment, the more questionable is their responsibility to refuse illegal orders.

Not all subordinates hold low ranks in the military hierarchy. An order that violates international law can come from a government or a high-ranking general; the subordinate might be a senior officer. Such subordinates may have more opportunities to evaluate the legality and morality of orders than those at lower levels.

Judges must consider all of these factors when deciding cases. A key question, however, is whether such circumstances should only be considered during sentencing or if they sometimes warrant an acquittal.

There are three main legal theories regarding the defence of superior order: (1) the Respondeat Superior Doctrine, which provides that only the superior is liable for the crime, not the subordinate; (2) the Absolute Liability Doctrine from the Nuremberg trials, which declares that superior orders are not a defence but may only serve to mitigate punishment; and (3) the Conditional Liability Doctrine related to war crimes and crimes of aggression in Article 33(1) of the Statute of the International Criminal Court ('ICC'), which specifies that subordinates are not exempt from criminal responsibility unless they were under a legal obligation to obey the superior's orders, were unaware that the order was unlawful, and the order was not manifestly unlawful.[2]

I analyse these legal theories through the lens of Western philosophical traditions. The philosophies of the Renaissance and Enlightenment promoted a new understanding of human freedom to choose and the resulting responsibility of individuals for their actions. But how can we interpret situations where individuals face intense institutional or superior pressure to follow orders, regardless of whether those orders are moral or lawful?

After World War II, existential philosophy refocused on concepts such as 'existence' (versus 'essence'), 'engagement' (versus 'detachment'), 'freedom' (acknowledging our responsibility for who we are and what we do), 'authenticity' (pursuing our projects based on our choices), and 'ethics' (assuming full responsibility for our decisions and helping others realize their freedom). Using these ideas, I analyse how well the theories of superior order defence align with existential philosophy's view of human existence and morality.

2 According to the Article 33(2) of the ICC Statute, 17 July 1998 (https://www.legal-tools.org/doc/7b9af9/), "orders to commit genocide or crimes against humanity are manifestly unlawful", leading to the conclusion that the ICC may acquit subordinates being ordered to commit 'war crimes' or 'crimes of aggression' if all three criteria are fulfilled.

I argue that joining and actively participating in a military organization never absolves an individual from moral responsibility for their actions on behalf of the organization. According to the existentialist perspective on freedom, if one remains morally responsible in all situations – including when following superior orders – does this support the Absolute Liability Doctrine of the Nuremberg trials? Alternatively, is the current tendency to condition or soften the Nuremberg Principles regarding the responsibility of subordinates based on a different view of human existence and morality than that presented by existential philosophy? Does the prevailing Conditional Liability Doctrine stand up to the scrutiny of existential philosophy?

1.2. The Individual as Subject and Duty-Bearer in International Law

International law has evolved significantly. Throughout the nineteenth century, it was believed that it concerned only states. This view has, at least since World War II, been replaced by doctrines emphasizing both individual rights and responsibilities under international law.

To clarify, international human rights law mainly requires states to respect, protect and fulfil individual rights. It allows human rights violations against individuals to be litigated internationally once domestic remedies are exhausted or considered unavailable. However, the situation is more complex. The key international human rights document, the 1948 Universal Declaration of Human Rights, refers in its Preamble not only to "all peoples and all nations" but also to "every individual and every organ of society", which bears a duty to promote respect for human rights. The 2011 United Nations ('UN') Guiding Principles on Business and Human Rights highlight the duty of certain non-state actors, specifically business enterprises. As specialized parts of society, these actors must follow all applicable laws and respect human rights.[3]

From early in the twentieth century, humanitarian treaties required states parties to enact legislation criminalizing violations of the treaties.[4] This indirect

3 UN Office of the Commissioner for Human Rights, "Guiding Principles of Business and Human Rights: Implementing the United Nations 'Protect, Respect and Remedy' Framework", 16 June 2011, p. 1.

4 For example, Convention of 1907 (X) for the Adaptation to Maritime Warfare of the Principles of the Geneva Convention of August 22, 1864, 18 October 1907, Article 27: "The signatory Powers likewise undertake to enact or to propose to their legislatures, if their criminal laws are inadequate, the measures necessary for checking in time of war individual acts of pillage and ill-treatment in respect to the sick and wounded in the fleet, as well as for punishing, as an unjustifiable adoption of naval or military marks, the unauthorized use of the distinctive marks mentioned in Article 5 by vessels not protected by the present Convention" (https://www.legal-tools.org/doc/193f74/). See also Article 29 of the Convention for the Amelioration of the Condition of the Wounded and Sick in Armies in the Field, 27 July 1929 (https://www.legal-tools.org/doc/c613cf/).

approach, which requires states to ensure individual accountability for violations of treaty law, remained dominant until World War II, when a more direct approach was introduced through the Nuremberg and Tokyo tribunals, which prosecuted individuals accused of war crimes, crimes against humanity or crimes against peace ('crimes of aggression'). These proceedings showed the world that individuals could be tried and convicted in an international court, bypassing national courts that had lost their independence and credibility during the Nazi dictatorship.

The Nuremberg trials and subsequent international legal developments confirmed that both states and individuals can be held accountable for international crimes. The Nuremberg Tribunal, among other things, stated that it has long been recognized "that international law imposes duties and liabilities upon individuals as well as upon States", refuting the argument that international law only concerns the actions of sovereign states.[5]

The International Court of Justice ('ICJ') noted in the *Bosnian Genocide* case that "duality of responsibility continues to be a constant feature of international law".[6] This is reflected in Article 25(4) of the ICC Statute, which states that "[n]o provision in this Statute relating to individual criminal responsibility shall affect the responsibility of states under international law".

The International Law Commission clarified in its commentary to the 2001 Articles on the Responsibility of States for Internationally Wrongful Acts, Article 58, that:

> Where crimes against international law are committed by State officials, it will often be the case that the State itself is responsible for the acts in question or for failure to prevent or punish them. […] the question of individual responsibility is in principle distinct from the question of State responsibility. The State is not exempted from its own responsibility for internationally wrongful conduct by the prosecution and punishment of the State officials who carried it out.[7]

---

5 Judgment of the International Military Tribunal, *Trial of the Major War Criminals before the International Military Tribunal, Nuremberg, 14 November 1945–1 October 1946*, vol. 1, Nuremberg, 1947, p. 223 (https://www.legal-tools.org/doc/388b07/).

6 International Court of Justice, *Application of the Convention on the Prevention and Punishment of the Crime of Genocide (Bosnia and Herzegovina v. Serbia and Montenegro)*, Judgment, 26 February 2007, (2007) Rep. 43, para. 173 (https://www.legal-tools.org/doc/5fcd00/).

7 "Articles on the Responsibility of States for Internationally Wrongful Acts", *Yearbook of the International Law Commission*, UN Doc. A/CN.4/Ser.A/2001/Add.1 (Part 2), 2001, pp. 142–143 (https://www.legal-tools.org/doc/e174dd/).

To summarize, international human rights law recognizes individuals as rights-holders and states as primary duty-bearers. States remain the primary actors, possessing legal personality and the capacity to enter into treaties, make claims, and be held accountable for violations. However, under certain conditions, individuals can file claims against states before international bodies such as the UN Human Rights Committee or the European Court of Human Rights. Soft law norms also require individuals and non-state actors, like businesses, to respect human rights. Some states and the European Union ('EU') have enacted legislation to enforce the duty of businesses to respect human rights. An advanced example is the 2022 Norwegian Transparency Act.[8]

International humanitarian law (for example, the 1949 Geneva Conventions) protects individuals and imposes obligations on states parties to control the members of their armed forces during conflicts. International criminal law, on the other hand, addresses norms directly at individuals who can be held accountable for crimes of aggression, war crimes, crimes against humanity and genocide under international law. However, states can also be held responsible for the same wrongdoing under principles of state responsibility.

The ICC is the leading organization promoting international justice when genuine justice is missing at the national level. The ICC Statute's complementarity principle partly supports the indirect approach by requiring States Parties to enforce justice, with the ICC acting as a fallback when national justice systems fail to provide genuine justice.[9]

In these ways, individuals are subjects of and duty-bearers under international law. The International Criminal Tribunal for the Former Yugoslavia ('ICTY', 1993–2017), the International Criminal Tribunal for Rwanda ('ICTR', 1994–2015), the ICC (a permanent court established in 2002), and several hybrid courts have enforced criminal responsibility in cases against individuals. The ICTY convicted 93 individuals for war crimes, crimes against humanity or genocide, while the ICTR convicted 62 individuals. As of June 2025, the ICC

[8] Norway, Act Relating to Enterprises' Transparency and Work on Fundamental Human Rights and Decent Working Conditions, 1 July 2022 (https://www.legal-tools.org/doc/9a1j1p5v/). In July 2014, the UN Human Rights Council adopted Resolution 26/9, UN Doc. A/HRC/RES/26/9, 14 July 2014 (https://www.legal-tools.org/doc/b9ce3f/), establishing an open-ended inter-governmental working group to develop a legally binding instrument to regulate business enterprises concerning human rights.

[9] The ICC Statute, Preamble and Article 1, see *supra* note 2, state that the ICC complements national criminal jurisdictions. This principle of complementarity is outlined in Article 17 concerning the 'admissibility criteria' for the ICC's jurisdiction and referred to in Article 53 regarding the Prosecutor's initiation of an investigation. The key criterion for the ICC is whether national authorities are willing and able "genuinely to carry out the investigation or prosecution". If they are not, the ICC can investigate and prosecute.

has convicted six persons of war crimes or crimes against humanity, five for witness tampering, and four have been acquitted. It has ongoing investigations in 12 situations, having concluded five. While both the ICTY and the ICTR convicted high-level political and military leaders, mid-level commanders, and low-level perpetrators or subordinates, the ICC has so far only convicted African militia leaders.[10]

This emerging international justice system faces numerous challenges, including a lack of universal membership. Major powers such as China, India, Russia and the United States have so far chosen to stay outside the system and, at times, have tried to undermine it.[11]

A related development is that the UN Security Council, the EU, individual states, or groups of states have imposed sanctions on states, business enterprises and individuals for breaches of international law, including serious human rights violations and core international crimes. The sanctions on individuals, often called Magnitsky or targeted sanctions, may include travel bans, asset freezes, and other measures that limit the sanctioned person's ability to operate internationally and profit from their illegal activities.[12]

1.3. Individual Rights and Responsibility Contributing to the Decline of Violence

To place these developments in a broader context beyond international law, one must recognize how attitudes toward violence and the use of force have become increasingly restrictive throughout human history. Data sets show a consistent trend: humans and societies have become less violent as civilization advances. This decline covers international and internal conflicts, although since the 2010s, there has been a new, harmful increase.[13]

---

[10] Information is taken from the court's or their residual mechanisms web sites.

[11] The ICC Statute has 125 States Parties, including 33 African states, 19 Asia-Pacific states, 20 Eastern European states, 28 Latin American and Caribbean states, and 25 Western European and other states.

[12] For an explanation of how Magnitsky (targeted) sanctions can contribute to justice by fighting impunity, see Parliamentary Assembly of the Council of Europe, Sergei Magnitsky and Beyond – Fighting Impunity by Targeted Sanctions, Res. 2252, 22 January 2019 (https://www.legal-tools.org/doc/m7pxnoqd/).

[13] The Armed Conflict Location and Event Data ('ACLED') Conflict Index provides a global assessment of how and where conflicts in every country and territory vary according to four indicators: deadliness, danger to civilians, geographic diffusion, and the number of armed groups. The Index is available on the ACLED's web site.

Many factors have contributed to this decline. Harvard professor Steven Pinker (1954–) highlights six major trends leading to reduced violence:[14] (1) the pacification process, where agriculture helped establish stable societies; (2) the civilizing process involves developing large kingdoms with centralized authorities and infrastructure for commerce; (3) the humanitarian revolution, during the Age of Reason and Enlightenment, saw increasingly strong movements opposed to sanctioned forms of violence such as despotism, slavery, torture, superstitious killing, sadistic punishment, cruelty to animals, and promoted pacifism; (4) the long peace after World War II was characterized by an unprecedented period during which major powers and developed nations ceased waging war against each other; (5) the new peace, after the end of the Cold War in 1989, resulted in a decline in organized conflicts worldwide – including civil wars, genocides, repression by autocratic regimes, and terrorist attacks; and (6) the rights revolution happened when the Universal Declaration of Human Rights became a rallying point for global and national organizations advocating against violence toward ethnic minorities, women, children, gay people, vulnerable groups, and animals.

Pinker discusses how trends influence the human mind through scientific analysis. He explains psychological systems that can lead to violence: – such as instrumentalization, dominance, revenge, sadism, and unrestrained belief in an ideology promising utopia – and those that may foster peace, like empathy, self-control, moral sense, and reason. Five historical forces have promoted peaceful motives and contributed to a decline in violence, connecting these trends with how the human mind functions. These forces are: (1) *The Hobbesian Leviathan*, that is, a state and judiciary with a monopoly on the legitimate use of force. Leviathan can "defuse the temptation of exploitative attack", "inhibit the impulse for revenge", and "circumvent the self-serving biases" that make all parties believe they represent the good; (2) *commerce*, which is a "positive-sum game in which everybody can win" and promotes the spread of technology, goods and ideas. It makes "other people become more valuable alive than dead" and "less likely to become targets of demonization and dehumanization"; (3) *feminization*, which is a process of increasing respect for the interests and values of women: "Cultures that empower women tend to move away from the glorification of violence and are less likely to breed dangerous subcultures of rootless young men"; (4) *cosmopolitanism*, which favours literacy, mobility and mass media and can help people to understand and sympathize with others, unlike themselves; and (5) *the escalator of reason*, which can force people to recognize "the futility of cycles of violence, to ramp down the privileging of their own

[14] Steven Pinker, *The Better Angels of Our Nature: A History of Violence and Humanity*, Penguin Books, 2011, pp. xxiii–xxvi.

interests over others', and to reframe violence as a problem to be solved rather than a contest to be won".[15]

Impressive data-sets and historical research support this outline of factors leading to the decline of violence. I will, however, not delve deeper into Pinker's explanations, but only highlight the role that human rights and humanitarian norms play in them. During a remarkable transformation in the seventeenth and eighteenth centuries, people began to dislike institutionalized violence, even if they did not know or were related to the person being tortured or executed by the authorities. Ideas and arguments that violent punishment should be minimized gained ground.[16] This was the humanitarian revolution, starting in Europe and gradually affecting much of the world.

Similarly, the rights revolutions after World War II led to significant progress in reducing official discrimination, reforming penal systems, and implementing policies that support marginalized groups. A key part of these changes concerned women's rights and the decline in rape and domestic violence. In many Western countries, laws that treated women as the possession of their husbands were repealed during the 1970s. Many nations also saw a general decrease in domestic and societal violence. Violence against women dropped most in countries that adopted international human rights standards.[17]

Pinker shows that human rights and humanitarian norms have decreased violence within and between nations. They have done this by promoting respect for everyone's rights, regardless of their traits or gender, supporting non-violent conflict resolution, and holding governments and officials responsible for violations.

As part of these developments, attitudes toward waging war as a legitimate tool for state leaders changed significantly. It might seem obvious that opposing violence would lead to opposing war. However, historically, many who were cautious about using violence domestically and within states were more accepting of fighting wars to promote national interests. Until recently, leaders were called 'Great' if they conquered territory and the people living there. Pinker bluntly states: "If Hitler's luck had held out a bit longer, he probably would have gone down in history as Adolf the Great".[18]

During the Age of Reason and Enlightenment, thinkers and movements argued that war was against reason and harmful to both sides. Why conquer land if you can buy and sell it for a profit? Few expressed this idea better than

---

[15] *Ibid.*, p. xvi.

[16] *Ibid.*, pp. 133–134.

[17] *Ibid.*, pp. 412 ff.

[18] *Ibid.*, p. 162.

Immanuel Kant (1724–1804), who foresaw one of the main ideas behind creating the EU: "It is the spirit of commerce that sooner or later takes hold of every nation, and is incompatible with war. [...] states [...] find themselves obliged to labor at the noble work of peace, though without any moral view".[19]

Many factors contributed to the development of humanitarian law in the second half of the nineteenth century, including the efforts of pioneers emphasizing the suffering of soldiers and civilians caused by the brutality of war. Their arguments, however, had an impact because people were already becoming sensitive to the suffering of their fellow human beings. The pioneers aimed to establish international legislation to combat the worst forms of brutality and to ensure that injured soldiers received proper treatment. The first Geneva Convention was adopted on 22 August 1864 to guarantee care for wounded soldiers.[20] The International Committee of the Red Cross ('ICRC') was established the previous year by a group of five Swiss citizens, including Henry Dunant (1828–1910), whose experience at the Battle of Solferino in 1859 inspired the creation of a neutral organization to aid wounded soldiers during war.

Although new laws were enacted in the following years, it soon became clear that the law's effectiveness depends on enforcement and the punishment of violations. This proved to be the most challenging part of creating an international law that can ensure violators face consequences. While there are early examples of leaders being held accountable when their subordinates commit atrocities, it was not until the Nuremberg and Tokyo trials after World War II that the world saw a systematic effort to uphold accountability. Twenty-two senior officials were convicted in Nuremberg and 25 in Tokyo.[21]

Nuremberg and Tokyo marked pivotal moments when significant international law changes occurred. These changes had a lasting influence because the UN General Assembly approved the 'Nuremberg Principles', enhancing the power of international norms. General Assembly Resolution 95(1), adopted on 11 December 1946, confirmed the principles of international law recognized by the Charter of the Nuremberg Tribunal and its judgment. This initiated a process

[19] Immanuel Kant, *Perpetual Peace*, The Book Tree, Los Angeles, 2008, p. 35. The original, *Zum Ewigen Frieden*, was published in 1795.

[20] Convention for the Amelioration of the Condition of the Wounded in Armies in the Field, 22 August 1864 (https://www.legal-tools.org/doc/59e0f5/).

[21] An overview of material related to the trials is available at "Prosecuting War Crimes after the Second World War: The Nuremberg and Tokyo Trials", *Cross-Files*, 22 May 2018. The ICC Legal Tools Database includes comprehensive collections of documents from the Nuremberg and Tokyo tribunals (https://www.legal-tools.org/).

of "turning the principles at issue into general principles of customary law binding on member States of the whole international community".[22]

The Nuremberg Principles eliminated immunity for heads of state (Principle 3) and expanded responsibility to include subordinates (Principle 4). This change meant that even foot soldiers could be held accountable for upholding morality and international law. Defence lawyers at Nuremberg argued that disobeying Hitler's orders carried the risk of execution. However, the Nuremberg judgment still emphasized the obligation to abide by the laws of humanity, not those of Nazi Germany.

The main issue is that imposing such a burden on individuals, as international criminal law does, might be necessary for its norms to reduce violence and influence behaviour effectively. Leaders and subordinates must follow these rules to protect and prevent attacks on human life, dignity and integrity. This constitutes the *utilitarian argument* for individual criminal responsibility, which includes those at the lowest levels of hierarchical military organizations. The argument is based on the evidence that holding individuals criminally responsible results in better life prospects for the majority by decreasing international crimes and human suffering.

The benefits of expanding the scope of those held criminally responsible can easily be overlooked. Many state leaders, even in democracies, may not be aware of or may dismiss the utilitarian argument. The experiences of extreme crimes, like those in concentration camps, the Holocaust, and the widespread neglect of human life by the Nazi regime, might be seen as unique in human history. Principles of justice developed in response to these events might not be justified in more typical situations. The Nuremberg Principles, in their strict form, can hinder recruitment because soldiers risk being prosecuted internationally. Furthermore, do the Principles ignore the realities of being a soldier in military organizations built on patriotism, discipline, and a culture of not questioning core moral or legal issues?

Perceptions of leaders' rights and responsibilities may be as old as humanity, but extending them to everyone represents a revolutionary and essential change. In his autobiography, the English philosopher Bertrand Russell (1872–1970) describes his grandmother as the most critical figure in his childhood after losing his parents early. In particular, he noted her "fearlessness, her public spirit, her contempt for convention, and her indifference to the opinion of the majority". She had given him "a Bible with her favourite texts written on the fly-leaf.

[22] A presentation of the Nuremberg Principles and their lasting effect on international law is provided in Antonio Cassese, "Affirmation of the Principles of International Law Recognized by the Charter of the Nürnberg Tribunal", in *UN Audiovisual Library of International Law*, 2009.

Among these was 'Thou shalt not follow a multitude to do evil' [Exodus 23:2]. Her emphasis upon this text led me in later life to be not afraid of belonging to small minorities".[23]

International criminal law expands this principle by emphasizing that one should not only avoid following a crowd, such as a group of soldiers driven by rage and exhaustion that commit crimes, but also steer clear of following a leader into evil, even if that leader is the one you have entrusted with your life.

1.4. Upholding Duties by Rights

Rights for all were initially regarded as 'natural rights' in eighteenth-century philosophies and declarations, influenced by ancient Stoic and Christian ideas, and later evolved into 'human rights'. As seen, international law established individual rights after World War II. The Nuremberg trials, the UN Charter's reference to human rights, and the Universal Declaration of Human Rights played the most critical roles in this change. The four 1949 Geneva Conventions also revised and expanded international humanitarian law in this direction, seeking to protect individuals during conflicts.

The introduction of individual human rights into international law faced widespread criticism. Critics argued that it focused too much on the individual and overlooked the significance of community, family and other collective identities in human life. The argument was that the conceptual framework and human-rights values reflected Western traditions, contrasting with community-focused traditions in Asia and Africa.

Another criticism was that human rights promised much but delivered much less. It took 28 years from adopting the Universal Declaration until the two legally-binding Covenants on Civil and Political Rights and Economic, Social and Cultural Rights came into force. The Covenants and various other human rights treaties require most of the world's states to respect and protect human rights, but many remain unwilling or unable to meet their obligations. This issue is also evident in regional human rights systems. Even if the UN and regional organizations like the Council of Europe play a prominent role in reviewing state policies, legislation and practice, the promise of human rights remains unfulfilled. One could even argue that in recent years, governments across every continent have moved away from human rights, primarily civil and political rights. The authoritarian shift in the 2000s has had its costs for human rights.

International criminal law presents a unique challenge. It aims to create a universal consensus on individual responsibility, which may involve holding people accountable even when they have limited control over military actions they are ordered to carry out or contribute to. Especially in complex cases where

[23] Bertrand Russell, *Autobiography*, Routledge, Abingdon, 2010, p. 16.

pressure to follow illegal orders increases, maintaining and clarifying individual responsibility can become difficult.

The role of leaders is clear concerning the crime of aggression, a so-called leadership offense. The basis of this crime "is the conviction that leaders bring their populations to war, not the reverse, and it is with leaders that responsibility should lie".[24]

Crimes against humanity and genocide, because of their definitional criteria, also entail a significant leadership role. Crimes must be part of a "widespread or systematic attack directed against any civilian population, with knowledge of the attack" to qualify as crimes against humanity. The definition of genocide requires that the crimes be "committed with intent to destroy, in whole or in part, a national, ethnical, racial or religious group, as such".[25]

It is unlikely that these crimes could happen without leadership orders and guidance, whether leaders have a formal (*de jure*) position as a political or military commander, planner or instigator, or an informal (*de facto)* role. The definition of war crimes does not include similar requirements. However, the jurisdiction of the ICC is somewhat limited to war crimes "committed as part of a plan or policy or as part of a large-scale commission of such crimes".[26]

Superiors' responsibility are most clear when they "order, solicit or induce" the commission of crimes. However, they can also be held criminally responsible for failing to "exercise control properly" to prevent or suppress their subordinates' crimes when they "knew, or consciously disregarded information" about their misconduct.[27]

Subordinates will inevitably be involved in all four categories of crimes, even if their roles vary. The key point is that crimes ordered by superiors cannot be conducted without obedient subordinates, except for the crime of "directly and publicly" inciting others to commit genocide.[28]

Given this pivotal role in committing crimes, a key question concerns the source of the subordinates' ethical and legal authority to refuse to obey orders they consider illegal or immoral. Of course, legal authority may come from international and national laws included in their contract with the military organization. They may also refer to international and domestic jurisprudence, which upholds this responsibility.

---

[24] Noah Weisbord, *The Crime of Aggression: The Quest for Justice in an Age of Drones, Cyberattacks, Insurgents, and Autocrats*, Princeton University Press, 2019, p. 2.

[25] ICC Statute, Articles 6 and 7, see *supra* note 2.

[26] *Ibid.*, Article 8(1).

[27] *Ibid.*, Articles 25 and 28.

[28] *Ibid.*, Article 25(3)(e).

However, my question here is whether there is an authority beyond the law that a soldier under pressure can, and should, turn to when refusing to torture a captured enemy soldier or civilian, or targeting civilian objects deliberately or indiscriminately, or committing any other war crime or aggression?

I referred to the utilitarian argument for criminal responsibility above. Over time and in specific cases, it leads to less violence and suffering. It serves the greater good. However, this argument might not be enough to persuade individual soldiers to obey international law when ordered to break it. Even if they agree that armed forces should follow humanitarian law and minimize violence and suffering among those not actively involved in the conflict, they may deny their responsibility and resist the suffering they might face if they refuse to obey orders.

Recognizing that both the individual and the potential victim have human rights represents an alternative perspective to the utilitarian approach. Because soldiers possess human rights, they are also obligated not to commit international crimes, so the argument would go. They maintain moral and legal agency, even as members of armed forces with hierarchical structures, and their internationally recognized human rights support this agency.

This argument can be presented in two opposing ways: *reciprocal* and *unconditional*. The reciprocal view holds that respect for the rights of enemy soldiers and civilians depends on the behaviour of the enemy armed forces. Simply put, the principle is that I will respect your rights as you respect mine. If there are signs that the enemy armed forces do not respect my rights by committing war crimes, I will then withhold respect for their rights.

The second perspective does not impose such a requirement. It argues that all human beings possess rights, and I should respect their rights regardless of whether they respect mine. This line of reasoning embodies the core of the first Nuremberg Principle, which states that "any person who commits an act which constitutes a crime under international law is responsible and liable to punishment".

The criticisms of human rights mentioned earlier may lessen their effectiveness. If rights are not seen as reflecting universal standards or having a limited impact, their ability to persuade soldiers to comply with international law could be constrained. Even if someone fully supports the principles upheld by human rights and humanitarian law and values their inclusion in international law, as this author does, they might also see the need for additional arguments to strengthen their influence.

For this purpose, I will turn to Western philosophical thoughts that underpin the unconditional value of human agency, freedom and responsibility.

1.5. The Breakthrough of the Concept of Human Agency in Renaissance Thought

Starting in the thirteenth century, the Italian Renaissance introduced the aspiration of the 'Renaissance man'. This ideal was developed in Italian cities, especially Florence, and was articulated by leading figures of 'Renaissance humanism' – a movement of philosophers, artists and political leaders during this period of rediscovering and studying Classical Greek and Roman philosophy and literature. Leon Battista Alberti (1404–1472) captured the essence of the new ideal by stating that "a man can do all things if he will". Renaissance humanism placed man at the centre of the universe while still recognizing the vital role of God as the creator, whom humans likened to. The reflection of God's image in every human being made us unique among living creatures.[29]

Humanism reshaped the understanding of human nature and core values, emphasizing how individuals could perfect themselves. This potential for perfection relied on their will to learn and fully develop their abilities. The '*studia humanitatis*', which included grammar, poetry, rhetoric, history and moral philosophy, were considered essential. This educational programme drew on Marcus Tullius Cicero's (106–43 BC) concept of '*humanitas*', an ideal at the movement's centre.[30]

Gifted individuals of the time aimed to develop their skills in knowledge, arts and sports. Alberti was skilled in architecture, painting, classicism, poetry, science and mathematics. He was also an excellent horseman, known for his physical feats. Yet Leonardo da Vinci (1452–1519) remains the most famous Renaissance man, excelling in art, science, music, invention and writing.

Humanism's defining traits as a lasting philosophical approach emphasize human experience, freedom and the responsibility to improve oneself. It was introduced as a contrast to the contemplative life and strict philosophical systems of 'scholasticism', promoting an active life in this world rather than a contemplative life preparing for eternity. It represented a syncretic, sometimes eclectic, approach to different philosophical and religious schools, highlighting that truth can be expressed in various ways.

This essay's focus on humanism dwells on its preoccupation with human dignity, freedom and responsibility. It replaced the Medieval ideals of a penance-filled life as the supreme form of human activity with efforts to depict, create and master nature. While initially an attempt to revive the ancient wisdom of Greek and Roman philosophies, it developed into a programme of exploring new knowledge through innovative philosophical, scientific and artistic pursuits.

[29] Robert Grudin, "Humanism", in *Encyclopedia Britannica*, 13 September 2025.

[30] *Ibid.*

The programme both embraced and strengthened ideas of human freedom and responsibility.

This programme's main expression is Giovanni Pico della Mirandola's (1463–1494) *Oration on the Dignity of Man* (1486). He contended that God did not assign fixed traits, specific roles within a hierarchical universe, or limits to humanity. As a result, humans are free to explore their place and shape their future. Not even divine dignity is beyond human reach. This perspective reflects his constant quest to understand different knowledge systems and reinterpret their truths. He did not support one system while dismissing others, as he believed all of them embodied philosophy's eternal, all-encompassing truth in their unique ways.[31]

To understand the novelty of Renaissance philosophy, a key idea is the principle of individuality. Starting from Aristotle's (384–322 BC) or Plato's (428/427–348/347 BC) ontologies leads to different conceptions. For Aristotle, individuality in things or persons combines 'matter' and 'form'. The form gives the individual its identity, while the matter makes it particular and unique. Pure forms do not exist independently, so individuals are the fundamental reality.

For a living body, the soul is its form. In humans, the soul includes rationality, which is unique to human individuality and allows individuals to pursue virtue, knowledge and the good life. The good life comes from following rules and practising a life of reason and virtue. Aristotle valued individuality, but emphasized that humans are 'political animals', meaning they realize their lives within communities.

Plato viewed forms (or ideas) as abstract concepts existing beyond the physical world we perceive through our senses. The world we experience is simply a shadow or imitation of these forms. The individual is an imitation of a form. Scholars are divided over how Plato regarded matter as 'space' or 'substance', where the form existed during its time on Earth. He described the soul as divided into three parts: 'reason' (the rational part), 'spirit' (the emotional or wilful part), and 'appetite' (desires and physical needs). Individuality arises from the unique balance of these parts within each person. Although humans share the same structure, the dominance of one part over the others influences personality, behaviour and individuality.

These different perceptions of individuality lead to diverse views on how humans can fulfil their societal roles and place in the Cosmos. During Medieval times, the system of thought developed by Thomas Aquinas (1225–1274) relied on Aristotelian concepts, while Bonaventure (1221–1274) and the Franciscan

[31] Johannes Sløk, *Tradition og nybrud: Pico della Mirandola* [*Tradition and Innovation: Pico della Mirandola*], Lindhardt og Ringhof Forlag, København, 1957, p. 26.

school he belonged to adhered to Plato, though with some nuances regarding the constitution of individuality. According to him, the specific relationship between matter and form results in individuality.[32]

The thinker who advanced the Plato-inspired ideas to their conclusion was Duns Scotus (1265/66–1308), who introduced the concept of '*haecceitas*' ('this-ness'), an irreducible category of being that represents the fundamental actuality of an existing entity. Therefore, individuality is a fundamental concept that cannot be equated with matter, form or their combination. While 'human' has a general form ('*qvidditas*'), each individual possesses their own form (*haecceitas*).

For Pico, the Renaissance thinker, as for us today, these discussions might seem abstract, although they influenced how human life and its true goals were understood. While Plato and the Neo-Platonism of Pico's era could lead to a contemplative life or a life focused on the highest eternal forms of 'Beauty', 'Goodness' and 'Truth', the Aristotelian approach might result in a more active engagement with political and social issues and possibilities. This is undoubtedly a simplification, and one must remember that the Catholic Church interpreted both Plato's and Aristotle's ontologies to support Christian thought and attempted to harmonize them.

The key change in Pico's philosophy is not that he finds a new solution to the old problem of individuation. His philosophy demands an entirely new concept of individuality. The problem that individualization now raises is not the traditional one – how the eternal idea or form can manifest in individual examples – but a modern one: the relationship between the eternal truth and its appearance in individuals. He sets a new fundamental task for humans. Their individuality requires them to become their own creators and builders; they should craft themselves. The essence of this thought is that life, in its content and truth, can only exist in an individualized form. Its individuality implies that it must be centred and structured, seen from a perspective, and developed within a context.[33]

According to the German Neo-Kantian philosopher Ernst Cassirer (1874–1945), Pico offers an anthropological reinterpretation of the new worldview that emerged after Nicolaus Cusanus' (1401–1464) mathematically inspired interpretations of 'infinity' and '*docta ignorantia*', and his critique of Aristotelian logic.[34] Aristotle did not incorporate a concept of 'infinity' into his logic, which

[32] *Ibid.*, p. 38.

[33] *Ibid.*, p. 90.

[34] Ernst Cassirer, "Pico della Mirandola", in *Journal of the History of Ideas*, 1942, vol. 3, no. 3, p. 322.

caused all contradictions to be seen as absolute. Aristotle relied on mundane experiences and could not comprehend the Cosmos, which requires the idea of infinity. In a universe without boundaries, there is no distinction between 'up' and 'down', and no place holds a privileged position. A circle with an infinite radius becomes a straight line.

These principles, which Cusanus had applied to nature, Pico now applies to the human world and the world of history. From this perspective, no historical epoch or society represents the truth. History loses its absolute character. No single epoch or historical creation can claim the truth as such or uniquely represent the world of humans. Humans are fundamentally free and can be understood only when history is considered in its total course.

Humanity, unlike animals, has a history. This is because they are not bound to a specific nature and must develop their existence within previously set limits. Nonetheless, one must also examine history in its full context to form an adequate understanding of man's essence; no epoch or creation should be left out of consideration.

According to Cassirer, human freedom for Pico means:

> [T]hat man is not enclosed from the beginning within the limits of a determinate being. It is this fact that raises him above even those beings that stand higher than himself in the hierarchical order. Upon the angels and the heavenly intelligences their nature and their perfection have been bestowed from the beginning of creation: man possesses his perfection only as he achieves it for himself independently and on the basis of a free decision.[35]

It also follows that each new epoch, and indeed each new individual, must not be reduced to simply representing a specific link in a series of developments. It is true that each epoch joins a continuum and continues an idea or content handed down from its predecessors. Nevertheless, each epoch begins, as it were, from the beginning. It must start, like the individual human being, in independence and freedom, from within and unencumbered by any authority, to shape its heritage and express the '*mundus humanus*'.

Such is human freedom, according to Pico. Humans' resemblance to God is not something given; it is something to which they can aspire. The risk, however, is that they can also stray from it. That is the essence of Pico's speech, as he eloquently describes it in the form of God speaking to humans:

> We have made you a creature neither of heaven nor of earth, neither mortal nor immortal, in order that you may, as the free and proud shaper of your own being, fashion yourself in the form you

[35] *Ibid.*, p. 323.

may prefer. It will be in your power to descend to the lower, brutish forms of life; you will be able, through your own decision, to rise again to the superior orders whose life is divine.[36]

1.6. Further Philosophical Foundations of Freedom and Responsibility

This description of human freedom and dignity laid the groundwork for further developments that justified treating every human as morally responsible, including those in positions of authority and subordinates within military organizations. Although several elements were absent, the humanist concept of a free and proud creator of one's own being offered a crucial starting point.

Indeed, pursuing human perfection could also enhance military capabilities. Some humanists, such as Federico da Montefeltro (1422–1482), were renowned for their intellectual talents and were also skilled soldiers. He was a mercenary known for winning battles and honouring his commitments, but he also invested the earnings from his military victories into moral, intellectual and practical advancements for his fellow Italians, caring for soldiers and their families, and constructing one of the largest libraries of his era.[37]

Niccolò Machiavelli (1469–1527) can also be considered a humanist, although he differed from most in key ways. He received a humanist education, being well-versed in Latin literature, Roman history, and Greek philosophy, and he incorporated ideas from Roman thinkers such as Cicero, Livy (59 BC–17 AD), and Tacitus (56–120) into his writings. However, while many humanists emphasize rational thought, they also refer to divine guidance and morality. This is absent in Machiavelli's works. He is familiar with the influence of the heavens on earthly actions, as described by astrology, but there is a lack of moral considerations. In his most famous work, *The Prince* (1513), he advocates pragmatism and realism as essential skills for a ruler, and he should not be unfamiliar with manipulation and ruthlessness, "according to necessity".

In *The Prince* and *The Art of War* (1520), Machiavelli explores ideas about politics as an independent activity, establishing the concept of powerful and autonomous states. His primary focus is not on what people should do based on Classical, Christian or humanist values, but on their behaviour. There seems to be no moral limits on rulers' conduct when pursuing their goals. Their most essential '*virtù*' is their ability to achieve and sustain power, regardless of ethical considerations.

He recognizes external forces beyond the ruler's control that could hinder ambitions, such as '*fortuna*' (chance or the influence of the universe), their

---

36 Giovanni Pico Della Mirandola, *Oration on the Dignity of Man*, trans. by A. Robert Caponigri, Gateway Editions, Regnery Publishing, Washington, D.C., 1956, p. 7.

37 Grudin, 2025, see *supra* note 29.

temperament, and the prevailing conditions. History is thus not solely the result of human actions – with kingdoms, republics and other institutions following a pattern of birth, growth and decline – but much depends on the rulers' ability to exploit events for their own benefit, whether they act within moral boundaries or not. Machiavellianism, which may oversimplify Machiavelli's complex views, became a doctrine that "the reason of state recognizes no moral superior and that, in its pursuit, everything is permitted".[38]

Machiavelli's realistic depiction of political power has impacted political philosophy and science. It became one of the two main strands in the ongoing debate between realism and idealism in international relations. The fact that both schools of thought were so strongly expressed during humanism's peak demonstrates the richness of its legacy.

However, the idealist humanist concept of human freedom required a significant revision to become a catalyst for societal and international change. Let me outline four key steps. *First*, humanism's appeal in theory included all people, but women, non-Europeans, and other vulnerable groups benefited little from its focus on human dignity. Evidence such as slavery, the inhumane treatment of labourers during industrialization, and the exclusion of women from large parts of society, education and leadership roles show that humanist ideals were not truly for everyone.

Although the French and North American revolutions in the late eighteenth century addressed some of these injustices, the slow and incomplete spread of humanist and human rights values shows how ideas can be far ahead of actual change.

Second, and interconnectedly, institutions that opposed ideas of human freedoms and responsibilities initially played a significant role. Only later did humanism develop social and institutional critique, which became essential to the Enlightenment's departure from the past. Enlightenment philosophers, such as Voltaire (1694–1778), were outspoken critics of the Catholic Church, condemning its intolerance and abuse of power and advocating for freedom of religion and the separation of church and state.

Jean-Jacques Rousseau (1712–1778) criticized the inequality built into social institutions, especially the monarchy and aristocracy. His concept of the 'general will' ('*volonté générale*') laid the groundwork for democratic theory. John Locke (1632–1704) challenged the divine rights of kings, arguing that legitimate government must be based on the people's consent. He also supported natural rights to life, liberty and property. Charles Montesquieu (1689–1755)

[38] Anthony J. Parel, "Niccolò Machiavelli", in Robert Audi (ed.), *The Cambridge Dictionary of Philosophy*, 3rd ed., Cambridge University Press, 2015, p. 621.

analysed political systems and identified the separation of powers as essential to preventing tyranny.

Enlightenment thinkers also criticized educational institutions and called for reform. A key point was that education should be based on reason and empirical knowledge rather than religious doctrine. These shifts away from religion and tradition toward secularism and science raised questions about the source of human dignity. Pico argued that humans are exceptional because they can resemble God if they work hard enough. They should use reason in these pursuits, but within the bounds of Classical and Christian doctrines. Now, philosophers turned to reason alone as the foundation of human dignity, rights and freedom.

Some argued that there may be a God, such as Thomas Paine (1737–1809), but we should not look to institutionalized religion or religious texts like the Bible to get his view about how we should live our lives.[39] Religion and religious texts have been used to enslave minds, monopolize power and promote cruelty. Institutions and texts are human inventions, often filled with contradictions, frequently promoting morally wrong behaviour. Paine instead promoted 'deism', a rational alternative to revealed religion, claiming that God is best understood through nature and reason, not scripture.

In these and other ways, institutions were criticized for hindering human development and freedoms, laying the ground for a rights-based approach to securing human dignity.

Third, as previously noted, the question of whether ethical norms and moral agency can be established solely through reason has become increasingly important in philosophy, leaving religion outside the moral sphere. If humans are not created by God, nor saved by Jesus, can reason uphold their dignity? Is there another unique quality that grants all humans dignity and agency? The concept of 'natural rights' is one such possibility, introduced by Enlightenment thinkers like Thomas Hobbes (1588–1679), Thomas Jefferson (1743–1826), Locke and Rousseau. Individuals are inherently born with natural rights, which are not granted by any government or authority. They are universal, inalienable and self-evident; applying to all people regardless of laws or customs.

However, most theories on natural rights still relied on reason as the foundation for the rights. Locke argued that humans have natural rights because they are rational beings and can discover natural law. Hobbes emphasized self-preservation as the most fundamental right, and reason was essential to finding the escape route from nature's violent and chaotic state by forming a 'social contract'. Reason also helps in applying natural rights in forming a government.

[39] Thomas Paine, *Age of Reason: The Definitive Edition*, Michigan Legal Publishing Ltd., 2014. The original was published in three parts between 1994 and 1807.

While early Enlightenment philosophers such as Locke and Baruch Spinoza (1632–1677), and prominent Enlightenment thinkers like Voltaire, Montesquieu and Denis Diderot (1813–1784) relied on reason as a trustworthy source for describing what is, causes, and effects, and as a tool to critique what should not be, they also believed that reason could establish norms for what ought to be. There was a firm conviction that a world of reason and progress was achievable for humans.

However, a few philosophers recognized fundamental issues with this approach early on. Rousseau proposed a more nuanced view of natural rights, emphasizing that they are based not only on reason but also on human freedom and moral capacity. His critique of social and political institutions was more profound than that of other Enlightenment thinkers. While they believed existing institutions required significant reform, he argued that the core problem with these institutions and civilization was more fundamental. Science, art and social institutions have not improved humanity, but corrupted its morals. The progress of knowledge has led to vanity, inequality and moral decline.[40]

He contrasted 'natural man' – free, peaceful and self-sufficient – with 'civilized man', corrupt, competitive and enslaved by social institutions. In the state of nature, humans were guided by pity and self-preservation, not greed or pride. Natural man is not the cruel and sinful individual you must kill or risk being killed by. The problem with civilized men is that they become *inauthentic*, constantly comparing themselves to others and seeking their approval.

Rousseau did not suggest that civilization is inherently evil, but that it has taken a wrong turn and become harmful. Inauthenticity was a social issue where societal expectations, vanity and dependence on others for recognition and status shaped individuals. Social and economic inequality among people leads to inauthenticity because individuals begin to value themselves in relation to others, not for their own intrinsic worth. It also affected morality, as it became a matter of social convention rather than inner conviction. People act as if to be seen as good, not because they are intrinsically good.

Roman Catholic writers shared such ideas, lamenting European culture's course since the Middle Ages. They shared Rousseau's hostility towards progress. However, they did not share his belief that people are inherently good. Nonetheless, this belief was the cornerstone of Rousseau's argument. Natural man and, on certain conditions, civilized man could act authentically.

[40] See Jean-Jacques Rousseau, *Discours sur les sciences et les arts* [*Discourse on the Sciences and the Arts*], 1750, and, *Discours sur l'origine et les fondemens de l'inegalité parmi les hommes* [*Discourse on the Origin of Inequality*], 1755.

Rousseau's concept of inauthenticity influenced philosophers like Friedrich Nietzsche (1844–1900), Karl Marx (1818–1883), and existentialists such as Jean-Paul Sartre (1905–1980), Martin Heidegger (1889–1976), and Albert Camus (1913–1960). The father of existentialism, Søren Kierkegaard (1813–1855), shared a deep concern about authenticity with Rousseau. Still, his approach focuses more on psychology and factors intrinsic to humans' relationships with themselves, not just on social aspects. Kierkegaard was not an admirer of Rousseau, seeing his secular and social approach to authenticity lacking in spiritual depth, grounding it in natural human goodness.[41]

Another philosopher presented a groundbreaking critique of reason as the source of dignity, understood as the capacity underpinning moral agency and freedom. David Hume (1711–1776) challenged fundamental principles of knowledge, basing his arguments on John Locke's empiricism. However, he considered himself chiefly a moralist. He characterizes moral goodness in terms of "feelings" of approval or disapproval that people have when considering human behaviour in light of its consequences to themselves or others.[42] This was based on his famous argument that we cannot derive moral judgments or how we ought to act from factual statements or what is. He observed that moral philosophers often move from descriptive statements, such as that people help others, to prescriptive statements, meaning that people ought to help others. The problem is that they do not explain how the leap from descriptions to prescriptions is justified.

Hume's solution is to base normativity on human nature, rooted in sentiments of 'approval', 'disapproval', 'sympathy' and 'benevolence'. We perceive specific actions as virtuous or vicious, which gives rise to moral obligations. He adds that qualities are valued either for their usefulness or their agreeableness, whether by their owners or others. Hume's moral system seeks both personal happiness and the happiness of others; however, he does not formulate a specific principle like "the greatest happiness of the greatest number", which Jeremy Bentham (1747–1832) and John Stuart Mill (1806–1873) later identified as the criterion for moral judgment. Concern for others is central to morality. Hume highlights altruism and sympathy as moral sentiments innate to humans. He contends that it is human nature to laugh with those who are laughing, to mourn with those who are grieving, and to seek the good of others alongside one's own.

---

41 Ciprian Turcan, "Rousseau and Kierkegaard: Authenticity of Human Existence", in *European Journal of Science and Theology*, 2017, vol. 13, no. 1, pp. 5–13.

42 Hume first outlined his moral philosophy in Book III of *A Treatise of Human Nature* (1739–1740). An *Enquiry Concerning the Principles of Morals* (1751) contains a reformulation and refinement of his earlier work, characterizing it as a "juvenile work".

While Hume denied that reason could justify duties and general moral rules, he pointed to a sense of duty among humans arising from their natural inclinations towards sympathy. He was sceptical not of morality, but of excessive theorizing about it. In important aspects, he dethroned reason. It can inform us about facts, but not motivate us to act morally. Normativity is not imposed by reason or divine command, but emerges from our psychological makeup and social interactions.

Fourth, reason made a robust comeback in the philosophy of morals by one of the most influential philosophers on modern thinking on normative statements, Kant. He developed 'deontological ethics', emphasizing duty and universalism. He referred to Hume's critique of reason as awakening him from his "dogmatic slumber". He realized that Hume had been right and that reason cannot establish that B must necessarily follow if A happens. Rationalism or empiricism cannot fully explain causality and our experience of an orderly world.

This prompted his 'Copernican Revolution' in philosophy. Instead of assuming that our knowledge reflects the world, he argued that the world conforms to the structures of our mind, such as 'space' and 'time', along with twelve fundamental concepts (categories), including 'causality'. Therefore, Hume was correct in his causality analysis; we do not perceive causality in the world, meaning that A necessarily causes B. We only observe repeated sequences of A followed by B. However, he was mistaken in claiming that causality, as a necessary connection between A and B, does not exist. He searched for it in the wrong place. Causality is not in the world; it is within us. It is a category of understanding that we impose on experience.

Similarly, Kant did not resolve the 'is-ought problem' by developing methods to bridge the fact-value gap. Instead, he reinterpreted the issue by grounding moral obligation not in empirical facts or sentiments, as Hume proposed, but in a 'pure practical reason'. Once again, he concurred with Hume's view that 'ought' cannot be derived from 'is'. However, normativity does not stem from Hume's human sentiments, which Kant hardly trusted, but from '*a priori* reason' or the structure of rational agency itself. Moral obligations do not originate from nature and cannot be based on experience. Instead, they are self-imposed by reason, arising from the form of a rational will. Kant's renowned 'categorical imperative' is a principle of reason applicable to all rational beings. You should only act according to a rule (maxim) that you, at the same time, want to become a 'universal law'.

In this way, Kant established a 'universalist test' for individuals to follow. He argued that to act freely is to act according to laws you create yourself through reason, which you can universalize without contradiction. Normativity is therefore inherent to rational agency, not something imposed from outside. At the same time, freedom does not mean acting in any way you wish but acting according to rules that have passed the universalist test of reason.

Individualism, reason and freedom are thus upheld. No one can evade their duty to act in accordance with moral law. Since that law is not articulated through detailed rules for specific situations but instead consists of the obligation to act only according to principles that can be universalized, it places moral responsibility on everyone. If a person happens to be a soldier, fighting on behalf of a state or a non-state hierarchical organization, they remain personally bound to uphold morality. This is not only through superior orders or national laws but also through a universal moral law, which, after the time of Kant, became reflected in principles of international law for superiors and subordinates to act within the bounds of respecting the dignity of their opponents.

1.7. Freedom and Responsibility in Kierkegaard

But did Kant help humans decide on complex ethical issues or provide guidance for acting in specific situations? No, was the reply of Georg Wilhelm Friedrich Hegel (1770–1831). Kant's categorical imperative is too abstract. Hegel also argued that the categories through which we understand the world are not *a priori* principles. Instead, they are part of a historical process he called 'spirit' (*Geist*). Our understanding of the world develops through the 'dialectical' process of the spirit. 'Dialectical' describes a logical process where categories relate to contradictions or incompleteness. To resolve a contradiction, one must examine it to see that the alternatives are compatible within a higher-order 'notion' ('*Begriff*'), which resolves or sublates their opposition. '*Aufhebung*' is Hegel's term for this process, a German word meaning 'to cancel', 'to preserve' and 'to raise up'.

According to Hegel, human freedom cannot be regarded merely as rational self-determination independent of external influences. The image of an isolated, self-conscious, self-determining individual – present in Kant and still influential in Western thought – requires revision. From the Kantian perspective, our relationships with others exist because they are created and willed into existence by individuals who are naturally separate from each other. In Kant, an unresolved conflict remains between 'duty', guided by reason, and 'inclination', which can lead us away from moral actions. However, according to Hegel, the categorical imperative was so formal and lacking in concrete content that it could not offer clear directives for action, for example, it could not endorse or prohibit specific actions. Moreover, it demanded a pure motivation that no human agent could fully embody.

Hegel's solution is to resolve the contradiction within what he describes as '*Sittlichkeit*' ('ethical life'). The term refers to humans integrated into modern social institutions that produce the tangible outcomes of rational will. These institutions – 'the family', 'civil society' (the economic sector of a capitalist society), and 'the state' – do not involve duties that potentially conflict with humans' substantive goals but are actualizations of their individual free wills. This implies that the perceived opposition between the state and the individual is sublated.

Hegel argued that the categories we use to understand the world and the norms we accept are products of a rational historical process. His thinking was, therefore, fundamentally historical. As the 'world spirit' ('*Weltgeist*'), reason drives history forward. Historical figures such as Napoleon are essential but can only unknowingly serve the world spirit. Hegel called this the cunning of reason in history. Humanity has attained higher forms of freedom, with modern society as its pinnacle, through the realization of reason *via* historical development. The truth is objective, unfolding through historical reason.

But even though Hegel charted the development of reason throughout history, he had little to say about what lay ahead. While many of his followers, including Marx, would endeavour to predict the direction of history, Hegel dismissed any attempt to form utopias. For him, philosophy always arrived too late – when a civilization was already in decline. It is an afterthought, but it can still legitimize the present situation of society.

For Kierkegaard, the Hegelian way of thinking represented grave danger. In *Fear and Trembling* (1843) and *Concluding Unscientific Postscript to Philosophical Fragments* (1846), Kierkegaard extensively criticizes Hegel's epistemology, philosophy of religion, and ethics. The key point is his insistence that as an 'existing' being, absolute truth is not attainable for humans through their reason, nor through society's embodiment of reason.

In the ethical traditions of Plato, Aquinas and Kant, humans had access to the 'Form of the Good', the 'Natural Law', or the 'Categorical Imperative' to guide them. Common to these thinkers was the belief that humans could access an eternal form or moral law through reflective or abstract reasoning. Kierkegaard knew these thinkers well and disagreed on essential points with them. His description of the ethical stage or life view is akin to Aristotle's conception of socialization (and not reason) as the basis of the ethical life.

In Kierkegaard's second major work, *Either/Or* (1943), a married and duty-bound judge named William embodies the ethical life. He exemplifies the Hegelian ethical model, rejecting Plato and building on Aristotle, where humans do not directly relate to the 'Good', but only access it "mediated through the laws and customs of one's people. *Sittlichkeit* (ethical life) signifies the social institutions that mediate the Good to the individual".[43] However, even if someone lives in the best of societies, Kierkegaard disagrees that its institutions and values represent the absolute good. At best, such laws and customs are approximations. I may have fulfilled all my duties and everything society requires, but I still have not fulfilled the infinite requirement, the infinite ethical demand, inherent in existence. In the Kierkegaardian language, this is expressed as "the upbuilding that lies in the thought that in relation to God we are always in the wrong".

In his first major work, his dissertation on *The Concept of Irony* (1941), Kierkegaard praised Socrates (470–399 BC) because he refused to make Athenian society the sole standard of his life. Notably, Socrates differed from the Sophists, who rejected society based on pre-ethical preferences. Socrates was connected to the eternal, which he sought to understand, although unsuccessfully. 'Socratic ignorance' meant that he knew he did not know. His wisdom was that he realized his lack of knowledge, unlike others who falsely believed they knew things they did not. It reflects a form of epistemological humility, which is present in later philosophical strands, including empiricist thought which demonstrates the limitations of our theoretical and moral knowledge.[44]

Socrates had a higher duty than merely serving Athens. This was not driven by romanticized personal preferences or speculation, as his difference from Plato demonstrated. As Kierkegaard describes it, Socratic subjectivity is a form of 'ethico-religious subjectivity', an alternative to the views of Plato, Hegel and those who believed humans could rely on absolute norms and societal practices. It must not be mistaken for 'subjectivism', which Kierkegaard criticized as an 'aesthetic' approach to life.

Kierkegaard criticized Hegel for a deeply personal reason. In the Hegelian system, religion was regarded as a preliminary expression of what philosophy could articulate much more effectively. Philosophy was the effort to transform "the whole content of faith into the form of a concept".[45] In this way, Hegel eliminated religion and established society as the only framework for an ethical and fulfilling life. On the contrary, Kierkegaard held that religion (embodied by

[43] Merol Westphal, "Kierkegaard and Hegel", in Alistar Hannay and Gordon Daniel Mariono (eds.), *The Cambridge Companion to Kierkegaard*, Cambridge University Press, 1998, p. 102.

[44] When Socrates' friend Chaerephon asked the Oracle of Delphi if any man was wiser than Socrates, the answer was, "There is none". When told about this, Socrates was "not flattered but puzzled. He eventually concluded that what the Oracle meant was that his wisdom consisted in knowing his own ignorance". Paul Johnson, *Socrates: A Man for Our Times*, Viking Penguin, 2011, p. 83.

[45] Søren Kierkegaard, *Fear and Trembling*, The Kierkegaard Collection, Blackmore Dennet, 2019, p. 10.

Socrates), particularly Christianity as he understood it, could not be subjugated by philosophy. For once, a philosophical system like Hegel's, with its all-embracing ambition, is not achievable for existing beings like humans. A round-up philosophical system of everything may be attainable for God in eternity, not for humans living in time. For them, the eternal truth is something they can only strive to attain.

Johannes Climacus, the pseudonym Kierkegaard used to author his philosophical works, defines truth in the following way: "An objective uncertainty, held fast through appropriation with the most passionate inwardness, is the truth, the highest truth there is for an existing person".[46] This means that Kierkegaard departs from Plato and those philosophers who believed humans could intellectually 'see' or 'deduce' the truth. Climacus adds that his definition of truth is "a paraphrasing of faith. Without risk, no faith. Faith is the contradiction (tension, incongruity) between the infinite passion of inwardness and the objective uncertainty".

Kierkegaard's revolutionary thought, which has precursors in Socrates, Blaise Pascal (1623–1662), and several other philosophers and theologians, was that abstract truths of philosophical detachment are always subordinate to the concrete truths of the individual in existence. This is a key point in establishing existentialism as a distinct philosophy. For Kierkegaard, the 'ethically existing subject', and not the 'cognitive subject', is the real subject.[47] In this conception of human existence, freedom is not mere autonomy or choice, but a profound and often troubling human condition. We cannot do away with ourselves as fundamentally free persons. Kierkegaard conducts a subtle and innovative analysis of how humans try to escape from freedom and the calling to become 'a self' in *The Concept of Anxiety* (1844) and *The Sickness unto Death* (1849).

Kierkegaard describes freedom as the ability to choose among possibilities. This causes anxiety ("angst") because it confronts the individual with the burden of responsibility and the unknown. Anxiety is thus a sign of freedom, the "dizziness of freedom". In the aesthetic stage, people live only for pleasure and avoid commitment. In the ethical stage, the individual begins to accept responsibility. However, for Kierkegaard, only religion can offer true freedom through a leap of faith and by accepting one's dependence on God to become an authentic self.

True freedom involves becoming a self, embracing individuality and responsibility before God. Being responsible for who you are is a burden, but it is

[46] Søren Kierkegaard, *Concluding Unscientific Postscript*, trans. by David F. Swenson and Walter Lowrie, Princeton University Press, 1968, pp. 203–204.

[47] *Ibid.*, p. 281.

also the entrance into true humanity. Therefore, Kierkegaard's main points can be understood within the framework of humanism, as Johannes Sløk (1916–2001), a Danish theologian, philosopher and Kierkegaard scholar, argues. Humanism, as the view that "ensures the dignity of the human being, the individual human being, as an independent, self-determining, and self-responsible being", captures the main ideas behind his manifold descriptions of human possibilities and how humans escape from selfhood. That does not mean, however, that he overlooks human dependencies of society and its prevailing cultural environment and their own inner preconditions.

As Kierkegaard framed it, humanist existentialism projects an understanding of humanity in which humans are adult beings who can take care of their own existence and stand up for themselves. They have only become human in the true sense when they have become the subject of their own decisions and actions and cannot be unambiguously described as the result of many influences. Because of this, humanism also means that man is his own ultimate purpose.[48]

1.8. The Existentialist Perception of Human Life

As an intellectual movement with its foremost spokespersons in mid-twentieth-century France, 'existentialism' is often portrayed as a historically contingent event that emerged against the backdrop of World War II. However, as indicated, 'existentialism' is a distinct strand of philosophical enquiry, developed by Kierkegaard, while Nietzsche and some other pre-twentieth-century thinkers contributed to major existentialist themes. However, in the post-war situation, existentialist themes came to the foreground due to the loss of meaning and direction caused by the tragedy of World War II. Existentialist concepts and views were reflected in literature, drama, painting and other artistic genres, in addition to theology and philosophy.

Heidegger's analysis of 'Dasein' in his seminal work, *Being and Time* (1927), was a main development in the philosophical sphere. His analysis applied a reinterpreted and transformed version of Edmund Husserl's (1859–1938) phenomenological method, the study of consciousness and direct experience. His main shift was to use the method to analyse the existential structure of Dasein, that is, the human being as a being who questions its existence. His method, often called 'hermeneutic phenomenology', and his descriptions of human existence became immensely influential. They formed with Kierkegaard the main inspiration for the post-war existentialist philosophies of Sartre, Simone de Beauvoir (1908–1886), Gabriel Marcel (1889–1973), Karl Jaspers (1883–1969), and other existentialists.

48 Johannes Sløk, *Kierkegaard: Humanismens tenker* [*Kierkegaard: Humanism's Thinker*], Lindhardt og Ringhof, København, 2016, p. 6.

In the following, only the central tenets of existentialism are presented.[49]

1.8.1. Existence

The central idea is that 'existence precedes essence'. Heidegger first introduced it with this statement: "The 'essence' of Dasein lies in its existence". It shares some similarities with Pico's description of humans, although the context differs. Heidegger and Sartre do not focus on explaining human dignity and God-likeness, but instead on providing a realistic view of the human condition. We exist for ourselves as 'self-making' or 'self-defining' beings. We are not entirely co-incidental with who we are, as we constantly shape ourselves by choosing among the possibilities our circumstances present. According to Sartre, this is "the first principle of existentialism", meaning "that man exists, turns up, appears on the scene, and, only afterwards, defines himself".

Indeed, certain situational factors limit us. Often called our 'givenness' or 'facticity', these include our embodiment, spatiality, appetites, desires and the socio-historical context. However, humans can 'transcend' these facts by relating, interpreting and understanding them. In Kierkegaard's words, human existence is "a relation that relates to itself". Therefore, tension exists between our facticity and 'transcendence', meaning we have the freedom to go beyond or surpass facticity.

Our nature or situation is not just something we are born into; it also raises questions and concerns. We can think about it and care about it. Through this process, we shape who we are. Being a soldier with a specific background, rank and other details does not fully define me. My relationship with and understanding of myself as a soldier influence who I am, regardless of the circumstances of my enlistment.

1.8.2. Freedom

The view that facticity can be overcome through our choices is fundamental to understanding the existentialist perspective on freedom. Our identity is shaped by the choices and actions we undertake. According to Sartre, the coward is not a coward because of an unstable childhood or genetic factors. Instead, they become a coward through their decisions.

---

[49] I base this short presentation on Kevin Aho, "Existentialism", in *Stanford Encyclopedia of Philosophy*, 6 January 2023. Johannes Sløk, *Eksistentialisme*, Lindhardt og Ringhof, København, 1983, provides a brief and readable introduction. Steven Crowell, *The Cambridge Companion to Existentialism*, Cambridge University Press, 2012, contains essays introducing the leading existentialist thinkers and their influence. A classical and recommendable work is Jean Wahl, *Philosophies of Existence: An Introduction to the Basic Thought of Kierkegaard, Heidegger, Jaspers, Marcel, Sartre*, Routledge, London and New York, 2019 (first published in 1959).

Free will exists because humans can make choices and take responsibility for their actions. As beings who exist, we imagine a specific life, shaping ourselves into who we are. However, freedom does not mean being able to do everything we want. We are placed in situations, and our existence is shaped by our limited ability to give meaning and direction to our circumstances through our choices and actions as our lives develop.

Like Kierkegaard, later existentialists often highlight the anxiety that arises from our discovery or experience of freedom. When we realize that there is no moral absolute, divine will or natural law to guide us or justify our actions, it becomes our own responsibility, and this can lead to anxiety. Sartre's famous phrase expresses this: "we are condemned to be free", because "there are no excuses behind us nor justifications before us".[50]

1.8.3. Engagement

As we have seen, Western philosophical traditions often prescribed the standpoint of theoretical detachment and objectivity to know the truth. Kant's achievement was to save the view that reason can help establish a criterion for ethical choices, even if Hume were right that we could not derive prescriptions from descriptions. However, his categorical imperative is another example of an abstract and detached ethical model that provides the guidance we need to act ethically in concrete situations.

Existentialism emphasizes our own 'situated', 'first-person experience'. We are initially thrown into existence and must navigate through it, as we do not have the luxury of addressing ethical questions *sub specie aeternitatis*. The human condition is described by examining how we engage with the world in our everyday lives.

For the existentialists, the possibility of breaking free from patterns of self-deception or making decisions in difficult situations is not achieved through detached reflection. When they refer to 'nausea' (Sartre), 'absurdity' (Camus), 'anxiety' (Kierkegaard), 'guilt' (Heidegger), or 'mystery' (Marcel), they are talking about affects with the power to shake us out of our complacency in a perceived secure and familiar world. These feelings force us to confront the question of existence and cause what we usually consider valuable and trustworthy to collapse.

These moods or deep feelings are essential to human experience. Although shocking and unsettling, they can open doors to personal growth and transformation.

---

[50] Jean-Paul Sartre, *L'Existentialism est un humanism* [*Existentialism is a Humanism*], 1946, in Charles Guignon and Derk Pereboom (eds.), *Existentialism: Basic Writings*, Hackett Press, Indianapolis, 2001, p. 296.

Thus, authenticity can be achieved not through detached reflection, but through engagement and openness to the seemingly negative feelings of lost meaning.

1.8.4. Authenticity

Kierkegaard believed that humans could become 'a self'. To do this, they must escape from "life in the crowd" and become authentic. He presents faith – specifically Christian faith – as the way to succeed. It is challenging, even if eternity or God is part of the synthesis that humans consist of. Humans can relate to God or eternity, not like Plato and other rationalist philosophers thought, because they can have knowledge of God, but only as an infinite demand for their existence. The demand does not ask for something specific from us, but the individual must express that they can do nothing themselves and are nothing before God. By honouring this demand, the individual becomes a self and can live in society without being subject to life in the crowd.[51]

Later existentialists took over Kierkegaard's depiction of inauthenticity as a significant problem in modern societies and showed how it could be explained from the structure of human existence. Inauthenticity is the tendency to conform to the norms and expectations of the public. It is not about honouring the laws of the land, but rather about fleeing from a responsible life. We "take pleasure and enjoy ourselves as they take pleasure. We read, see, and judge about literature and art as they see and judge [...] we find 'shocking' what they find shocking".[52]

This lifestyle can be comfortable, creating illusions that we live well because we do the same things and share the same opinions. Sartre and Beauvoir describe inauthenticity as 'bad faith' (*mauvaise foi*), where we deny one of the two aspects of human existence, 'transcendence'. However, we may also deny 'facticity' by rejecting our past actions and the fact that our choices are limited and constrained.

Existentialists argue that this kind of inauthenticity is not just a problem of our time. As self-deception, it is a fundamental part of being human. Because human existence is ambiguous, made up of facticity and transcendence, we can change our circumstances and are responsible for our lives. In Kierkegaard's words, existence is about becoming and movement. However, humans may resist these possibilities.

[51] This is Knud Ejler Løgstrup's interpretation of Kierkegaard in Knud Ejler Løgstrup, *Kierkegaard's and Heidegger's Analysis of Existence and Its Relation to Proclamation*, trans. by Robert Stern, Oxford University Press, 2020.

[52] Martin Heidegger, *Sein und Zeit*, 1927, trans. in English as *Being and Time*, General Press, 2023, p. 247.

Inauthenticity is connected to the tendency to accept only facticity as our human condition. In modern societies, the institutional setup, fashion and expectations about how we should behave can make it challenging to break free from inauthenticity. At the same time, modern societies may provide more opportunities for individuals to become authentic than in earlier times. They promote fundamental freedoms for everyone. However, this freedom can be challenging because humans fear freedom – and responsibility.

1.8.5. Ethics

Existentialism does not preach nihilism, even if it rejects moral absolutes or universalizing judgments about ethical conduct. A moral, responsible life is possible for everyone. It is one where we recognize ourselves as free to choose and accountable in all situations. We should also act in such ways that we help others realize their freedom.

Beauvoir admits that human beings have no reason to will themselves. "*But* this does not mean that it cannot justify itself, that it cannot *give itself* reasons for being that it does not *have*." Human existence "makes values spring up in the world on the basis of which it will be able to judge the enterprise in which it will be engaged".[53]

There is thus an account of ethical responsibility inherent in freedom. This responsibility does not result from universal principles or commands, but is an expression of transcendence and the obligation to help others realize their freedom. Others, recognizing their freedom, have the potential to assist me in realizing mine. However, this is not an ethics of mutual conditionality: I will help you if you help me. Instead, it is based on the acknowledgment that, as freedom is the essence of my existence, it is the essence of others. There is an intertwinement of my freedom and the freedom of others.

Sartre put this point eloquently: "We want freedom for freedom's sake and in every particular circumstance. And in wanting freedom, we discover that it depends entirely on the freedom of others, and that freedom of others depends on ours […]. I am obliged to want others to have freedom at the same time that I want my own freedom".[54]

Much more can be said about existentialist ethics. However, I will restrict myself to only rendering one point, often made by existentialist philosophers. In inauthenticity, human tends to objectify each other. In this state, they can effectively undermine the freedom of others, not help them realize it. In the authentic being-for-others, there is instead a reciprocity that involves "the mutual

[53] Simone de Beauvoir, *Pour une Morale de l'ambiguïté*, 1947, trans. by B. Frechtman, Open Road Integrated Media, New York, 2018, p. 14.

[54] Sartre, 2001, p. 306, see *supra* note 50.

recognition of two freedoms […] [where] neither would give up transcendence [and] neither would be mutilated".[55]

In this way, authenticity and morality are linked, creating a shared responsibility to help each other become free, so that you and I can take ownership of our lives. In Kierkegaard, a practising Christian who demonstrates love – including love for neighbours and enemies – should help others become Christians and love in the same way. Heidegger describes a kind of care ('*befreiend Fürsorge*'), which aims to free the other from self-deception so that they can create their own existence. However, when we care in this way, we must resist the temptation to "leap in" ('*einspringen*') for the other, as if she is an object that needs protection from existence.

The same point is underlined by the Danish theologian and philosopher Knud Ejler Løgstrup (1905–1981), who states that the ethical demand inherent in human existence's interdependency with others never asks us to take the responsibility away from them. In his seminal book, *The Ethical Demand* (*Den etiske fordring*) (1956), he describes the demand as a radical, unspoken, and one-sided calling that arises when one meets others. In every human encounter, we hold something of the other person's life in our hands. There is an unspoken trust that the other person places in us simply by being vulnerable in our presence. The ethical demand asks us to care for the other person's well-being in light of this trust.

While Løgstrup's conception of the ethical demand represents a critique of Kierkegaard, there is also much continuity. The demand is not codifiable in laws or moral rules; it is situational and must be responded to with openness to the specific needs of the other person. We cannot choose whether to accept the demand or not. It is part of human existence, imposed on us by the fact of human interaction. In short, for Løgstrup, ethics is about existence, not primarily about rules or consequences.

Unlike other existential thinkers, Løgstrup emphasizes that helping others is not primarily about aiding their realization of freedom, but about doing what we believe is best for them in any situation.

1.9. The Existentialist Test

Since Pico and the humanist breakthrough, Western thought has presented diverse philosophies about how humans can become authentic and responsible moral agents. As recorded above, there is significant disagreement on how this can be achieved, whether agency is based on ethical principles accessible through reason (Plato, Kant), human nature (Hume), applying reason to

[55] Simone de Beauvoir, *Le Deuxième Sexe*, 1949, trans. by H.M. Parshley in English as *The Second Sex*, Knopf, New York, 1952, p. 667.

calculate consequences (Bentham, Mill), adhering to the norms of society (Hegel), or faith (Kierkegaard, *et cetera*).

I have presented the existentialist approach in more detail because I believe it can be an effective partner in evaluating responsibility issues in international criminal law. It can shed light on the defence of superior orders and the three main principles for tackling the inherent conflicts facing military personnel ordered to commit illegal or immoral actions.

Objections to this approach do exist. First, some might argue that we cannot expect ordinary soldiers or superiors to be educated in Western philosophical traditions. If they disobey orders, it is probably because they believe or feel the actions are morally wrong. Of course, they might also be aware of humanitarian law and choose to refrain from actions they view as violating its provisions. However, if their objections are solely based on feelings, it does not necessarily mean their concerns are grounded in well-thought-out philosophical principles.

This objection misses the point. There is clearly a question of how well-informed and grounded their feelings are; however, everyone can understand the conditions of human existence from their own life. That is precisely the point of existentialism: we can recognize freedom, right and wrong through our own experiences as living humans.

There are many real-life stories about commanders or ordinary soldiers refusing orders. A revealing example is Wehrmacht commander Captain Josef Sibille who, along with two other commanders, had been ordered to shoot all Jews in his area of command on the Eastern Front during World War II. While the other commanders obeyed (although one hesitated slightly), Sibille maintained his objection and never carried out the order. Knowledge about his motivations from his family indicated that this refusal was based not only on professionalism (arguing that it was outside the duty of soldiers to commit such killings), but also on a deeper moral objection rooted in part in religious beliefs.[56] He would, however, probably not have been able to give a comprehensive philosophical justification for his disobedience.

The objection also misses the point because philosophy challenges not only individual soldiers, but also the principles of law and military organizations. Any law is based on philosophical assumptions, including values that protect

[56] Neither he nor other service members in the Wehrmacht, SS or police seemed to have faced serious consequences because of their disobedience. Of the 85 documented cases of refusal to shoot Jews or Soviet prisoners of war, 49 experienced no consequences, 15 were reprimanded, 14 were transferred, five were investigated, and three were sent to combat units at the front, but only one was imprisoned. See Jody Prescott *et al.*, "Ordinary Soldiers: A Study in Ethics, Law, and Leadership", United States Holocaust Memorial Museum and Center for Holocaust and Genocide Studies at West Point, 2017, p. 16.

humans from suffering. A philosophical enquiry into the foundations of such values and whether the institutional and moral set-up of military organizations adheres to those values is of paramount importance. Such enquiries and assessments can lead to legal reform and improve recruitment and training for greater norm efficacy.

Another objection could be based on a scientific understanding of how military organizations operate and suppress soldiers' ability to refuse illegal orders. Equally important is how combat environments over time influence the "normative competence" necessary for a soldier to consider ethical issues, verify information, and recognize permitted behaviour. Another faculty that may be diminished if you are under battle pressure for protracted periods of time is your power to control yourself. The question is, how relevant are peacetime moral considerations in extreme circumstances, such as in combat?[57]

My answer is that circumstances may cause humans to act with lower morals, but that should not result in watering down principles and values. As long as war remains a frequently occurring human institution, we should strive to uphold the principles of humanity despite war's brutalizing effects. That does not imply that our primary goals should be anything but doing our utmost to prevent war.

1.9.1. The Respondeat Superior Doctrine

The doctrine states that only those who give an order are responsible for its illegality and the unlawful conduct of subordinates who carry it out. It is a doctrine of strict military discipline. It has a long history and "reflects a basic tension between the importance of the principles of international law and those of military discipline". This was the original doctrine, although even by the late nineteenth century, there were signs that it had been replaced by the rule that orders only protect a subordinate if they were 'manifestly illegal'. After World War I, the Conditional Liability Doctrine became dominant.[58]

---

[57] For a description and assessment of such factors, see Song Tianying, *Legal Construction of Common Humanity: Human Agency in a Cosmopolitan War Crimes Law*, Torkel Opsahl Academic EPublisher, Brussels, 2025, Chapters 5–7 (https://www.toaep.org/ps-pdf/46-song/). Arne Willy Dahl adds important aspects which I have not dealt with in this chapter, such as a tendency to treat one's own people in the dock differently than aliens charged with war crimes or other core international crimes. He argues that not all ICC war crimes are manifestly unlawful. Therefore, "it would not make much sense [in some cases] to go after individual soldiers who have put illegal orders into effect". Arne Willy Dahl, "Equality Before the Law? Some Reflections on the Defence of Obedience to Superior Orders", in *Israel Yearbook on Human Rights*, 2020, vol. 50, pp. 1–16.

[58] Robert Cryer *et al.*, *An Introduction to International Criminal Law and Procedure*, Cambridge University Press, 2007, pp. 342–346.

The doctrine fundamentally derives from the subordinates of moral agency. As discussed, existentialism describes 'bad faith' or inauthenticity as inherent in human existence; people tend to identify with their 'facticity' and ignore 'transcendence'. Absolute military discipline is equivalent to depriving service members of transcendence. This, in turn, replaces 'human existence' with 'military institutional existence' and transforms humans into mere tools of the military organization.

Therefore, the doctrine fails the existentialist test and has few, if any, supporters in the legal community today.

1.9.2. The Absolute Liability Doctrine

This is the doctrine outlined in Article 8 of the Statute of the Nuremberg Tribunal. A superior order shall not free a defendant from responsibility, "but may be considered in mitigation of punishment if the Tribunal determines that justice so requires". The Nuremberg Tribunal added a requirement that "moral choice was in fact possible". This was the prevailing doctrine (although not unequivocally) until the ICC Statute reintroduced the 'manifest illegality' test inherent in the Conditional Liability Doctrine. The statutes (Articles 7(4) and 6(4) respectively) and the case law of the ICTY and ICTR applied the Absolute Liability Doctrine, which is also stated in Article 2 of the 1984 Convention Against Torture.[59]

The existentialist view of the human condition considers humans to be fundamentally free and responsible for their actions. This doctrine best reflects that perspective. Humans are moral agents not because of their autonomy or reason, as Kant explains, but because they can transcend 'facticity' in any situation. In general, humans are placed in situations, and existence is shaped by our limited ability to give meaning and direction to them through the choices and actions we take.

However, given soldiers' unique situation, military discipline, combat training and practice, facticity may be challenging to overcome. They may be overwhelmed by circumstances, which strip away their normative competence, moral agency and ability to control themselves. If they lose these, are they still responsible?

Yes. Existentialism supports this challenging conclusion for at least two reasons. Even if you are overwhelmed, you are not free not to be free. Freedom is unavoidable. When you enlist in a military organization, you knowingly place yourself in a situation where your freedom will be limited. However, it will not

[59] Convention Against Torture and Other Cruel, Inhuman or Degrading Treatment or Punishment, 10 December 1984, Article 2(3) (https://www.legal-tools.org/doc/326294/): "An order from a superior officer or a public authority may not be invoked as a justification of torture".

be entirely taken away. You will always be responsible for defining yourself as the soldier you want to be.

Secondly, you always face a 'moral choice' to see the enemy as a human with freedom and moral agency. Upholding the moral agency and dignity of the enemy obviously presents a significant challenge during combat. Nevertheless, it remains a moral obligation. Disobeying orders that would degrade human dignity in violation of international or moral law may be necessary.

The Nuremberg trials did not clarify the qualification, "whether moral choice was possible". The judgment decided on the mitigation of punishment based on the defendant's knowledge of illegality, but there was no detailed discussion on the meaning of moral choice. It could relate to the issue of 'coercion', or knowledge of 'illegality' or 'manifest illegality' or whether this should only serve as a principle for mitigating punishment or also apply in the decision on guilt.

It is therefore fair to say that the Nuremberg principle of absolute liability for subordinates introduced some ambiguity, which remained unresolved during the trials. This ambiguity became even more apparent in the subsequent proceedings held by the United States and France in their respective zones in Germany.[60]

However, from the perspective of existentialism, the principle in its purest form, accepting superior order defence only in the context of mitigating punishment, best expresses the role freedom and responsibility play for existing humans.

1.9.3. The Conditional Liability Doctrine

At the end of this inquiry, I will not focus on whether the ICC Statute's conditional liability principle violates customary law by diverging from the Nuremberg principle. Instead, I question whether its formulations, returning to the 'manifest illegality' test of the pre-World War II era, constitute a refinement akin to the existentialist view of human existence.

The answer is that, based on what has already been said, one may conclude without much discussion that introducing such conditions as in Article 33(1) of the ICC Statute for accepting the superior order defence departs from existentialism's central tenets.

An objection might be raised that the Absolute Liability Doctrine reflects a unique situation. The world had experienced the most devastating war in human history, and Nazi ideology and Hitler's orders had led to acts of extreme

[60] Hiromi Sato, *The Execution of Illegal Orders and International Criminal Responsibility*, Springer-Verlag, Berlin, p. 71.

brutality. It can also be added that the existentialist view of human existence was further developed and gained significant attention because of the war.

This argument ignores that if the formulation of the absolute liability principle was motivated by the world's shock over the crimes ordered by the Nazi regime and committed by ordinary service members, then this could actually strengthen the principle instead of weakening it. It is not necessarily true that peacetime reflections provide the best understanding and answers to wartime excesses.

We can all acknowledge that much about existentialism. Its emphasis on human freedom and responsibility in every situation was a realistic and essential response to the war. But it was much more than just that. Kierkegaard identified and accurately described the danger of the constant problem of inauthenticity, which can lead to severe forms of moral corruption. Existentialism was not just a reaction to the war, but a timely response and mobilization against it.

A soldier does not need to carry a library of international law to understand the exact meaning of Article 33(1) or how to align that article with post-war international jurisprudence, including ICTY and ICTR case law, which apply the absolute liability principle. It is enough for him to know from his first-hand existential experience what one should not do to others, even as a soldier. ICC crimes are clearly recognizable as unlawful and morally wrong.

1.10. Conclusion

In accordance with existentialism, it would be better if Article 33(1) of the ICC Statute had not reintroduced the 'manifest illegality' test. That would not have rendered irrelevant the questions of whether the subordinate was under a legal obligation to obey an order,[61] whether he or she did not know that the order was unlawful, or whether the order was manifestly unlawful. It would still be for the judges to consider if answers to such questions should result in a more lenient punishment.

[61] This is the case in all states, although in some states this only applies to lawful orders. Cryer *et al.*, 2007, p. 344, see *supra* note 58.

2

Broader Normative Bases for Religious Leaders to Prevent Hate Speech*

2.1. Introduction

A quote by China's most famous teacher, Confucius (551–479 BC), states that you should not do unto others what you do not want to be done unto you. Similar teachings – often phrased positively as 'do to others as you would like them to do to you' or 'love your neighbour as yourself' – are included in the ethical doctrines of most world religions and belief systems. They are often not limited to people of the same creed, but refer to any human being. Sometimes even to enemies.

Illustrating the positive ethical contributions of world religions, in 1947, aimed as a contribution to the drafting process of the Universal Declaration of Human Rights, the United Nations ('UN') Educational, Scientific and Cultural Organization ('UNESCO') Philosophers' Committee received 56 answers to their questions on views on human rights from diverse religious and philosophical thinkers. In their answers, Chinese, Islámic, Hindu, Christian philosophical, scientific and political thinkers gave reasoned opinions on human rights principles. According to the Committee, overall, the results were encouraging, indicating that the leading human rights principles were present in several cultural and religious traditions.[1]

Later scholarship indicates that the UNESCO survey may have failed to comprehensively represent non-Western religious traditions' views and that its authors overplayed global consensus on human rights principles.[2] There is also a critical underpinning question of whether the universality of human rights can

---

* This chapter was first published as Chapter 17 of Morten Bergsmo and Kishan Manocha (eds.), *Religion, Hateful Expression and Violence*, Torkel Opsahl Academic EPublisher ('TOAEP'), Brussels, 2023 (https://www.toaep.org/ps-pdf/41-bergsmo-manocha/).

1 Mary Ann Glendon, *A World Made New: Eleanor Roosevelt and the Universal Declaration of Human Rights*, Random House, New York, 2001, p. 76. For a critical account of the narrative that the 1947 UNESCO survey "demonstrated the universality of human rights through empirical evidence", see Mark Goodale, "The Myth of Universality: The UNESCO 'Philosophers' Committee' and the Making of Human Rights", in *Laws & Social Inquiry*, 2018, vol. 43, no. 3, pp. 596–617.

2 Extensive material and comments related to the UNESCO Survey on Human Rights are presented in Mark Goodale (ed.), *Letters to the Contrary: A Curated History of the UNESCO Human Rights Survey*, Stanford University Press, 2018.

be constructed by such empirical research. In any case, it remains an indisputable fact that religion remains both a source and a target of hate speech and violence, in stark contravention of human rights principles and values. At the same time, it can contribute to reconciliation and building of bridges between conflicting parties by mobilizing norms and behaviours to that effect.

There are several complications related to religion as a source of hate speech, such as believers invoking scriptures or revelations of God's will which may be interpreted as justifying hatred for a group. It may be hard for courts and targeted people to know if they should take the quoted passages as a literal expression of the believer's view. Another complication is that religious beliefs are often deeply rooted and part of a shared culture. Believers may experience censorship by the state as an affront to their dignity and the standing of their group.[3]

Taking these complications into account, this chapter discusses normative bases for religious leaders to prevent hate speech and violence in the name of religion. Religious leaders may have considerable impact on preventing hate speech. They can probably be more influential than secular authorities or outside persons criticizing such abuse, especially if they can refer to esteemed teachers within their religious tradition or other respected teachers who aspire to create universal ethical bases for adherents belonging to different religions or life-stance traditions.

By 'religious leaders', I refer to persons recognized within a particular religion as having authority. The authority may be based on *formal* recognition by a prescribed body to persons that perform specific roles, such as priests, imams, preachers and so on. However, the authority may also be based on *informal* recognition by a group of persons, that is, granting a person *de facto* leadership.

Where can such leaders find norms to prevent hate speech and violence? First, norms against hate speech and violence are expressed in founding texts, religious discourse, religious philosophies and efforts at systematizing the religions' ethical teachings. Importantly, there exist religiously inspired inquiries that strive to establish *universal* moral teachings that adherents of different faiths can accept. I outline the approaches of Danish protestant Christian philosopher Søren A. Kierkegaard (1813–1855) and Knud E. Løgstrup (1905–1981). They were the two most influential Danish philosophers in the nineteenth and twentieth centuries.

While not addressing hate speech and violence in the name of religion specifically, they analyse foundational ethical demands inherent to human existence that consider 'care for the neighbour' the primary duty of human beings. Their

3 Richard Moon, *Putting Faith in Hate: When Religion is the Source or Target of Hate Speech*, Cambridge University Press, 2018, pp. 115–116.

account of human existence and the ethical demand is inspired by Christian conceptions, but aims to be valid for all human beings, regardless of their religious or philosophical outlook. They point to how religion may be used for ideological purposes, ossifying its proclamation into political and sometimes intolerant doctrines, instead of challenging individuals to believe in and serve God and their neighbour.

Second, while the discussion of Kierkegaard and Løgstrup is the main contribution of this chapter, I briefly point to other normative bases. In addressing hate speech, religious leaders may refer to norms about religious tolerance, freedom, spiritual- and life-view diversity, and epistemology of religion.

Third, they may refer to common messages by religious leaders of diverse creeds on human dignity, love for your neighbour, compassion and other values that can prevent hate speech. Part of this approach would be to refer to dialogue between representatives of religions to tackle hate and hate speech by or against members of religious groups. Values of dialogue, mutual respect, love and the ability to agree to disagree have been repeatedly expressed in the encounters of the fourteenth Dalai Lama (1935–) and the late South African Archbishop Desmond Tutu (1931–2021).

Another example is the Council for Religious and Life-Stance Communities in Norway, established in 1996 to promote equal treatment of religious and life-stance communities and respect and understanding among them through dialogue. The Council arranges meetings of senior religious leaders and has proved to be an effective tool in addressing sensitive issues and preventing conflicts among religious and life-stance communities.[4]

Fourth, religious leaders may refer to internationally recognized human rights as norms that protect freedom of religion or belief as embedded in a comprehensive set of rights to protect the integrity, dignity and well-being of all human beings. Reading the Universal Declaration of Human Rights as it was meant to be read by its framers, namely as a whole, makes it become "a common standard that can be brought to life in different cultures in a legitimate variety of ways". It was never intended as "a kind of menu of rights from which one can pick and choose according to taste".[5]

Referring to lesbian, gay, bisexual, transgender or intersex ('LGBTI') persons, persons belonging to religious minorities, or other groups at risk of discrimination and hatred as having the same rights as any other member of society may become a potent weapon against hate speech in the mouth of religious

[4] More information about the Council for Religious and Life Stance Communities in Norway is available on its web site.

[5] Glendon, 2001, p. xviii, see *supra* note 1.

leaders. In the words of Eleanor Roosevelt (1884–1962), who led the UN drafting process of human rights, the Declaration may, in their practice, become "a bridge upon which we can meet and talk".[6] However, many religious leaders are sceptical about human rights, and one may need to find novel ways to start a conversation with them.

Fifth, religious leaders may refer to norms prescribing prudent relationships between religion and politics. Many examples of religious movements becoming a source of hate speech and violence against certain groups of individuals, organizations or even foreign states originate from abusing religion and religious institutions by politicians or religious leaders that operate like politicians. There may also be temptations for religious institutions that receive financial and other benefits from political leaders to compromise spiritual integrity. However, norms of prudence can guide religious leaders to avoid becoming 'useful tools' for politicians seeking to mobilize support for politics of conflict.

2.2. Understanding Religious Hate Speech

Religious hate speech is a sub-group of hate speech. A starting point for understanding such speech is a provision of the 1966 International Covenant on Civil and Political Rights ('ICCPR'), obliging States Parties to prohibit by law "[a]ny advocacy of national, racial, or religious hatred that constitutes incitement to discrimination, hostility, or violence". The 1965 International Convention on the Elimination of All Forms of Racial Discrimination ('ICERD') similarly obliges States Parties to "declare an offence punishable by law all dissemination of ideas based on racial superiority or hatred, incitement to racial discrimination, as well as all acts of violence or incitement to such acts against any race or group of persons of another colour or ethnic origin, and also the provision of any assistance to racist activities, including the financing thereof".[7]

The definition of hate speech inherent in these international provisions is *the advocacy of hatred that constitutes incitement to discrimination, hostility or violence*. Many states have enacted laws against hate speech, including incitement. Canadian law prohibits public statements that incite "hatred against any identifiable group where such incitement is likely to lead to a breach of the peace", while Danish Law prohibits comments "by which a group of people is threatened, derided, or degraded […]".[8]

---

[6] Eleanor Roosevelt, "The UN and the Welfare of the World", in *National Parent-Teacher: The P.T.A. Magazine*, June 1953, vol. 47, p. 14.

[7] ICCPR, 16 December 1966, Article 20 (https://www.legal-tools.org/doc/2838f3/); ICERD, 21 December 1965, Article 4(a) (https://www.legal-tools.org/doc/43a925/).

[8] The quotation is from Jeremy Waldron, *The Harm in Hate Speech*, Harvard University Press, 2012, p. 8.

The words 'deriding' and 'degrading' signifies another essential element, which is made clear in German law, prohibiting attacks on "the human dignity of others by insulting, maliciously maligning, or defaming segments of the population".[9]

Hate speech may then be characterized as *speech that attacks human dignity and incites discrimination, hostility or violence*. Racial and ethnic groups constituting minorities of the population are among the targets. In national laws, religious groups and some other minorities are also frequently protected. The Norwegian Penal Code defines hate speech as a "discriminatory or hateful statement" (which includes the use of symbols) that is "threatening or insulting a person or promoting hate of, persecution of or contempt for another person based on his or her a) skin colour or national or ethnic origin; b) religion or life stance; c) homosexual orientation; and d) reduced functional capacity".[10]

While hate speech in its most dangerous forms may contain all elements, it is not necessarily so with all forms of hate speech. Hate speech may attack the dignity of targeted groups without an explicit incitement element.[11] Understanding hate speech is, however, not only about knowing its elements. An equally important question is: what is the intended purpose of *speech that attacks human dignity and/or incites discrimination, hostility or violence against certain groups*?

Slogans such as "do not trust Muslims", "Muslims are about to take over our land, and they are even prepared to use violence to achieve that goal", or "Muslims are full of hate, violence, and murder and are incapable of living peacefully among non-Muslims" clearly intend to mobilize defensive actions and in the end may be understood to signal that Muslims deserve ill-treatment.[12] However, the underlying message to members of the targeted group may be best summarized as 'they should not feel safe here, they do not belong, they do not deserve the same rights as us and they had better leave'.

Jeremy Waldron (1953–) summarizes this inherent messaging of hate speech well:

> Don't be fooled into thinking you are welcome here. The society around you may seem hospitable and non-discriminatory, but the truth is that you are not wanted, and you and your families will be shunned, excluded, beaten, and driven out, whenever we can get

[9] *Ibid.*

[10] Norway, Penal Code, 20 May 2005, Section 185 (https://www.legal-tools.org/doc/aa2cee/).

[11] UN Office on Genocide Prevention and the Responsibility to Protect, *Plan of Action for Religious Leaders and Actors to Prevent Incitement to Violence that Could Lead to Atrocity Crimes*, 14 July 2017, p. 2 (https://www.legal-tools.org/doc/8723g7/).

[12] Examples are from Moon, 2018, p. 9, see *supra* note 3.

> away with it. We may have to keep a low profile right now. But don't get too comfortable. Remember what has happened to you and your kind in the past. Be afraid.[13]

For persons belonging to a targeted group, pressing questions will be: How many people feel this way about our presence here? Is the number increasing? And importantly, what do the government, the police and other powerful institutions think?

Discussions on how to react to hate speech may start from two opposing assumptions. It may be argued that, as disturbing as it may be for targeted persons, hate speech is mainly about people needing to express their frustrations and distorted views of certain social groups. Characterizing slogans as *hate speech* mainly refers to it as "a way in which one or another racist or Islámophobic element "lets off steam", as it were, venting the hatred that is boiling up inside".[14]

Or the argumentation may instead, more convincingly I think, take as a starting point that hateful expressions are mainly about rallying support for actions intended to drive certain people away, expel them or threaten them in such a way that they withdraw from society. Based on this assumption, hate speech should be understood as *speech that attacks human dignity and incites discrimination, hostility or violence against certain groups to drive them away or underground.*

Supposing that this understanding of hate speech is correct; how then to understand *religious* hate speech? The term 'religious' clearly indicates that religious belief plays a substantial role for those who express hate or that their role as representatives of religious institutions, religious leaders or adherents plays a part. The hate speech must be motivated, propagated or framed by persons in their capacity of belonging to a religious group or belief system. Typically, a monk, a minister or an imam express religious hate by attacking members of other religions or different interpretations of their religion or groups of society that adhere to lifestyles they deem to be sinful, such as members of LGBTI communities.

It may also take the form of attacking those who criticize, make caricatures or ridicule religion, as illustrated by the *Jyllands-Posten Muhammad cartoons controversy* in 2005–2006. The Danish newspaper Jyllands-Posten published 12 editorial cartoons on 30 September 2005, depicting the Prophet Mohammad. The newspaper presented this as a contribution to the debate about criticism of Islám and self-censorship. Muslim groups in Denmark complained and there

---

13 Waldron, 2012, p. 2, see *supra* note 8.

14 *Ibid.*

were worldwide protests, which included hate speech, deadly violence and riots in some Muslim countries.

One of the publications that printed the cartoons was the French satirical magazine *Charlie Hebdo*. On 7 January 2015, two gunmen attacked the Paris offices of the magazine, killing 12 people, including senior editorial staff members, in retribution for the magazine's provocative portrayals of the Prophet.[15]

Another prominent example is the *fatwá* (legal opinion) against the Indian-born British writer Salman Rushdie (1947–) because of his depiction of a character modelled after the Prophet Mohammad in his novel *Satanic Verses* (1988). On 14 February 1989, the spiritual leader of Iran, Ayatollah Ruhollah Khomeini (1902–1989), publicly condemned the book and issued a *fatwá* against Rushdie. A bounty of USD 3 million was offered to anyone who would execute him. Even though the Iranian government stated, in 1998, that it would not enforce the *fatwá*, a quasi-official foundation added USD 500,000 to the bounty in 2012.

In August 2022, Rushdie was attacked and seriously injured in Chautauqua, New York. The attacker, Hadi Mater, 24 years of age, motivated his actions by referring to Rushdie as "someone who had attacked Islam, he attacked their beliefs, the belief systems".[16] The official reaction by the Iranian government was to deny any link to the attack, while underlining that freedom of speech did not justify Rushdie's insulting of Islám:

> In this attack, we do not consider anyone other than Salman Rushdie and his supporters worthy of blame and even condemnation.
>
> By insulting the sacred matters of Islam and crossing the red lines of more than 1.5 billion Muslims and all followers of the divine religions, Salman Rushdie has exposed himself to the anger and rage of the people.[17]

Since religious leaders may play important political roles, alongside being authorities on religious matters, religious hate speech can have substantial political repercussions. As has been the case in Myanmar, India, and current conflicts between Russia and Ukraine, religious leaders may play the role of political ringleaders, mobilizing support for violent or military actions to chase away

[15] Nicki Peter Petrikowski, "Charlie Hebdo Shooting", in *Encyclopedia Britannica*, 19 September 2025.

[16] "Sir Salman Rushdie attack suspect 'only read two pages' of Satanic Verses", *BBC News*, 18 August 2022.

[17] Statement by Iran's foreign ministry spokesperson Nasser Kanaani, quoted in "Salman Rushdie: Iran Blames Writer and Supporters for Stabbing", *BBC News*, 15 August 2022. According to some observers, the *fatwá* against Salman Rushdie contributed to radicalizing an entire generation of Muslims, both Shí'ah and Sunní. See Kunwar Khuldune Shahid, "Iran's Rushdie Fatwa Radicalized an Entire Generation of Muslims", *Haaretz*, 15 August 2022.

or subjugate targeted groups. Muslims have been targeted by Buddhist nationalists in Myanmar and Hindu nationalists in India.[18] Despite Hindus constituting 81 per cent of the population in India, Hindu hate speech is becoming increasingly widespread,[19] claiming that "Muslims pose an imminent threat to Hindus in India, and seek to undermine Hindu interests through several conspiracies. Thus, Hindus must unite against their common enemy, that is, Muslims".[20]

In the Russia–Ukraine conflict, Russian Orthodox leaders have supported military action against Ukraine while denouncing the establishment of an independent Ukrainian Orthodox Church. In a sermon on 6 March 2022, Russian Orthodox Patriarch Kirill depicted the ongoing war in spiritual terms: "We have entered into a struggle that has not a physical, but a metaphysical significance". He contended that some of the Donbas separatists were suffering for their "fundamental rejection of the so-called values that are offered today by those who claim world power". According to him, this unnamed world power is posing a "test for the loyalty" of countries by demanding they hold gay pride parades to join a global club of nations with its ideas of freedom and "excess consumption".[21]

Throughout history, hate speech and violence against members of different interpretations or representatives of independent institutions within the same religion happened frequently. The conflict between the Moscow and Kyiv Patriarchates is a new chapter in that long and brutal history.

Is religious hate speech different from hate speech motivated by non-religious ideologies or racist ideas? There may be a few factors that make preventing and remedying religious hate speech especially hard. Since religious beliefs are often deeply rooted and part of a shared culture, it may be exceedingly

[18] Amresh Lavan Gunashingham, "Myanmar's Extreme Buddhist Nationalists", *The Interpreter*, 21 September 2021. Sameer Yasir, "As Hindu Extremists Call for Killing of Muslims, India's Leaders Keep Silent", *The New York Times*, 24 December 2021.

[19] See Madan B. Lokur and Shruti Narayan, "Reflections on Freedom of Expression, Hate Speech and Sedition in India", in Morten Bergsmo and Kishan Manocha (eds.), *Religion, Hateful Expression and Violence*, TOAEP, Brussels, 2023, pp. 167 ff. (https://www.toaep.org/ps-pdf/41-bergsmo-manocha/); Medha Damojipurapu, "Patterns and Risks in Contemporary Religion-Based Hate Speech in India", in *id.*, pp. 209 ff.; and Usha Tandon and Harleen Kaur, "Religion-Based Hate Speech or Free Speech: Indian Courts in a Quandary", in *id.*, pp. 279 ff.

[20] Medha Damojipurapu, "Language, Themes and Responses to Hate Speech in India", Policy Brief Series No. 132 (2022), TOAEP, Brussels, 2022, p. 4 (https://www.toaep.org/pbs-pdf/132-damojipurapu/).

[21] Jonathan Luxmoore, "After Supporting Ukraine Invasion, Russia's Patriarch Kirill Criticized Worldwide", *National Catholic Reporter* ('*NCR*'), 15 March 2022; and Peter Smith, "Russia's Patriarch Kirill Defends Invasion of Ukraine, Stoking Orthodox Tensions", *NCR*, 8 March 2022. See also Jason Horowitz, "The Russian Orthodox Leader at the Core of Putin's Ambitions", *The New York Times*, 21 May 2022.

difficult to convince adherents to change their course. Religious leaders are often highly respected, making it hard to persuade followers that they are wrong. Even secular courts and governments may find it difficult – and sometimes wrong – to go against religious leaders. Criticism from outsiders may be dismissed simply because religious leaders perceive it to be against religion and spiritual values.

2.3. Searching for Solutions

The role of religion in conflicts is nuanced and complex, depending on the context. Other factors may play more prominent roles in escalating disputes and violence. There exists, nevertheless, a widespread realization that religion matters in many of today's conflicts, both as conflict drivers and in efforts to solve them. Religion, it seems, can be a part of both the problem and the solution.

Linked to this realization is a second one concerning the understanding of religion as such. Religion is doctrine and values upheld by leaders, institutions, authoritative interpretations of scriptures, as well as efforts by theologians at adaption of core doctrines to new circumstances. A 'functional' one supplements this 'substantive' aspect of religion, that is, how doctrine, ritual, procedural rules and loyalty to a religious community affect individual or group behaviour, thoughts and choices.[22] It follows that religious leaders may need not only to understand religious doctrine and criticize misinterpretations, but must also excel in knowing community dynamics, loyalties and power structures within religious networks to confront hate speech effectively. The role of religion in conflicts may depend as much on its 'functional' as its 'substantive' aspects.

Another critical issue is the relationship between 'modernity' and 'religion'. In analysing religious fundamentalism, Ernest Gellner (1925–1995) defined it as the view that "faith is to be upheld firmly in its full and literal form, free of compromise, softening, re-interpretation or diminution. It presupposes that the core of religion is a doctrine, rather than ritual and that this doctrine can be fixed with precision and finality, which further presupposes writing".[23] The secularization thesis held that religion would gradually lose its influence in modern industrial societies, soften its edges progressively and lead to the religious doctrine being adapted to scientifically rooted life views; this, however, has not happened. Fundamentalism in the name of Islám has gained substantial popular support, in several cases in the form of intolerant and sometimes violent political ideology, based on particular and in no way uncontested interpretations of

---

[22] Sara Silvistri and James Mayall, *The Role of Religion in Conflict and Peace Building*, British Academy, 2015, p. 6.

[23] Ernest Gellner, *Postmodernism, Reason and Religion*, Routledge, London, 1992, p. 2.

Islám.[24] Other world religions also have their versions of fundamentalism, often leading to intolerance, conflict and sometimes violence.

Arguably, the collapse of communism during the late 1980s and the early 1990s has given religion a new upspring in former Soviet and East European countries. Under the slogan of defending 'traditional values', signifying anti-gay, family values and stigmatization of sexual and gender minorities, many governments in Europe, Asia, Africa and the Americas have used religion to mobilize support for policies that leads to increased intolerance. Such policies are often presented as a defence against globalization and harmful foreign influence, strengthening national sovereignty and revising the global order.

Russia has been a regional and global promotor of traditional values, including in the UN Human Rights Council, creating new coalitions of actors in opposition to sexual and gender rights and making respect for human rights dependent on 'responsible behaviour'.[25] In the words of Swedish political scientist Emil Edenberg,

> [t]he idea of Russia as an international beacon of "traditional values" echoes older missionary narratives of Russia's role in the world, such as the pre-revolutionary idea of Moscow as a "Third Rome" embodying true Christianity after the fall of the Roman and Byzantine empires, as well as the Soviet rhetoric of liberating workers across the world […]. [T]he Russian state's turn to "traditional values" does not merely represent a defensive and inward-looking reaction to globalisation and perceived threats to established norms of gender and sexuality. On the contrary, this move constitutes an element of an activist and revisionist foreign policy, a soft power initiative that sends a message about Russia's importance in world affairs, as a purported leader in a transnational conservative axis.[26]

These developments point to significant challenges for human rights-based approaches to mobilizing religious leaders against hate speech, as pointed out in Morten Bergsmo's concept note for the Centre for International Law Research

[24] Marit Tjomsland, "A Discussion of Three Theoretical Approaches to Modernity: Understanding Modernity as a Globalising Phenomenon", CMI Working Paper No. 2 (1996), Chr. Michelsen Institute, Bergen, 1996, p. 10. See also, Mustafa Akyol, *Islam Without Extremes: A Muslim Case for Liberty*, W.W. Norton & Company, New York, 2013.

[25] For an account of Russia's attempts to redefine human rights in the UN Human Rights Council, see Maggi Murphy, "'Traditional Values' vs Human Rights at the UN", *OpenDemocracy*, 18 February 2013 (available on its web site).

[26] Emil Edenberg, "Homophobia as Geopolitics: 'Traditional Values' and the Negotiation of Russia's Place in the World", in Jon Mulholland, Nicola Montagna and Erin Sanders-McDonagh (eds.), *Gendering Nationalism*, Palgrave Macmillan, 2018, p. 78.

and Policy's research project on 'Religion, Hateful Expression and Violence'.[27] Fundamentalists, nationalists or specific schools of conservative religious leaders may not share the values and principles of human rights. Convincing them to become religious human rights defenders may prove exceedingly difficult. Such leaders may perceive international human rights as Western, secular and alien to their faith. Religious leaders embracing human rights are easier to attract, but their impact may be limited to those who already refrain from hate speech.

An alternative or supplementary approach, to be presented in the following, would be to mobilize *internal* normative bases against hate speech, assuming that world religions contain interpretative resources to fight hate directed against non-believers, those who believe differently or those who adhere to perceived sinful lifestyles. Detecting such resources may be an essential first step and fertilize the ground for introducing comprehensive human rights approaches at later stages.

For any approach, misuse of religion by political leaders remains a significant obstacle. Autocratic political leaders who use religion to build support for conflict-oriented and intolerant policies may meet religious leaders who actively prevent hate speech with hostility. Most democratic states restrict hate speech by law, particularly incitement to violence or discrimination. At the same time, courts in these countries try to strike a proper balance between such restrictions and legal norms to uphold freedom of expression. In authoritarian environments, religious leaders cannot rely on state authorities to comply with such norms, playing their part in restricting hate speech while upholding the right to freedom of expression.

The UN and other intergovernmental organizations have invested heavily in developing a human rights approach to fighting religious hate speech and violence, including the involvement of religious leaders in developing action plans and measures to prevent the misuse of religion. However, these plans do seldom challenge religious leaders to refer to broader normative bases outside human rights to act.

2.4. Broader Normative Bases

In the following sections, I discuss a few examples of such normative bases.

[27] Centre for International Law Research and Policy (CILRAP), "Religion, Hateful Expression and Violence: 'CILRAP Concept and Programme, 220408-09 Conference (as of 220405)'", p. 2 (https://www.cilrap.org/events/220408-09-florence/). See also UN Office on Genocide Prevention and the Responsibility to Protect, "Plan of Action for Religious Leaders/Actors from the Asia-Pacific Region to Prevent Incitement to Violence that Could Lead to Atrocity Crimes", 7 December 2016 (https://www.legal-tools.org/doc/lc4g5j/).

2.4.1. Internal Normative Bases Against Hate Speech

The Western Enlightenment period introduced a lasting shift in the role of religion. It is true that the death of religion (or God), as proclaimed by Friedrich Nietzsche (1844–1900), never occurred. Religion has survived despite philosophers' and scientists' critical assessments of its foundations and role in society. As stated by Morten Bergsmo, "rather than solemnly burying God, sixty-six years after Nietzsche's madman pronounced God dead, nations of the world raised a normative shield by declaring that 'everyone has the right to freedom of [...] religion'" in the 1948 Universal Declaration of Human Rights.[28]

However, an enduring result of the Enlightenment and the rise of science is that Christianity gradually lost its status as the provider of *moral knowledge* in the Western world. Development took place, which resulted in the fact that there currently exists no moral *knowledge* or a 'science of ethics', as framed by American philosopher Dallas Willard (1935–2013).[29] He insists that even if many persons can provide clear outlines of their moral convictions, moral questions do not make up the subject matter of any systematic discipline that extends our moral knowledge by appealing to reason and evidence. Unlike scientific disciplines concerning non-normative issues, there is no institutional home for objective moral inquiry.

This situation is different from previous times. As late as 1903, the great English moral philosopher George E. Moore (1873–1958) compared disagreements in ethics to those in arithmetic. We are not surprised, he pointed out, when there is a disagreement about the solution to a problem in arithmetic. We assume that there was a mistake somewhere and seek to locate it. It is similar in ethics, according to Moore. When we disagree, "though [...] we cannot prove that we are right, yet we have reason to believe that everybody, unless he is mistaken as to what he thinks, will think the same as we", once we have clarity on the question being asked.[30] The only difference is that in ethics, "owing to the intricacy of its subject matter, it is far more difficult to persuade anyone either that he has made a mistake or that that mistake affects his result".[31]

Moore's ethical-philosophical programme thus presupposed that the science of ethics existed. Knowledge of moral reality was achievable by sensible and thoughtful people, a conviction he shared with other philosophers at his time.

[28] CILRAP, 2022, p. 2, see *supra* note 27.

[29] Dallas Willard, Steven L. Porter, Aaron Preston and Gregg A. Ten Elshof (eds.), *The Disappearance of Moral Knowledge*, Routledge, New York, 2018.

[30] G.E. Moore, *Principia Ethica*, Dover Publications, Mineola, 2004, p. 123.

[31] *Ibid.*

This conception is not around any longer and has not been for some time. During the twentieth century, ethics and its foundations became increasingly fragmented in the West and, due to Western influence, in other parts of the world. The role of Christianity and philosophy as sources of a compelling moral theory gave way to a plurality of approaches influenced by political ideologies and diverse philosophical or religiously inspired doctrines. The closest one that comes to a *universally* accepted set of norms today may be international human rights, interpreted not only as a body of legal norms, but as a statement by the international community of binding moral values.

When a compelling body of rational and evidence-based knowledge of morality does not exist, the risk is that too much is left to demagogues and interest-based approaches. Over time, this situation may have unfortunate consequences. A quotation from the preface to Willard's book on the disappearance of moral knowledge by Scott Soames (1945–) summarizes the situation well:

> Because morality is central to human life, we will always be concerned with it. The issue isn't whether we will pursue what we take to be moral, but how we will do so. Without the discipline and humanity forced on us by rational, evidence-based inquiry, we too easily become blind to our own moral limitations and intolerant of those who don't march in lockstep with us. As a result, purported answers to contentious moral questions come to be treated as moral certainties about which there can be no debate. Since no single moral perspective dominates all the others in society, intimidation, coercion, and condescension fill the gap left by the absence of moral reasoning.[32]

How we ended up in this situation is a complex story. The shift from the firm belief held by philosophers from Socrates, Plato and Aristotle to George E. Moore and shared by theologians and politicians until the twentieth century, holding that moral knowledge existed and should guide the actions of individuals and societies, did not give way to the present disbelief due to specific discoveries or the presentation of definite arguments. Willard suggests several factors that led to a gradual change in perceptions that resulted in the current situation, such as the abdication of God as a guarantor of morality, the realization that moral principles and behaviour vary according to culture and shifts in perceptions of the human self, which is no longer seen as an integrated and rational agent capable of being the subject of moral knowledge.[33]

The French Enlightenment philosopher Marquis de Condorcet (1743–1794) predicted that a moment would come when the Sun only shines over "free

[32] Willard, 2018, p. viii, see *supra* note 29.

[33] *Ibid.*, pp. 8–18.

people, who will not have any other master than their own reason".[34] His utterly optimistic view about the future of human society and well-being included progress in science and technology as well as in morals and in creating peaceful societies. Everything he detested would be overcome, such as slavery, repression and inequality. Medicine would keep humans healthy and society would be rid of friction and conflicts. Knowledge about how one can avoid conflicts and achieve results that benefit all would be incorporated into the laws and disseminated to the citizens.

Looking at today's world, one must conclude that only half of Condorcet's vision has come true. Science and technology ('hard' Enlightenment) have even outperformed his imagination of what would be achieved, while developments in morals and society ('soft' Enlightenment) lag far behind.[35] This is the broader picture that must be considered when pointing to the need for religious leaders to mobilize against hate speech and violence in the name of their religions. They must be specific in addressing hate speech, but they must also consider how they can contribute to a wider strengthening of a shared morality against hate and violence. They must mobilize the ability to see the humanity and dignity present in all human beings.

Based on the above outline of the disappearance of moral knowledge and the failure of 'soft' Enlightenment, I argue that religious leaders should refer to religiously inspired universalist ethical teachings in addressing expressions of hate and violence. They should not only refer to scriptures and teachings specific to their religion, but to teachings that present fundamental ethical values valid for all.

Doing so, they help build that 'bridge upon which we can meet and talk'. They may also, in this way, provide elements for that 'science of ethics' which is much needed to confront abuse of religion in formulating slogans and hate speech.

---

[34] Marquis de Condorcet, *Esquisse d'un tableau historique des progrés de l'esprit humaine*, Masson et Fils Libraires, Paris, 1822, p. 271. The full quotation in French reads: "Il arrivera donc ce moment où le soleil n'éclairera plus sur la terre que des hommes libres, et ne reconnaissant d'autre maître que leur raison".

[35] Sven-Eric Liedman, Swedish historian of ideas, has called the two aspects of Condorcet's vision of human progress 'hard' and 'soft' Enlightenment. Condorcet conceptualized the Enlightenment project "as an indissoluble unity. In reality, however, hard enlightenment can work without the soft one". Sven-Eric Liedman, *Den moderne verdens idéhistorie: I skyggen av fremtiden* [*The Modern World's History of Ideas: In the Shadow of the Future*], Dreyers forlag, Oslo, 2016, p. 27.

2.4.2. Religiously Inspired Universalist Ethical Teachings

The essential values to be mobilized in preventing hate speech include respect for 'humanity' or 'dignity' inherent in every human being, treating neighbours and foreigners well, and tolerating people or communities who adhere to different beliefs or lifestyles. Such values promote equal treatment of human beings in some fundamental respects, although not all. Refraining from hate speech and violence does not mean that you must treat all humans equally in all respects, although this maximalist ideal is inherent in some religious teachings.

In the following, I present two protestant theologians and philosophers who contributed decisively to developing *ethics of individual responsibility and integrity*, inspired by Christianity but presented within the realm of philosophy and thus intended to be valid for anyone – religious or non-religious.[36] Inherent in their thinking are criteria to detect abuse of religion – by religious institutions, politicians and demagogues.

2.4.2.1. Søren Kierkegaard's Analysis of Existence

Danish religious philosophy has a personalistic and nearness-to-life approach as one of its most noticeable characteristics. Søren Kierkegaard is a great representative of this type of criticism and the prevailing thinking of his time (that is, the first part of the nineteenth century) which centred around state, church and society membership as the way for the individual to attain a meaningful life and salvation. 'Being Danish equals being Christian and in alignment with God' is a somewhat simplified summary of this mode of thinking. At the elite level in the Church, academia and among a wider circle of intellectuals, the sentiment was heavily influenced by Georg W.F. Hegel's (1770–1831) philosophy and conception of religion as a form of self-consciousness and a pre-stage to the absolute form of knowledge attained in philosophy.

Kierkegaard's philosophy is complex, explicated in an impressive sequence of books published between 1838 and 1855 by many pseudonyms and sometimes in Kierkegaard's name, either as an author, editor or publisher.[37]

---

[36] The analysis of human existence to be found in Kierkegaard, and later in Martin Heidegger's (1889–1976) work *Sein und Zeit* [*Being and Time*], 1927, was influenced by the New Testament of the Bible, St. Augustine (354–430), and Martin Luther (1483–1546) and their accounts of the Christian proclamation. K.E. Løgstrup, *Kierkegaard's and Heidegger's Analysis of Existence and Its Relation to Proclamation: Translated with an Introduction and Notes by Robert Stern*, Oxford University Press, 2020, p. 75. The book was based on lectures held by Løgstrup at the Freie Universität in Berlin and first published in German as *Kierkegaards und Heideggers Existenzanalyse und ihr Verhältnis zur Verkündigung*, Erich Blaschker Verlag, Berlin, 1950.

[37] The whole spectre of Kierkegaard's authorship, including both his published and unpublished books, his extensive journals, notes and papers is available online on the web site of Søren

Extremely well-written as his books are, they nevertheless represent severe difficulties for the reader to fully apprehend their meaning and significance. He is not a philosopher who presents a view and then argues in favour of it. Instead, his texts include a variety of styles and the different pseudonymous authors refer to and argue with each other. 'Indirect communication', is Kierkegaard's term for this authorship practice, which is inspired by Socrates' (470–399 BC) way of challenging his fellow Athenians by asking uncomfortable questions to detect misconceptions and inspire awareness of what can be known and what cannot. One of the results is that scholarship on, and influence by Kierkegaard, is vast and presents conflicting interpretations.

In the following, I restrict myself to focusing on Kierkegaard's analysis of human existence, including his concepts of the 'philistine' ('*Spidsborger*', from the German '*Spiessbürger*'), 'aesthetic', 'ethical' and 'religious' stages on life's way ('modes of existence', 'archetypes' or 'life views', as scholars tend to term them). Kierkegaard tells stories and stages various archetypical figures to show the reader how life can unfold, depending on which life view one has. The multiple characters' foremost task is to elicit self-knowledge in the reader, not to teach a lesson. There is no necessity to develop from one stage to another. However, there is no doubt that the religious stages in Kierkegaard's view represent the possibility for the individual to attain selfhood and escape from 'life in the crowd'. However, acquiring a new life view is always based on the individual's decisions and passionate striving to attain the truth.[38]

The precondition for Kierkegaard's expositions is his conception that humans are born with the possibility of becoming human beings entirely or becoming 'a self', as he explains in *The Sickness unto Death* (1849). He defines humans as a synthesis of 'soul' and 'body', the latter including the whole physical environment, which they are conscious of in 'reflection'. But humans are also a synthesis of 'infinity' and 'finitude', 'eternity' and 'temporality'. The self as a synthesis of body and soul refers to humans beings aware of their dual nature. In contrast, the relation between infinity and finitude refers to how the individual, through their *actions*, 'relates itself to itself'. In its actions, the individual responds to an *infinite demand*, which is how 'eternity' is present in

Kierkegaards Skrifter. His published and unpublished writings as well as his journals and notebooks are available in English translation, *inter alia*, in the Princeton University Press series *Kierkegaard's Writings* and *Kierkegaard's Journals and Notebooks*. For further information, see "Søren Kierkegaard", Princeton University Press.

38 The 'aesthetic' and 'ethical' stages are presented by the pseudonymous author and publisher Victor Eremita in *Either/Or: A Fragment of Life* (1843) and by Hilarius Bogbinder, publisher of *Stages on Life's Way* (1844). The religious stage is presented in *Fear and Trembling* (1843) by Johannes De Silentio. Both the publishers and the authors of different parts of these books are pseudonyms. The real author is Søren Kierkegaard.

human existence and by which a human being can become a self. It is through the self's response to the infinite demand, in a decision to obey or disobey it, that its relation to the infinite, God, is determined.[39]

Humans' relationship to God or eternity is not about cognition, as in speculative philosophy, but about action. Being a human means not only being conscious or knowledgeable, but rather that your existence is of fundamental concern to you. It is about being an ethical individual, placed in a decision-making situation by relating to the infinite demand. The demand does not come from outside the person; rather, it is a part of being human. It is, therefore, inescapable.

According to Kierkegaard, humans are metaphysically ambiguous beings. He is not alone in holding this conception of humans as having an inherent connection to eternity, as Platonism and various theological strands maintain. In the Bible, conceptions of humans being created by God include that eternity still has a place in their hearts, despite their sinful state. Genesis 1:26 teaches that every human being possesses the image of God. Ecclesiastes 3:11 declares that God has "set eternity in the hearts of men", while in Luke 17:21, Jesus proclaims, "The kingdom of God is within you". The apostle Paul teaches that every human being possesses an immaterial soul-spirit and that it is this part of us that connects with God (Hebrews 4:12).

However, Kierkegaard's view is that eternity's presence in human beings is not in the form of the knowledge of God, but as an infinite demand for our existence. This demand has not the form of a command, that is, God telling humans to do certain things. The infinite demand does not have a specified content; it is rather *a demand that the individual expresses in existing, that they can do nothing themselves but is nothing before God.* Only by honouring this demand can the individual become a self and regain his life in society without being subject to life in the crowd.

The *philistines*, however, have not realized the possibility of becoming a self. Their way of life is characterized by never questioning whether life or society could be different. They are not aware of their choices, but let society's values and norms determine which path they choose to take. They flow with the flow and live up to the environment's expectations, doing like the others. The philistines think they have made their choices, but they have not. They are simply a product of the society they are part of. They cannot choose and are not aware that they have a choice. They let circumstances choose for them, are unaware of themselves, and live their life without passion and genuine commitment.

[39] Løgstrup, 2020, Chapter 2, see *supra* note 36.

The *aesthetes* have realized that they have a choice and depart from the philistine way of life. However, according to Kierkegaard, their life is still marked by the despair of not wanting to be themselves, not choosing themselves "in their eternal validity", as he phrases it.[40] They are not bound by the norms of society, but consider life and others with an ironic distance. Despite all the cultural events they attend, they are eventually plagued by boredom and despair. They choose based on desire, sensuality, possibilities and the projected exciting outcome of their adventures. They cannot or will not make binding choices. Instead, they choose based on what they feel like in a given moment. Preoccupied with the exterior, beauty, fun and enjoyment, they stage themselves in different roles about what they want to achieve. They do not concern themselves with their actions' moral and ethical aspects, living a non-committal life without engaging with others or taking responsibility for the society of which they are a part. Love relations are based on lust and desire rather than commitment and responsibility.

The *ethicists*, on the other hand, perceive life as a task and have discovered life's inner and ethical dimensions. They choose out of duty and take responsibility for themselves and their choices without leaving out feelings, passion and love. Such unstable emotions, however, need support and direction by decisions based on duty. They stand by their choices and live a committed, moral, meaningful and duty-fulfilling life without hidden agendas for their surroundings and those closest to them.

The ethicists commit to themselves, their families, work and the community. They enforce the rules and norms around which society is built because they choose to participate actively in the culture of which they are part. In their view, God is behind its norms and provides for their validity.

Even for ethicists, however, life is not without anxiety and despair. They are, in a way, desperate to be themselves and fulfil their responsibilities. They are anxious about the consequences of their choices because they stand alone with the duties and responsibilities for themselves and their actions. There is a risk that the norms and responsibilities will crush them. They realize that it is difficult to live up to all the demands they set on themselves. They feel guilty about their mistakes and that there are things in the world they cannot change.

Ultimately, the ethicist may enter the *religious* stage, taking comfort in the idea that we are always wronged against God. The *religious* see themselves as created by God, the greatest all-embracing love that stands above society's norms. They see themselves as part of something bigger. God forgives and loves

[40] Victor Eremita (pseudonym of Søren A. Kierkegaard), *Either/Or: A Fragment of Life, 1843, Abridged, Translated and with an Introduction and Notes by Alastair Hannay*, Penguin Classics, London, 1992, p. 499.

man unconditionally when he chooses to perceive himself as created by God and receive life as a gift and task.

The religious person leaps into the 70,000 fathoms of water and starts believing that God is the possibility in the impossible and that humans are created by something greater than themselves. God can forgive guilt and creates coherence and peace in their lives. God is the foundation the ethicists sought when they realized they could not change the world's cruelties. Neither the many rules they set up for themselves nor sublime humour was enough for them to step into character as themselves.

For Kierkegaard, the paradox of faith is that the individual is higher than the general. On this point, he opposes Hegel, who places the individual under society's norms and rules, as the ethicist exemplifies in his version of the Hegelian concept of '*Sittlichkeit*', or living according to the prevailing social norms.[41] These social norms are used to justify or prohibit actions within a community. For Kierkegaard, Christian faith is a matter of individual subjective passion, which cannot be mediated by the clergy, human artefacts or thinking. Faith is the most critical task for a human being because only based on faith does an individual have a chance to become an authentic self, to escape from living in the crowd. This self is the lifework that God judges for eternity.

The individual is thus subject to a heavy burden of responsibility. Humans are not only responsible for validating the prevailing norms through their primordial choice as the ethicists prescribe. The existential choice or leap of faith, without proof or even against reason, "by virtue of the absurd", as Johannes De Silentio (the pseudonymous author of *Fear and Trembling* (1843)) terms it, determines one's eternal salvation or damnation.

The concept of faith as holding certain dogmas to be true is thus replaced by Kierkegaard as a 'way of life', as 'a form of the will'. In *Fear and Trembling*, the emphasis on acting rather than thinking or reasoning is highlighted by the sheer irrationality of Abraham's faith, his belief, 'by virtue of the absurd', that he will get Isaac back when God asks him to sacrifice him.[42] Thus, faith cannot be reduced to a form of preliminary expressions of knowledge that philosophy or science can express better and more coherently. Kierkegaard believed that Christian civilization had effaced the true meaning of Christianity. Becoming a

41 See William McDonald's description of 'The Ethical stage' in "Søren Kierkegaard", in Edward N. Zalta (ed.), *The Stanford Encyclopedia of Philosophy*, Winter 2017 Edition, 2017; and Merold Westphal, "Kierkegaard and Hegel", in Alastair Hannay and Gordon M. Mariono (eds.), *The Cambridge Companion to Kierkegaard*, Cambridge University Press, 1998, Chapter 4.

42 Johannes De Silentio is referring to the story of Genesis 22:1–18.

Christian had once entailed significant risk, but over time it had been reduced to merely being born to Christian parents in a Christian nation.[43]

Anxiety or dread ('*Angest*'), as outlined in *The Concept of Anxiety* (1844), is the presentiment of this freedom and responsibility when the individual stands at the threshold of momentous existential choice, as well as the Christian concept of 'sin', which together with 'absolute guilt' characterizes human standing in relation to God. The individual creates, through temporal choice, a self, which will be judged for eternity. Anxiety may be seen as the *symptom* of this freedom to choose oneself, not in a fantastic way, but within the social context and the human capabilities given to a specific person. 'Despair', another important Kierkegaardian concept outlined in *The Sickness unto Death* (1849), is when we instead attempt to be rid of ourselves.

Underpinning Kierkegaard's analysis is, as already noted, the view that in order to become a self, the individual must avoid "living a life that is governed by others and so is inauthentic, trapped within the humdrum and the mundane – a life in the crowd".[44] A person living in the crowd "finds being himself too risky, finds it much easier and safer to be like the others, to become a copy, a number, along with the crowd".[45] In this way, the person has allowed himself to be "cheated of its self by 'the others'".[46] Kierkegaard uses value-laden words about this situation, underlining that the person in this way may gain "all that is required for a flawless performance in everyday life, yes, for making a great success out of life. Here there is no dragging of the feet, no difficulty with his self and its infinitizing, he is ground as smooth as a pebble, as exchangeable as a coin of the realm".[47]

This happens because temporal and worldly interests imprison human beings. Going under in the crowd presupposes that the human being is bound to the earthly in an immediate way, in which their whole life goes on. They put themselves in "an absolute relation only to relative ends", as stated in Kierkegaard's seminal philosophical work, *Unconcluding Scientific Postscript* (1946).

From this, it follows that one can never make a proper decision in this life. That decision, which is essentially only to be found in the individual, is sought after outside the self, in the opinion of the social environment, in public opinion and village gossip. In this life, there is only *action without any decision*, an

43 See Ronald M. Green, "'Developing' Fear and Trembling", in Hannay and Mariono (eds.), 1998, Chapter 10, see *supra* note 41.

44 Robert Stern, "Introduction", in Løgstrup, 2020, p. xviii, see *supra* note 36.

45 Søren Kierkegaard, *The Sickness unto Death*, Penguin Books, 2004, p. 61.

46 *Ibid.*

47 *Ibid.*

action whose only point is that something in a superficial sense is accomplished as an undertaking.

2.4.2.2. Kierkegaardian Takeaways

Kierkegaard's analysis of human existence and the possibilities for humans to become a self puts some constraints on any religious proclamation, life or worldview. As Enlightenment philosophers put constraints on religions based on science and reason, Kierkegaard presents correspondence with the formal structure of human existence as preconditions for humans to become adherent freely and based on their comprehension of the proclamation. While in earlier times, philosophy made constraints on religious proclamation in the name of reason, Kierkegaard made it in the name of existence.[48]

Existence puts humans in a decision situation. They may choose to run away from this or to live as there is no demand on them. But living in this way is life in the loss of oneself. Humans may refer to their place in society, serving important institutions, or being members of religious or political movements as sufficient determinations of their meaning of life. But according to Kierkegaard, this is despair or not wanting to accept human life as it is, a life of responsibility, becoming, movement and repetition of choices.

While humans may become part of religious practices by being introduced to them and trained as children, they must still answer individually about why they adhere to a particular religion. In Kierkegaard, being religious by default does not exist. Everyone must choose for themselves.

While the content of religion cannot be demonstrated, it must nevertheless be comprehensible. The fundamental relationship between philosophy and religion in Kierkegaard is that:

> the content of [religious] proclamation [must] correspond to the purely formal structure of human existence, that it lets itself be understood in the formal/empty determinations that result from the analysis of the structure of human existence. If that is not the case, if the proclamation is not comprehensible in the sense that the inner structure of existence is graspable, then the receiving or accepting of a proclamation would either involve allowing others to impose it upon one or imposing it on oneself. Faith without understanding is not faith, but coercion; the individual then imposes the proclamation on themselves not because they take it up and accept it for the sake of its content, but for other and therefore illegitimate motives. If a proclamation is not comprehensible in the sense that it corresponds to the structure of human existence, what would the

[48] Løgstrup, 2020, p. 75, see *supra* note 36. In the following, I render the main points of Løgstrup's interpretation of how philosophy and religion relate in Kierkegaard.

> difference then be between proclamation and obscure superstition? Philosophy as the analysis of existence can therefore serve to distinguish between faith and coercion.[49]

If there is an argument for the truth of Christianity in Kierkegaard, it is precisely based on his description of how its proclamation corresponds to the formal structure of human existence. Its truth cannot be objective and certain, but rather is paradoxical and even absurd. A religion presenting itself as objectively certain would make the existence wholly indifferent. The point here is, however, not to render Kierkegaard's argument for Christianity comprehensible, but to show how his philosophical analysis of existence puts forward constraints on any religion or life-view.

These constraints can be expressed in a series of questions:

1. Does the religious proclamation "leave the individual at the mercy of the crowd, or does it insist that the person who receives it lives their life as an individual"?[50]
2. "Does the proclamation seduce the human being into committing themselves to what has been realised, or does its content insist that the addressee remain true to the character of their existence as becoming and possibility"?
3. Does the proclamation let "the relation of the individual to the absolute [God] be hidden from the outsider, from the third"?
4. Does the proclamation "give human beings an absolute certainty in their life and actions", or does it make "clear to the individual that they must live their life in uncertainty, in their responsibility, and their own guilt"?

If the proclamation does not leave the individual in uncertainty, having to rely on their understanding of how to realize their relationship with the absolute or God,

> the absolute and radical would become transformed and garbled into an idea, a principle, and a value; in other words, it would then be something thought, the product of reason or thought. And as thought, it would be a system, and ideology or a utopia.

Subordinating existence to thought effectively eliminates the human as an existing being. Instead, they would become mere tools for realizing a programme or a belief system. Their insight, humanity, personal commitment and the decision of the existing person would be put out of play. In short, there is a risk of the total dehumanizing of human beings, who become mere agents. If we let thought 'override existence' in this way, everything "can proceed wholly mechanically; only a purely technical calculation is necessary". The absolute and

[49] *Ibid.*, p. 74.

[50] This and the following quotations are from *ibid.*, pp. 75–79.

radical must remain beyond thinking; it must be given with human existence and "cannot be a freely thought-out idea, ideology, utopia, or freely thought-out principle".[51]

In other words, to be true to their existence as decisions, becoming and movement, humans must use their own understanding, insight and humanity to make clear to themselves what to do. There is plenty for thinking and insight to be involved with the "understanding of existence as a becoming, as a permanent possibility, and the connected understanding that the situation is always new and requires new decisions keeps thinking alive".

An important consequence of subordinating existence to thinking is contempt for the other human being. If one's existence is disregarded for the sake of realizing an idea which has been thought out once and for all, then the existence of the other person will be ignored as well. The subordination of one's own existence will lead to subordination in general. Only if thinking remains subordinate to existence and its infinite demand will thinking stay in the service of finding out what best serves the other. A final question to religious proclamation should therefore be posed:

5. "In proclamation, is the existence of oneself and the other there for the sake of thinking, or is thinking there for the existence of oneself and the other"?

The main takeaway from the Kierkegaardian analysis of existence is a consequential challenge to any proclamation in the name of religion: does it pretend that 'the absolute', 'God' or any other word one uses for the highest authority, can be realized in "an absolutely definite action, where one can see that it has been performed in obedience to the absolute because the absolute is a thought-out-ideology or utopia, that subordinates oneself and the existence of other human beings to thinking"?

The alternative, which Kierkegaard and Løgstrup present, is that individuals remain "true to the character of their existence as becoming and possibility". In doing so, they know that what they say and do, in virtue of their relation to the absolute, is said and done on their own responsibility and in complete uncertainty. They make efforts by thinking about how to best act for the sake of their own existence and other human beings. But they can never be sure that they did what was the best.

This is the way of thinking behind Kierkegaard's attack on the Danish Church's proclamation of his time. He criticizes it for leaving the individual to live in the crowd, complaining that it preaches it to be sufficient for someone to be Christian that they are born in a Christian nation, that nothing is disturbing in being Christian because we are all Christians by default. He also charges that

[51] *Ibid.*, p. 78.

ministers of the Church use 'aesthetic' categories in their Christian lectures without distinguishing them from ethical-religious categories.[52]

An important question remains as to whether religious leaders and thinkers should accept that philosophy in this way presents constraints on religious proclamation. Løgstrup presents Kierkegaard's analysis of existence as being influenced by Christian proclamation in the first place and opts for not simply accepting it as authoritative. Instead, a debate should be underway between philosophy and theology: "Ultimately, it is the same human existence, whether it is centred on philosophy or theology. The concern they share ought to allow fruitful interaction to seem wholly natural".[53]

Suppose that religious leaders reject the possibility of a philosophical critique of religious proclamation because the latter is based on revelation or holy scripture. In that case, they then assume that revelation does not need to correspond to the structure of human existence. They thereby claim that the proclamation must neither be rationally nor existentially comprehensible. Then, however, the difference between faith and coercion is annulled.

While Kierkegaard and Løgstrup are wrestling with this question within a Christian context, their conclusion is valid for everyone. If there is no understanding in faith, if it does not correspond to the formal structure of human existence, it is impossible to distinguish it from coercion, brainwashing or superstition.

For Løgstrup, the implication of the philosophical analysis of existence for the relationship between religion and politics is obvious: "Every political use of Christianity, for example, is open to critique by philosophical existence analysis, where Christianity is used as the reason or argument for a particular policy".[54] Of course, religious persons may engage with political issues, but the point is that they cannot deduce their *political* views from their religion. Any human being must use their reason and experiences to arrive at their opinions. Every mixing of religion and politics, each assertion that a specifically Christian, Muslim, Hindu, Buddhist, *et cetera* policy ought to be put forward, is open to criticism based on the philosophical analysis of existence.

The same goes for any purported religious ethics, which must pertain to the same considerations and disagreements as any other ethical knowledge. Religious leaders who assert to have special authorization from God to promote

52 Kierkegaard's series of pamphlets against the Danish Church called 'Øieblikket' ('The Moment') is available in English translation by Howard V. Hong and Edna H. Hong (eds. and trans.), *The Moment and Late Writings: Kierkegaard's Writings, XXIII*, Princeton University Press, 1998.

53 Løgstrup, 2020, p. 80, see *supra* note 36.

54 *Ibid.*, p. 81.

certain principles make God into something given and their relationship with God into a fact, which others may inspect and certify. However, the ethical demand asks us to serve the other person based on our insight and reason. In arguing for what we say and do to be ethically sound, we must refer to our reasons and not to an intention of fulfilling the ethical demand. Our relationship to God and the fulfilment of the ethical demand is a private affair, hidden from others.

Of course, religious leaders may claim that they represent the religious message or the ideals and values derived from that message. But they then make religion into an ideology "that is at one's disposal and can be directly applied and immediately realised".[55] Suppose that one thinks that religion can be reduced to a given set of messages or system of ideas without considering one's relation to them. In that case, religion is "ossified into an ideology that can be applied". The risk is that leaders or adherents start to believe that they are in a position to speak and act with absolute or divine certainty. To be religious would amount to being able to go beyond one's human limitations and to cut themselves off in political and ethical matters from the non-religious or adherents of other religions.

Ossifying religion into ideology includes a great risk that organized religion establishes itself as a political front and supports political leaders that purport to represent the ideology. By way of the analysis of existence and its constraints on religion that I have presented, we have now come to a point where we can address some of the main problems we observe today. Religion is made into an ideology applied to separate and build fronts between people of different creeds and to build political power. Individual responsibility in relationship with God is replaced by responsibility for realizing an ideology which cannot be criticized or debated. Not only is one's own existence disregarded, but also the existence of the other human being, which is subordinated to that which is thought out once and for all.

A further unsound consequence of applying religion in this way, as an ideology that often involves coercion, is that one's conscience may remain completely clean: "it is after all the absolute, for which one bears responsibility that is realised".[56] The limits in our responsibility for others drawn by Kierkegaard and Løgstrup in their existential analysis, based on the fact that each individual has the task to live their lives as individual persons, are disregarded. According to these limits, responsibility for others can never consist in taking away their responsibility. We are all placed in the same human condition, to remain responsible for our own words and actions. From that follows that we have to respect

[55] *Ibid.*, p. 82.

[56] *Ibid.*, p. 84.

that others are responsible for their lives, even though we care for them and want to help them according to our understanding of what is best for them.

In short, humans can never act as God's representatives.

2.4.3. Knud E. Løgstrup's Disclosure of the Ethical Demand

The analysis of human existence by Kierkegaard, Løgstrup and other philosophers inspired by them may help define constraints on religion and the way religion can be abused in politics and ethics. Løgstrup aims, however, to go a step further. He presented Kierkegaard's (and Heidegger's) existential analysis in a book from 1950, on which I have based the previous section.[57] In this book, it was clear, however, that as much he shared Kierkegaard's view that human existence includes an inherent ethical demand, he was not content with how Kierkegaard framed and explicated the demand.

According to Kierkegaard, every human being is a synthesis of temporality and eternity. Eternity is present in existence as an infinite demand, which we relate to either in obedience or disobedience. Unlike Heidegger (and Emmanuel Levinas (1905–1995), with whom Løgstrup has some affinities), Løgstrup agrees with Kierkegaard on this critical point. But while Kierkegaard maintains that the ethical dimension is primarily linked to the individual's relationship with God, for Løgstrup, the ethical demand confronts humans in their social, interdependent and vulnerable life with other human beings. The demand arises from situations where we are responsible for larger or smaller parts of fellow human beings' lives, as he demonstrates in his ground-breaking analysis of primordial 'trust' in encounters between individuals.[58] The demand states that we should care for the other for their own sake, not basing our acts or words on our interests.

Løgstrup's philosophical account of this foundational demand inherent in human existence is expounded in his main work, *The Ethical Demand*, originally published in Danish in 1956.[59] His starting point is – in continuity with

---

[57] See *supra* note 36.

[58] K.E. Løgstrup, *The Ethical Demand: Translated with an Introduction and Notes by Bjørn Rabjerg and Robert Stern*, Oxford University Press, 2020, pp. 67–75 ('*The Ethical Demand*').

[59] The book made Løgstrup 'world famous' in Denmark and the Nordic countries. It is, however, only recently that authoritative translations into English of this and some of his other seminal works on ethics have been published. Oxford University Press publishes a series entitled 'Selected Works of K.E. Løgstrup', which currently consists of four volumes: *Kierkegaard's and Heidegger's Analysis of Existence and its Relation to Proclamation*, see *supra* note 36; *The Ethical Demand*, see *supra* note 58; *Ethical Concepts and Problems: Translated with an Introduction and Notes by Kees van Kooten Niekerk, Kristian-Alberto Lykke Cobos*, Oxford University Press, 2020; and Bjørn Rabjerg and Robert Stern (eds.), *Controverting Kierkegaard*

Kierkegaard and Heidegger – that for a religious proclamation to be relevant and comprehensible, it must correspond to features in our existence. We may be unaware of those features, so we need the proclamation to disclose them. But as soon as we have been made aware of and comprehended them, we can recognize them ourselves without needing a proclamation. We may even accept the features of our existence disclosed by the proclamation while rejecting the proclamation itself. In this way, the religious proclamation has both philosophical contents, revealing features of human existence that can be recognized by anyone regardless of their belief and a purely religious message which is up to everyone who hears it to believe or not.[60]

According to Løgstrup, the proclamation of Jesus of Nazareth touches on one feature of human existence in particular, namely our relation to other human beings. It is this feature that Løgstrup sets out to analyse, "what attitude to the other human being is implicit in Jesus's proclamation?".[61] While there is a content of Jesus' proclamation that "in a wholly ordinary and vague sense of the word is religious", there is also at play "an attitude to the other human being, which, although it is contained within the religious content of the proclamation, could still be formulated in purely human terms".[62]

The attitude that you should love your neighbour and even your enemy, as illustrated by the story about the Good Samaritan, is put in a purely religious context in Jesus' proclamation. It states that the individual's relationship with God is decided through their relationship with another human being. Life is a gift from God, and God wants other human beings to be cared for. However, a precondition for this close relationship can be described in purely human terms, namely that we live our lives in interdependence and entanglement with each other. In Martin Luther's words, we are the 'daily bread' in one another's lives.

In disclosing the ethical demand and its origin in the interdependence of human existence, Løgstrup makes use of the phenomenological method he learned from the German philosopher Hans Lipps (1889–1941), who belonged to the famous Philosophical Society of Göttingen that gathered around Edmund Husserl (1859–1938) and Adolf Reinach (1883–1917). Lipps understood philosophy as a hermeneutics of reality, which is tied up with ordinary language. It is through language that reality, both in terms of objects and human beings, is revealed. The philosophical investigation must therefore follow the hints toward meaning and distinctions embodied in ordinary words and speech, clarifying

---

('Opgør med Kierkegaard', 1968), Oxford University Press, 2023. Throughout this chapter, I refer to these translated versions of Løgstrup's books.

60 *The Ethical Demand*, p. 60, see *supra* note 58.

61 *Ibid.*, p. 62 (*sic.*).

62 *Ibid.*

those hints and explicating the understanding they contain. In contrast to Husserl's theory of the 'ideal unities of significance', Lipps emphasized the undetermined meaning of words and concepts whose exact meaning changes according to the context of the speech situation.[63]

According to Løgstrup, humans tend to treat the world and other human beings as mere means to their ends. We take undue credit for our achievements, but in fact, the features and deeper value structures of human existence can be known to us. Phenomenology, rather than scientific methods, can disclose our misconceptions of who we are and what the world really is. Just as the Christian proclamation can disclose our dependency on others and how we fail to take proper care of them, this can also be made sense of philosophically by applying a phenomenological method.

Løgstrup's short formulation of his undertaking is thus to make "the distinctions that are necessary in order to understand the silent, radical, one-sided, and unfulfillable character of the demand which is contained in the proclamation of Jesus".[64] In other words, his aim is to disclose the ethical demand as a feature of human existence in a way that can be understood independently of any religious proclamation.

He does that by outlining how our mutual interdependence and vulnerability put us under each other's power. That power can be used to do good or ill for the other person. We then fall under a demand to do good. Understanding the demand in this way, including providing it with specific content, honours Kierkegaard's concern that the individual becomes a self, living his or her life in a society without being subject to life in the crowd. The demand must not be confused with the requirements put on us by convention or ethical and legal requirements prevalent in the society where we live. It is neither to be identified with what the vulnerable person asks of us. To genuinely care for the other, therefore, we may have to go against their expressed wishes, instead using our own understanding of what is best for them. It therefore isolates and makes us responsible.

The demand being *unspoken* or *silent* in this way, leaving it to ourselves to decide how to act on it, results in a risk that we intrude on the other. There are, therefore, limits to be respected. We should neither make others the master of our deeds to take care of them, reducing us to mere tools in their hands, nor should we subjugate them to our understanding of life as a form of intrusion and encroachment.

---

63 Løgstrup's philosophy of language presented in *Vidde og Prægnans: sprogfilosofiske betragtninger* [*Width and Meaning: Philosophical Considerations of Language*], Gyldendal, Copenhagen, 1976, is inspired by Lipps. Løgstrup followed Lipps' lectures in the early 1930s and reiterated his dependency on his method throughout his works.

64 *The Ethical Demand*, p. 64, see *supra* note 58.

In this way, "we are caught in a conflict between a consideration for others that is in fact indulgence, compliance, and flattery on the one hand, and on the other hand lack of consideration for others which in the interests of our understanding of life becomes an intrusion and an encroachment".[65] Addressing this conflict in a balanced way includes avoiding taking away a person's responsibility for themselves while at the same time not just doing what the other person asks of us. Including in the notion of 'respect' that individuals ultimately remain responsible for themselves, even if they depend on our help, is to appreciate that they may have another understanding of life.

Unlike social norms, the ethical demand presupposes that we act selflessly for the other person's good. We do not fulfil it for the sake of avoiding sanctions or to look good. Thereby lays the *radical* nature of the demand. Prevailing morality and law also often give rise to specific prescriptions or prohibitions of actions, while the demand leaves it to our understanding, insight and experience to decide how we should act. Moreover, the radical nature of the demand also includes other essential aspects. It does not only cover situations where it is pleasant for us to fulfil the demand. It also includes situations where we have our enemy's life, fate or well-being in our hands. Our enemy may also be dependent on us:

> Is not my enemy dependent on me to some degree, and on the manner in which I come to meet them? How much thinking is taken up with focusing on the enmity between us? Isn't a human being as dependent on whom they hate, and often much more than on whom they love? The demand therefore consists in taking care of that part of the life of the other person which has been delivered up to me, regardless of whether they are someone who is closest to me or a stranger, and regardless of the manner in which they have been delivered up to me, whether it is through a trust that I welcome or through an enmity which arouses me to self-assertion.[66]

While other demands or requirements may involve *rights* claims, as they are established through contracts or are adopted by legitimate assemblies, the ethical demand is not grounded in such processes. The other person cannot present a claim that I fulfil the demand or fulfil it in a certain way. The demand must not be confused with the more or less well-founded claims we present on each other, based on past achievements or services we have provided. It must also be separated from views that our responsibility is limitless, regarding things which are not in our power to accomplish. Such views may, on the contrary, be

[65] *Ibid.*, p. 83.

[66] *Ibid.*, p. 104.

a product of selfishness, an attempt to give significance to our own lives, or result in overzealous control over the lives of others.[67]

Given our tendency to disregard the ethical demand and act selfishly, we need social norms of 'law, morality, and convention' to protect us against each other and stabilize our lives and societies. They function well precisely because they, different from the ethical demand, do not require that we act selflessly. As long as we adhere to these norms, our motivations do not matter so much. They can therefore be enforced through threats of punishment or promoted by the promise of reward. As written or customary norms, they also require less engagement in terms of personal assessment and judgment on our side.

We may then ask if we need an ethical demand independent of the prevailing social norms of the society where we have our lives. Løgstrup offers some compelling answers to this key question:[68]

- Even if social norms are prescriptive, many are not completely determinate, and will still require some judgment from our side, including on what is best for the individual whose life is influenced by the fulfilment of the norms.
- In personal relations, acting only based on what is required by social norms, may severely reduce my ability to act properly. Without the attitude of love or care for the other (required by the demand), obeying social norms may not make my spouse or my children or wider family happy. Acting in loveless manners results in a feeling that I am not present in or behind my deeds myself.
- If we dropped the ethical demand, we would lose the compass we need to assess the social norms and see if they result in good or not. Social norms need constant assessment as they can be damaging as well as beneficial to a good life. They vary according to time and place, and the ethical demand provides us with the capacity to assess them.

There is another key feature of the demand to care for the other's life in a way that best serves the other, namely that it is non-reciprocal or *one-sided*. There are many ways we can protest the demand, based on conceptions that it would be unreasonable to demand that we always put our own best interests aside to help the other. After all, life is conducive to basic rules of 'give and take'. Why should I act for you without ensuring that I get something in return? Løgstrup's answer is that the demand requires an understanding of life as a gift:

> For this reason, a human being has no basis in their existence on which to make a counterdemand to another human being. In view

[67] *Ibid.*, p. 105.

[68] *Ibid.*, pp. 115–120.

> of the fact that what a human being owns is something that they have received, no counterclaim can be issued. The individual is a debtor, not by first committing some wrong, but simply because they exist and have received their life.[69]

The Christians as well as adherents of other religions that teach the world and humans to be created by a merciful God have an explanatory framework to make sense of this aspect of the demand. However, Løgstrup argues that atheists and those who do not share a belief in creation will also find enough fundamental phenomena in their lives that they cannot claim to have created themselves or be created by other humans to accept that 'life is a gift'. The primary examples are understanding, openness, love and compassion, which he in later works characterizes as 'sovereign expressions of life'.[70] The point is that these phenomena are pre-ethical and in some fundamental meaning given so that we can fulfil them or distort them, but not take credit for them.

These phenomena provide important elements in the account of life as a gift, namely, that their

> ethical structures are not something we bring about for ourselves but are a normative order in which we always already have our place. This then allows Løgstrup to make a clear distinction between the goodness of life itself, and the harm that we then bring to life by imposing our own self-created distortions upon it, as we turn trust into reservation, and love into selfishness.[71]

The ethical demand is *unfulfillable* in a fundamental sense. While the demand may arise out of natural love, the problem with the latter is that it often fails. It can easily dissipate, friends and loved ones losing the attraction they once had. A more fundamental problem, though, is that natural love is selective, only extending to some people but not all. In these circumstances, the ethical demand creates an obligation to replace love by doing what love would have done without being obliged to do it. In love as a pre-ethical relationship, there is no need for an ethical demand. Love is a 'given' for us; so, if we are capable of genuine love, this comes from the goodness of life itself, as a gift. However, our selfishness tends to distort love. In Løgstrup, there is an ontological

69 *Ibid.*, p. 174.

70 In his final critical account of Kierkegaard's understanding of Christianity, *Opgør med Kierkegaard* [*Controverting Kierkegaard*], Gyldendal, Copenhagen, 1968, one of Løgstrup's main arguments is that Kierkegaard overlooks such spontaneous and life-upholding phenomena as love, trust and compassion, and therefore creates a false dichotomy of either love in relation to God as an infinite idea or conformity ('life in the crowd'). There is a third option, according to Løgstrup, and that is a life where one responds to the claim of the sovereign expressions of life.

71 Robert Stern, *The Radical Demand in Løgstrup's Ethics*, Oxford University Press, 2019, pp. 91–92.

optimism "concerning the goodness of human life and anthropological pessimism concerning the wickedness of human beings".[72]

The demand is thus unfulfillable in the sense that if I need to be told to do what is best for the neighbour, I have already failed to act out of love. Ethically demanded acts replace in this way the natural goodness and love that are inherent in human existence. The demand is thus not unfulfillable because it asks too much of us, but because it should not have been necessary. The Good Samaritan did not act after recognizing a demand to help, but did so spontaneously. In replacing this spontaneity, the demand also lets in other motives to help, such as self-righteousness and proving to others that we care.

In the final chapters of *The Ethical Demand* (Chapters 10–12), Løgstrup discusses whether his conception of the demand is compatible with science, anti-metaphysical philosophy (positivism of some sort), how it relates to poetry and finally how Jesus' proclamation related to the demand.

Science may give explanations for why we fail to love others, referring to biological factors, our upbringing or our environment, thereby taking away our responsibility. Løgstrup's response is that if we think of ourselves as selves at all, we must take responsibility for making the demand unfulfillable. But to think that we are to blame in this way is to go beyond any scientific or anti-metaphysical conception of life, so there remains an inevitable conflict with science. When it comes to the problem of determinism, Løgstrup argues similarly to Luther and Calvin that, as long as the concept of the self is kept, a person can still be held responsible.

In Chapter 11, Løgstrup refers to poetry as an ally in helping to pay attention to often forgotten features of our existence. While "[p]hilosophy can at best make an understanding clear. Poetry can make it present".

In the book's last chapter, Løgstrup returns to the proclamation of Jesus. The question is whether Jesus is solely a teacher who taught us about the ethical demand, which we otherwise can understand in purely human terms, or whether he represented something more. The answer is that Jesus offers forgiveness to us for our failure to respond to the other with love. Here Jesus speaks with a particular kind of divine authority. In Løgstrup, as in Christianity, Jesus here speaks for God, and puts us in the decision situation of faith: do we believe him to be the son of God or not?

All the rest is made sense of in philosophical enquiry and open for every human being to understand, debate, criticize and *apply*.

[72] Bjørn Rabjerg and Robert Stern, "Introduction", in *The Ethical Demand*, p. 43, see *supra* note 58.

2.4.4. How Can Religious Leaders Make Use of Kierkegaard and Løgstrup?

There are several ways religious leaders can make use of Kierkegaard's and Løgstrup's analysis of human existence in mobilizing against hate speech and violence in the name of religion.

Firstly, as already outlined above, the analysis provides a set of criteria for religious leaders to scrutinize religious teaching. Concepts such as 'holy land', 'holy religion' or 'holy war', for that matter, fail the test. They represent distortions by absolutizing ideas that humans have thought out and put into action. By making their own religion into an ideology, religious leaders may also be prone to attacking adherents of other religions on the basis that they are agents of rival religious ideologies with an aim to take over the land. The result may be religious hate speech, which denies others the right to stay and practise their religion.

Hate speech in the name of religion may in some circumstances be an unavoidable consequence of making religion into ideology, that is, a set of finalized ideas on how society should be organized as a fulfilment of religious doctrines. In this way, a front against the others is established. The others are portrayed as threats to the implementation of the ideology and should either leave or possibly convert. In attacking, conspiracies that the others have plans to take over the land and replace us are frequently used. An argument may be presented that, 'if we do not act decisively, others may do and it will be the end of us'.

Secondly, religious leaders should teach that individual responsibility always remains in religion. It is true that religious beliefs are often deeply rooted and part of a shared culture, but an important insight of the analysis of existence provided by Kierkegaard and Løgstrup is that the decisions to relate to God in one's life cannot be taken once and for all. Existence is movement and decisions must be repeated or changed on one's own account.

An argument may be presented that non-Western cultures are prone to putting the collective at a higher place than Western cultures do. However, while respect for the elderly, a sense of belonging to the family or a clan, as well as adherence to social norms may vary, becoming a self always includes taking responsibility for the cultural specificities one is placed under. There is no exit from this kind of responsibility in the life of humans if they decide to leave life in the crowd.

Thirdly, religious leaders should engage in and refer to conversations about the kind of universalist approach inherent to Kierkegaard and Løgstrup. Philosophers today have limited influence on policies and the way people think. In many contexts, religious leaders may play more decisive roles in placing the need for 'soft' Enlightenment on the agenda, that is, the need for moral knowledge that can challenge the way religious as well as non-religious communities and movements relate to ethical issues. Fragmentation of ethics is a dangerous route for everyone, and religious leaders should rather promote respect for our shared humanity as exemplified in Kierkegaard and Løgstrup than insist on exclusively religious ethics. The decisive point is not whether one accepts any of their accounts of human existence and its inherent ethical demand, but whether one engages with them and with similar projects in a serious and honest conversation.

In the above reference to American philosopher Dallas Willard's diagnosis of Western culture, I referred to his claim that moral knowledge has disappeared. His prescription of how moral knowledge can return, by presenting *a model of the good person*, underlines the contributions to ethical thinking of Løgstrup and Levinas. They present, according to Willard, descriptions of 'primitive personal interactions', attempting to describe (often overlooked) experiences of moral obligation. Løgstrup focuses on natural trust in human relationships while Levinas focuses on the experience of the human face and of human need beyond all classifications of the one in need. They do not make efforts of establishing rules or general principles but leave it to the individual to mobilize their own insight and understanding when meeting the other's face or being called to action by the ethical demand.[73]

Religious proclamation often refers to 'good' or even 'holy' persons and tells stories of human interactions to exemplify good and evil. If Willard's prescription is right, religious leaders may play an important role in debating the main characteristics of good persons, based on experiences and tested values.

Last, but not least, both Kierkegaard and Løgstrup refer to 'love' as the fundamental expression of life in humans. Their conceptions are far from any Hollywood-style romantic cliché story. They rather represent a realistic analysis of life without overlooking the way human selfishness and hate may distort relations and even lead to deadly conflict and war.

Their understanding of life was nurtured by religion. They experienced plenty of challenges in their own life – Kierkegaard experienced the death of all his siblings but one brother in spite of him being the youngest, and Løgstrup experienced the breakdown of European culture during both world wars – but kept faith in life as a gift and love as the primary expressions of life.

This may also be an important inspiration for religious leaders, to talk about love, not only for adherents of their religion, but for humans.

[73] Willard, 2018, pp. 362–63, see *supra* note 29.

2.5. Religious Tolerance, Freedom, Diversity and Epistemology

There are several ethical norms that can be found in religions as well as in reflections on diversity and the epistemology of religion, which can help religious leaders to confront hate speech and violence in the name of religion. I will mention just a few.

According to a survey by Pew Research Center, Indians feel their country has lived up to its post-independence ideals of creating a society where followers of many religions can live and practise freely. India's population, at the time of the survey of about 1.4 billion, consisted of 81 per cent Hindus, 12.9 per cent Muslims and 2.4 per cent Christians, as well as significant groups of Sikhs, Buddhists, Jains and other religions.[74]

The survey finds that Indians of all religious backgrounds overwhelmingly feel free to practise their faith. They see:

> religious tolerance as a central part of who they are as a nation. Across the major religious groups, most people say it is very important to respect all religions to be "truly Indian". And tolerance is a religious as well as a civic value: Indians are united in the view that respecting other religions is a very important part of what it means to be a member of their own religious community.[75]

A remarkable feature discovered by the survey is that not only do most Hindus (77 per cent) believe in *karma*, but so do an identical percentage of Muslims. Further, 32 per cent of Christians and 81 per cent of Hindus say they believe in the purifying power of the Ganges River. However, despite sharing certain values and beliefs, members of different religious communities often do not feel they have much in common with one another. The survey found that 66 per cent of Hindus see themselves as very different from Muslims, and 64 per cent of Muslims return the sentiment. While a few of the smaller communities feel they have a lot in common with Hindus, people in the major religious communities tend to see themselves as very different from others and prefer to live with, have friends with and marry people from their own communities. In fact, 36 per cent of Hindus stated that they did not want to have Muslim neighbours.

While overwhelmingly expressing support for religious tolerance, most Indians seem to prefer segregation along religious divides. For example, 82 per cent of Hindus say they value tolerance, but do not want interreligious marriages of Hindu women. There is also a strong identification among Hindus of being

[74] The survey was based on nearly 30,000 face-to-face interviews of adults conducted in 17 languages between late 2019 and early 2020. Neha Sahgal *et al.*, "Religion in India: Tolerance and Segregation", *Pew Research Center*, 29 June 2021. In the following, I render the main points of the survey.

[75] *Ibid.*

'truly' Indian and Hindu (64 per cent) and speaking Hindi (59 per cent). These groups also mainly support the ruling Bharatiya Janata Party ('BJP'), led by Prime Minister Narendra Modi (1950–), known for its Hindu nationalism. According to observers, the BJP's electoral success is largely attributed to Modi's charisma and the politics of religious polarization and strident nationalism.[76]

Based on this background, an important question is what 'tolerance' really means in the Indian context. Adding to a somewhat confusing picture, according to the survey, 65 per cent of Indians say violence between religious groups is a 'very big problem'. How can widespread tolerance go hand in hand with the wish for segregation and frequently occurring interreligious violence?

Religious tolerance has been defined as "the forbearance and the permission given by the adherents of a dominant religion for other religions to exist, even though the latter are looked on with disapproval as inferior, mistaken, or harmful". In contrast, religious 'liberty' or 'freedom' is understood as the recognition of equal freedom for all religions without discrimination. Toleration is something a ruler can easily withdraw, while freedom is harder to cancel.[77]

The concept of tolerance had its breakthrough in the European eighteenth century Enlightenment in order to overcome religious conflicts and wars. The Enlightenment was usually seen to include, among its defining achievements, reason, civility, tolerance, commerce and freedom. Traditionally, research has pointed to the role of so-called *philosophes*, living in Paris, who tried to change the world with their writings, and in particular to take on the Catholic Church or religious fanaticism to introduce a modern, scientific and philosophical approach to developing society.

Later scholarship has, however, to a degree redefined Enlightenment as an *Atlantic* and not a French or Western European phenomenon with a variety of national contexts and characteristics. The philosophy-centred research has given way to research on the many forms of Enlightenment culture. The black-and-white understanding of the Enlightenment as a secular and anti-religious movement has given way to perceptions that stress that several religious trends played important roles within the Enlightenment. There was a religious or Christian Enlightenment and even a Catholic one. The Enlightenment, therefore, is now seen as "a spectrum of many different, and even opposed, 'lights'. The Enlightenment is giving way to 'the Enlightenments'".[78]

[76] Soutik Biswas, "The Secret Behind Success of India's Ruling Party BJP", *BBC News*, 2 December 2020.

[77] Perez Zagorin, *How the Idea of Religious Toleration Came to the West*, Princeton University Press, 2003, pp. 5–6.

[78] Juan Pablo Domínguez, "Introduction: Religious Toleration in the Age of Enlightenment", in *Journal of History of European Ideas*, 2017, vol. 43, no. 4, pp. 273–74.

While there is still considerable support for the view that science, political freedom, human rights and religious tolerance all have their origin in the Enlightenment, some modern scholars tend to complicate this perception. They have, *inter alia*, shown that the ideal of religious toleration "long preceded the Enlightenment, that religious persecution continued in many parts of Europe throughout the eighteenth century, and that Enlightenment thinkers not only held a vast range of religious and political ideas but also often advanced arguments for *both* tolerance and intolerance".[79]

However, while Enlightenment philosophers adhered to different views on many topics, they may all have shared a view that the principal enemy was of a religious nature: the 'abuse of spiritual authority', in the words of Jean le Rond d'Alambert (1717–1783), or 'ecclesiastical despotism' as Immanuel Kant (1724–1804) called it. They were not fighting religion as such; they "rather aspired to reform churches and beliefs so that they ceased to be an obstacle to political stability, social harmony, economic growth, and intellectual development".[80] In this endeavour, they were united with reform-oriented men inside the churches as well.

In our context, it is important to note that tolerance was from its inception a narrower concept than religious freedom. The idea of toleration was used to differentiate between 'enlightened, acceptable citizens and intolerable fanatics'. Counter-Enlightenment could therefore point to their opponents being inconsistent, denying toleration to Catholics and advocating repression of atheists. Religious freedom, on the contrary, was closer to how religious people in opposition to the church thought, namely that every person should be permitted to decide on their religious views and adherence.

As illustrated by the Pew Research Center survey on India, supporting religious tolerance does not preclude Indians from supporting segregation, being against interreligious marriages and violence between religious groups remaining widespread. I, therefore, argue that religious leaders should aim at promoting 'religious freedom' rather than 'religious tolerance'. Tolerance is, of course, better than intolerance, being motivated by considerations on how to make society more peaceful even if it is divided along religious lines. Its solution is that we should simply accept 'others', while we do not have to make efforts to understand them better or interact with them.

Religious freedom goes deeper. It is aligned with existential analysis as presented above, underlining that the individual must take their own decision on how to relate to the religious proclamation. While Enlightenment philosophers

[79] *Ibid.*, p. 275.

[80] *Ibid.*

were primarily concerned about religious institutions being subjugated to civil authorities, religious figures such as William Penn (1644–1718) propagated "the need to stop the persecution he and his fellow Quakers suffered at the hands of *civil* authorities".[81]

There may be discerned a different attitude to religious diversity in attitudes dominated by tolerance compared to attitudes dominated by freedom. While the tolerant reluctantly accepts diversity even if they do not like the 'others', those who profess religious freedom may even appreciate that in religious matters there can be no consensus, at least not without coercion.

There are three main views on religious diversity, the *pluralistic*, *exclusivist* and *inclusivist* theories. While pluralist approaches state that, within bounds, one religion is as good as another, exclusivists underline that one religion is uniquely valuable. Inclusivist theories agree with exclusivism that one religion has the most value but adds that others also have significant religious value.[82] While the concept of religious pluralism in some contexts is simply referring to a tolerant and sympathetic view of the various religions, it can also function as a normative principle, stating that people of different religions should be treated the same. Religious leaders should, at least, by reflecting on religious diversity be cautious in judging those who believe differently, also taking into account that it may be impossible to prove that one belief is truer than others.

The question of evidence or proof adds an additional basis for religious leaders to promote religious freedom and confront intolerance. It comes from the fact that the *epistemology* of religious belief differs from other areas of human understanding. Contemporary epistemology of religion asks whether some sort of *evidentialism* applies to religious beliefs, or whether we should instead adopt a more permissive epistemology. Evidentialism says that a belief is justified only if "it is proportioned to the evidence".[83] However, religious belief is seldom if ever based on *the graduation of the likeliness that the religious propositions are true based on an assessment of evidence.*

Adherents of religious belief are hardly ever heard to be saying, when confronted with why they believe that the evidence they base their belief on justifies, for instance, a 60 per cent certitude, that their religion is true. Rather we believe based on a comprehensive interpretation of life experiences, and sometimes after listening to convincing preachers. Or the situation may be like Kierkegaard explained, there is no compelling evidence, but I mobilize my inner passion and

81 *Ibid.*, p. 278.

82 Dale Tuggy, "Theories of Religious Diversity", in *Internet Encyclopedia of Philosophy* (available on its web site).

83 For a short introduction, see Peter Forrest, "Epistemology of Religion", in Edward N. Zalta (ed.), *The Stanford Encyclopedia of Philosophy*, Winter 2017 Edition, 2017.

fulfil the leap of faith. There may also be many adherents who did not seriously question why they believe because religion for them is more about belonging to a community and culture than questioning the truth of their faith.

Admitting this subjective dimension to religious belief, religious leaders should promote respect for individuals that chose differently.

2.6. Religious Dialogue and Human Rights

In confronting hate speech and violence against members of other religious communities, religious leaders may refer to norms and practices of dialogue. 'Dialogue' refers to ways of meeting and interacting with those who have other opinions, or with whom one has a conflict. It is a way of solving conflicts or at least understanding each other better through conversations that may be more or less structured.

Dialogue norms may vary, and even be subject to adoption in an initial phase of a specific dialogue. The following proposal for cross-cultural dialogue rules contains in my experience some of the most frequently referred to norms:[84]

- Try on ideas. If someone expresses an idea, opinion or point of view new to you or different from your own, try it on; try to see it from within that other person's perspective.
- Practise 'both/and' thinking. We often practise 'either/or' thinking, believing that ideas, situations, plans and so on can only be 'this way' or 'that way'. What happens if both ideas – more than one plan or situation or perspective – can be meaningful, valuable or true?
- It is permitted to disagree, but not to shame, blame or attack another person.
- Use 'I' statements, speaking from your own personal experience rather than speaking of another's experience or generalizing about a group, whether that group is your own or another's.
- Take responsibility for your own learning: if there is something that you do not understand, ask for clarification. Seek out sources of new learning. Come to the conversation with an 'intent to learn', rather than an 'intent to control'.
- Respect confidentiality: it is good to share our learnings and experiences from dialogue with others, but it is not permitted to share another's story and to name that person unless that person gives specific permission to do so.
- It is allowed to be messy. Real dialogue, especially when it takes place across various kinds of differences, will be messy – inconclusive,

[84] "Suggested Norms for Cross-Cultural Dialogue", *Harvard University* (available on its web site).

sometimes uncomfortable or unclear. Welcome the messiness as a sign of authenticity and honesty. Practise bringing to the conversation a spirit of compassion and flexibility.

- Step up or step back: if you are a person who often remains silent in group conversations, step up to share your experience and perspectives. If you are someone who often speaks in such conversations, step back to leave space for others. Be intentional about both contributing to the conversation and sharing the 'air space'.

Such norms distinguish dialogue from *discussions*, *debates* or *deliberations*. In the latter, the emphasis is on agreeing on decisions, while debates involve argumentation in which two or more opposing sides on an issue make a case for their position. Discussions are informal and unstructured conversations without a goal to achieve specific outcomes. In dialogues, the aim may be to agree on decisions, but it can also be a collective act of sharing and listening to increase understanding of each other's perspectives and positions.

2.6.1. The Messaging of the Dalai Lama and Desmond Tutu

The encounters between the fourteenth Dalai Lama, Tenzin Gyatso, and the late Archbishop of Southern Africa Desmond Tutu were full of dialogue. Eventually, they became friends and published a book together on how joy in life can be achieved despite suffering and other troubles on life's way.[85]

They differ vastly in their background and religious outlook. The Dalai Lama is the spiritual leader of the Tibetan people and of Tibetan Buddhism, travelling extensively and promoting a message of kindness and compassion, interfaith understanding, respect for the environment and world peace. Aligned with the approach presented in this chapter, he has been a passionate advocate for a secular universal approach to cultivating fundamental human values. He has lived his life in exile in Dharamsala, India.

Desmond Tutu was a prominent leader in the struggle for justice and reconciliation in South Africa. In 1994, he was appointed Chair of the Truth and Reconciliation Commission, where he pioneered new ways for countries to address abuses, civil conflict and oppression. He was the Founding Chair of The Elders, a group of global leaders that promotes peace and human rights. He lived in Cape Town, South Africa.

From their different backgrounds, they had common experiences of struggles against powerful adversaries. As religious leaders, they have important political functions. And they have much to say on how humans and societies can

[85] The Dalai Lama, Desmond Tutu and Douglas Abrams, *The Book of Joy*, Hutchinson, London, 2016.

deal with issues that for most people would seem insurmountable obstacles to progress on peace and human development. This is, however, not the point here. The point is that they both represented a deep understanding of what connects people of all creeds. They look to the deep respect for humanity in each person which religious belief, at its best, can instil. Religion has opened their eyes to what unites people on a very basic level, not to those articles of faith which may divide them.

After all, it is, as Løgstrup noted, the same human existence that religions, as well as philosophical thinking, refer to. In recommending how people should receive their message, they advised that:

> You don't need to believe us. Indeed, nothing we say should be taken as an article of faith. We are sharing what two friends, from very different worlds, have witnessed and learned in our long lives. We hope you will discover whether what is included here is true by applying it in your own life.[86]

They are outstanding persons whom religious leaders can learn and draw inspiration from.

2.6.2. Institutionalized Dialogue, an Example From Norway

Inspiration to adhere to norms of tolerance or freedom in religious matters may come from outstanding leaders. But it can also come from successful institutionalized dialogue and co-operation on developing common views and fighting hate and extremes across religious and life-view divides. I will present but one of the many examples of such dialogue around the world, the Council for Religious and Life Stance Communities in Norway, established in 1996.[87]

The Council's member communities include Bahá'í, Buddhists, Christians, Humanists, Hindus, Jews, Muslims and Sikhs. The main goals of the work of the Council are to promote equal treatment of religious and life-stance communities in Norway and to promote respect and understanding among religious and life-stance communities. In this way, the Council unites engagement for equal rights, and dialogue to increase understanding between the different communities. In addition to a national council, there are local councils in seven Norwegian towns.

The Council has been active on a range of political issues in education, workplaces, health institutions, detention centres, the military and graveyards. It is also developing common views on a number of ethical issues, such as

[86] *Ibid.*, p. x.

[87] More information about the Council for Religious and Life Stance Communities in Norway is available on its web site. All quotes in this section are from this web site.

protection of the environment, biotechnology, gender equality, sexual harassment within religious communities and the rights of refugees.

In its decision-making, the Council applies the principle of consensus, so that the opinion of each of the members has the same weight regardless of the size of the community. The Council can, however, make statements even if not all members agree, making explicit which religious or life-stance communities do not support a specific opinion. The Council provides advice and consultation to the Norwegian government.

There are some specific features, which may have contributed to the importance of the Council and made its prevention of hate speech and conflicts between religious communities effective. First, it provides co-operation among both religious and secular communities. Second, it provides a forum where both majority (the Protestant Church of Norway) and minority communities can take part on equal feet in defining and pursuing common political goals such as equal treatment of religious and life-stance communities. Third, the Council includes both Shí'ah, Sunní and Ahmadiyya communities, as well as different Christian communities, having different groups of Muslims and Christians sit at the same table. Fourth, the Council has run projects to document and counter hate speech and discrimination based on religion or life-views. In this way, it has increased awareness of the problems and effectively promoted larger responsibility within the communities to counter such practices.

Another important factor is that the Council facilitates regular meetings of senior religious leaders. According to its own assessment,

> the level of mutual knowledge, trust and cooperation established within and supported by the Council, has proved to be an effective tool to address sensitive issues in the field of religious pluralism and has worked as a tool for conflict prevention in Norway among religious and life stance communities.

2.6.3. Freedom of Religion or Belief as a Human Right

The most relevant UN instrument for the topic of this chapter is the 1981 Declaration on the Elimination of All Forms of Intolerance and Discrimination Based on Religion or Belief.[88] It underlines in its Preamble that religion and belief is one of the fundamental elements in the 'conception of life' of anyone who professes either and "that freedom of religion should be fully respected and guaranteed":

[88] Declaration on the Elimination of All Forms of Intolerance and Discrimination Based on Religion or Belief, UN Doc. A/RES/36/55, 25 November 1981 (https://www.legal-tools.org/doc/hexdsg/).

> it is essential to promote understanding, tolerance, and respect in matters relating to freedom of religion and belief and to ensure that the use of religion or belief for ends inconsistent with the Charter of the United Nations, other relevant instruments of the United Nations and the purposes and principles of the present Declaration is inadmissible [...].

The duty-bearers and potential perpetrators are, according to Article 2(1), both state and non-state actors ("any State, institution, group of persons, or person"). However, the operational provisions of the Declaration are addressed to states, which shall "take effective measures to prevent and eliminate discrimination on the grounds of religion or belief" (Article 4(1)), "enact or rescind legislation where necessary to prohibit any such discrimination" and take "appropriate measures to combat intolerance on the grounds of religion or other beliefs" (Article 4(2)).

A resolution of 12 April 2011 by the UN Human Rights Council adds substantial flesh to the Declaration's call for "effective measures".[89] The Declaration has been followed up by a series of resolutions in the Council and concretized in the so-called Rabat Plan of Action of 2012.[90] In addition to calling upon states to respect and protect freedom of religion or belief for all, the resolution presents a list of eight recommended measures, including the creation of collaborative networks for dialogue and action in the fields of education, health, conflict prevention, employment, integration, media education, creating a mechanism within governments to address potential areas of tension between different religious communities and assisting with conflict prevention and mediation.

Several recommendations concern outreach to religious communities and encouraging religious leaders to discuss within their communities the causes of discrimination and how to counter these causes. State representatives should speak out against intolerance and religious hatred, and criminalize incitement to imminent violence. Other measures include education, awareness-building and "open, constructive and respectful debate of ideas, as well as interfaith and intercultural dialogue at the local, national and international levels".

---

[89] Combating Intolerance, Negative Stereotyping and Stigmatization of, and Discrimination, Incitement to Violence and Violence Against, Persons based on Religion or Belief, UN Doc. A/HRC/RES/16/18, 12 April 2011 (https://www.legal-tools.org/doc/0a86d2/).

[90] Rabat Plan of Action on the Prohibition of Advocacy of National, Racial, or Religious Hatred that constitutes Incitement to Discrimination, Hostility, or Violence: Conclusions and Recommendations emanating from the Four Regional Expert Workshops organized by the Office of the UN High Commissioner for Human Rights in 2011 and adopted by experts at the meeting in Rabat, Morocco, on 5 October 2012, UN Doc. A/HRC/22/17/Add.4, 11 January 2013 (https://www.legal-tools.org/doc/oymwge/).

These and other international initiatives endeavour to make religious leaders partners in fighting religious hate speech, but the question is whether their human rights- and state-oriented approach succeed. As referred to above, conservative religious leaders may acknowledge the benefits of the prohibition of discrimination and some other human rights for their own group, but are far more sceptical of the principled view that all human rights should be protected for everyone – regardless of their religion or belief, ethnicity, sexual orientation or gender identity. They may perceive international human rights as Western, secular and alien to their faith, aiming at emancipating people from religion, not within religion.

So how can a conversation with them on human rights start?

I think the first step should be to point to internal normative bases that reinforce the value placed on all humans – in religions, philosophy, as well as in human rights.

As modern scholarship has nuanced the view of the Enlightenment, pointing to the role of religious reformists in promoting religious tolerance and freedom, Samuel Moyn's research on 'Christian human rights' has nuanced the view on the role of religion in the drafting of the Universal Declaration. Conservative Catholic and Protestant Christians had before and during World War II adopted a concept of 'dignity' that applied to all humans and not only privileged people. Their main motivation, according to Moyn was not to defend human emancipation in the tradition of the Enlightenment, but rather to defend a 'reinvented conservatism' inspired by personalism and religion – against both liberalism and totalitarian communism. Such ideas played, according to Moyn, a bigger part in the drafting of the Universal Declaration of Human Rights than previously admitted. The breakthrough of human rights in its secular form, and as an expanding part of international law, took place only in the 1970s.[91]

Moyn's thesis is not uncontroversial,[92] but it nevertheless illustrates how one may enter human rights from a variety of standpoints and motives, including from conservative religion. The point is that if one starts the conversation on human rights by introducing conceptions found in religion, which support human dignity, tolerance and freedom, one can create ownership and provide for an open discussion. Starting from external and perceived secular norms may close doors.

In line with this, the second step should be to ask religious leaders to do more than UN action plans usually ask them to. They should be asked to respect

---

91 Samuel Moyn, *Christian Human Rights*, University of Pennsylvania Press, Philadelphia, 2015.

92 See Ronald E. Osborn, "Conservatism by Other Means", in *The Hedgehog Review*, 2016, vol. 18, no. 1.

human rights by refraining from hate speech themselves and criticizing those who do. However, they should in addition be challenged to develop their own views on how hate speech and violence can be addressed based on broader normative bases. Part of that discussion should focus on how they can prevent religion from becoming a political front, an ideology.

From there, the conversation can take many different directions. By following this approach, however, the view that less religion is the solution to the problem of religious hate speech and violence is left out. Instead, the discussion will facilitate views on *how religious leaders can be more ambitious in fighting hate speech* and teaching religious tolerance, freedom and respect for diversity.

2.7. Religion and Politics: Norms of Prudence

Few have stated the demarcation between religion and politics as clearly as Pope Francis (1936–2025). The Pope, in a conversation on 16 March 2022 with Russian Orthodox Patriarch Kirill (1946–), told the Patriarch, who is a crucial supporter of President Vladimir Putin's aggressive war against Ukraine:

> Brother, we are not state clerics, we cannot use the language of politics but that of Jesus. We are pastors of the same holy people of God. Because of this, we must seek avenues of peace, to put an end to the firing of weapons. […] The patriarch cannot transform himself into Putin's altar boy.[93]

Kirill was elected in 2009 as the Patriarch of the Russian Orthodox Church, which has more than 100 million followers. Orthodox Christianity is the dominant faith both in Russia and Ukraine. Still, after Russia invaded Eastern Ukraine in 2014 and then attempted the invasion of the whole country starting on 24 February 2022, the Russian Orthodox Church has contributed to a rift between Moscow and Kyiv and between the Russian and the Ukrainian Orthodox churches.

In April 2022, Patriarch Kirill called on Russian soldiers to "love our fatherland […] protect it, as only Russians can defend their country". He described those affected by the conflict in Ukraine as "people of Holy Russia. They are our brothers and sisters". He has lauded military service as "an active manifestation of evangelical love for neighbours".[94]

The relationship between Patriarch Kirill and President Putin helped justify the war. President Putin used the language of faith to support his political and military ambitions, while Patriarch Kirill used sermons to back the campaign on

[93] Timothy Bella and Sammy Westfall, "'Don't Be Putin's Altar Boy', Pope Warns Russian Orthodox Leader", *Washington Post*, 4 May 2022.

[94] *Ibid.*

spiritual grounds, underlining Russia's broader struggle with Western countries that supports Ukraine and represent a decadent and God-less culture.

Patriarch Kirill's support for President Putin's latest war led to strong criticism within his church and internationally. Nearly 300 Russian priests and deacons signed an open appeal calling for a cease-fire.[95] In Ukraine, more than 320 priests signed a letter accusing the Patriarch of "heresy" and "moral crimes by blessing the war against Ukraine".[96]

The Pope's demarcation did not imply that religious leaders should not interfere in politics. Instead, he underlined that when doing so, they should use religious language, which is a language of peace and respect for human life. He also implied that the church must refrain from being instrumentalized by political power.

I did not find a more to-the-point criticism of Patriarch Kirill than the one expressed by the Pope, probably the world's most influential religious leader. The norms underlying his criticism are based on centuries of mistakes and struggles to define the demarcation of religion versus politics.

2.8. Conclusions

There are several bases where religious leaders can find norms against religious intolerance, hate speech and violence.

I have pointed to universalist ethical approaches inspired by religious proclamation, as outlined by Kierkegaard and Løgstrup. Based on their philosophical analysis of human existence, they argue that the religious proclamation must correspond to human existence's structure and central features. If there exists no correspondence, religion becomes superstition, ideology and coercion. As such, it can lead to escalation of conflicts, abuse in the name of God and spreading of hate against those who represent other religions or beliefs or are excluded because of ethnicity, sexual orientation or other grounds.

The risk of religion developing into intolerant ideology can be effectively addressed by religious leaders, referring to the examples of open-minded and dialogue-oriented religious personalities such as the Dalai Lama and Desmond Tutu, religious traditions of tolerance, freedom and love for your neighbour, to diversity and epistemology of religion and to examples of institutionalized dialogue between religions and secular life-views. They can engage in debates about universalist ethical approaches and how to re-establish moral knowledge.

---

95 Jeanne Whalen, "Russian Orthodox Leader Backs War in Ukraine, Divides Faith", *Washington Post*, 18 April 2022.

96 "'Don't Be Putin's Altar Boy', Pope Warns Russian Orthodox Leader", 4 May 2022, see *supra* note 93.

Religious leaders are frequently urged by the UN and other international organizations to abide by human rights norms and to refrain from using hateful expressions and criticize those who do. But they must also be challenged to mobilize internal normative bases to fight abuse of religion.

3

Jeremy Bentham's Legacy: A Vision of an International Law for the Greatest Happiness of All Nations*

Jeremy Bentham (1748–1832), English Enlightenment philosopher, political and legal reformist, coined pivotal English legal terms and created a vision of rationally reformed legislation at the national and international levels as primary instruments of human progress, civilization, and peace.

This study outlines Bentham's positions on the main intellectual currents of his time, distancing himself from what he perceived as a backward-looking emphasis on religion and tradition as well as from protagonists of natural rights and natural law as a basis for reforming law, government and relations between nations. He argued in favour of carefully *codified* laws, based on what he perceived to be a rationally and empirically sound basis, namely, the 'utility principle' or the principle of maximization of pleasure and minimization of pain for the largest possible number of affected persons.

Bentham's texts on international law – including his influential *An Introduction to the Principles of Morals and Legislation* (1789), *Of Laws in General* (1782, rediscovered in 1939) and four articles dealing specifically with international law written between 1786 and 1789 – argue in favour of the law-like quality of international law. Admitted, the 'moral' or 'religious' sanctions, as he called them, for breaches of international law were seldom of great efficacy. But still there was enough to international law that was law-like to let one call it law.

He defined international law as the law on inter-state relations, and proposed ways to strengthen its role in preventing wars and improving inter-state relations. His idea of codifying an international legal code also led him to see the need for an international court able to decide on disputes between states.

This study discusses foundational concepts, the role and the limits of international criminal law, considering Bentham's ideas and arguments about law. His vision of international law as a vehicle for peace, replacing wars with legal

* This chapter was first published as Chapter 12 of Morten Bergsmo and Emiliano J. Buis (eds.), *Philosophical Foundations of International Criminal Law: Correlating Thinkers*, Torkel Opsahl Academic EPublisher, Brussels, 2018 (https://www.toaep.org/ps-pdf/34-bergsmo-buis/). The author extends his gratitude to Natalia M. Luterstein and Martín H. Barros for very useful comments and observations during the final revision of this text.

decisions, is part of his legacy. In situations where peace fails, however, Bentham's zeal for perfecting and codifying laws as well as subjecting judicial processes to the test of efficiency and the principle of utility may also be of lasting relevance. These ideas may have a bearing on contemporary discussions about effects and justification of international criminal law and the prosecution of international crimes.

Bentham was influenced by Enlightenment thinkers, as well as by his opposition to William Blackstone (1723–80), famous law professor and teacher of English common law. His ideas have been influential up to the present, including on important thinkers such as John Stuart Mill (1806–1873), John Austin (1790–1859), and the pivotal twentieth-century legal positivist H.L.A. Hart (1907–1992).

While many took inspiration from Bentham's framing of legal concepts, his rejection of natural law and scepticism towards unwritten law, fewer followed him in his idealistic vision that a world guided by law would be a world without war. However, this may be his most important and lasting contribution.

3.1. Introduction

Jeremy Bentham coined terms like 'international law', 'codification' of unwritten laws, and 'maximization' and 'minimization' of happiness and pain, respectively. He developed a range of proposals for reform of the way England and other states at his time were governed, on how to improve the ways laws were drafted and enacted, on how to effectively fight corruption in government, and on how to improve penitentiaries, the care for poor people, and the overall functioning of the economy. He even spent time in Russia in 1786–1787 to influence the reform-minded Empress Catherine II, though with little success.

Even though many of his ideas became influential at his time – in European countries like France, Spain, Portugal, and in several American countries – Bentham remained frustrated by his lack of success in efforts to gather support for reform in his native England. The rejection of his proposal for a model prison, the 'Panopticon', by the English government in 1803 was a serious disappointment. After Parliament had adopted his plan in 1794, he had drafted thousands of pages of detailed plans for a prison that, in his view, would lead to less suffering among the inmates, rehabilitation of criminals, and more happiness for the society.

Bentham scholars maintain that his frustration with the government's rejection of his prison plan was pivotal in leading him to adopt ideas of representative democracy in the years after.[1] Long before this experience, however,

[1] There exists, though, different views on what led Bentham to become a political radical, campaigning for abolition of the British monarchy and the House of Lords, the replacement of the

Bentham as a young law student was initially reacting to what he perceived as lack of consistence and accessibility of England's legislation, which often existed only in the form of customary laws presented by lawyers, prosecutors and judges in unpredictable ways. He argued that for law to become a tool for improving society and preventing crime, it had to be codified based on sound principles, and foremost among them, the 'principle of utility'.

After the government rejected the Panopticon and other reform proposals, Bentham realized that legislators did not always care for the well-being of society, but rather for their own interests and the interests of a group of benefactors. His democratic breakthrough seems to have come from his realization that those in power were informed by 'sinister interests', rather than by the utility principle. He first applied the concept of sinister interest to the legal profession and then to the political establishment to explain their interest-based resistance to legal and political reform.

Even though Bentham found the task of legislating too complex for ordinary people, he considered that they (including women) should have a final say over who would represent them in drafting laws that benefitted society. It would also follow that people had to be given the option to scrutinize the way the government and the Parliament operated to make informed choices among candidates.

This is how Bentham the 'legal reformer' (the 'Enlightenment Bentham' of the eighteenth century) and Bentham the 'democrat' (the 'radical Bentham' of the nineteenth century) are connected. To legislate well is for expert legislators to accomplish; often based on proposals from external experts like himself. However, if legislators did not have the well-being of the people in mind, the people should have the power to replace them.[2]

As important as his utilitarian-based legal and political reform proposals were, Bentham had much more to offer. He was not only a legal and political reformist, but contributed to defining new foundations of ethical and legal philosophy ('jurisprudence'), as well as presenting influential ideas in political science, philosophy of language and logic.

Much inspired by progress in the natural sciences at his time, Bentham considered his own efforts of developing and applying foundational principles of legislation and morals as parallel to developments in physics and medicine.

common law with a codified system of law, the 'euthanasia' of the Anglican Church, and for universal franchise. The influence of James Mill (1773–1836), John Stuart Mill's father, and other liberals may also have played an important role. For a detailed account, see Phillip Schofield, *Utility and Democracy: The Political Thought of Jeremy Bentham*, Oxford University Press, 2006, Chapters 5–6.

2 See *ibid.*, p. v.

His main contribution would be to lay out the details of the 'principle of utility' in law and politics, as he outlined in his most known work, *An Introduction to the Principles of Morals and Legislation* (1789).[3]

It could be said that Bentham devoted the first part of his long career as philosopher and publicist to developing proposals for reform of legislation, detecting obstacles for sound reforms to be implemented, and devising strategies to overcome them. From the second decade of the nineteenth century, he devoted much of his attention to proposals for democratic reform in England. During the same period, he also developed extensive contacts with legislative authorities in a range of countries to promote a rationalized code of law which could serve as a model for all nations with liberal opinions.

The present chapter outlines some of Bentham's main ideas, and applies them to contemporary debates about the foundations of international criminal law. Benthamite concerns may – even though international law of his time was lacking important characteristics of current international criminal law – still have some bearing on current debates and efforts to develop sound foundations of this branch of international law, and strengthening consensus on both the legal norms and the institutions established to uphold them, such as the International Criminal Court ('ICC').

3.1.1. The Principle of Utility

Bentham formulated the 'principle of utility' in 1769 while he was still a young man. Among those he took inspiration from were contemporary philosophers such as Claude-Arien Helvétius (1715–1771), David Hume (1711–1776) and Joseph Priestley (1733–1804). According to the principle, *the greatest happiness of the greatest number* is the only proper measure of right and wrong and the only proper end of government. In Bentham's mind, however, even if the fundamental goal for the science of legislation and politics was fixed, the science itself was complex. To succeed, one must constantly consider information and ideas as to how the defined end might best be achieved.[4]

Until his death, Bentham remained convinced that the principle of utility, along with supporting principles, constituted sufficient foundation for a scientific approach to morals, legislation and politics.

His faithfulness to moral reasoning based on this principle is well illustrated by his acting in the last hours of his life. On 6 June 1832, he said to a

3 The first edition of the book was printed in 1780, but published only in 1789. A new version, corrected by the author, was published in 1823: Jeremy Bentham, *An Introduction to the Principles of Morals and Legislation*, printed for W. Pickering and E. Wilson, London, 1823.

4 See James Steintrager, "Bentham", in Geraint Parry (ed.), *Political Thinkers*, Vol. V, Routledge, London, 2004, p. 110.

friend that was with him, "I now feel that I am dying; our care must be to minimize the pain. Do not let any of the servants come into the room, and keep away the youths; it will be distressing to them and they can be of no service. Yet I must not be alone; you will remain with me and you only; and then we shall have reduced the pain to the least possible amount".[5] Not much happiness was achievable at such a moment; however, making efforts to minimize the pain was still within Bentham's power.

Bentham introduced the 'principle of utility' in the form of a metaphor:

> Nature has placed mankind under the governance of two sovereign masters, *pain* and *pleasure*. It is for them alone to point out what we ought to do, as well as to determine what we shall do. On the one hand the standard of right and wrong, on the other the chain of causes and effects, are fastened to their throne. They govern us in all we do, in all we say, in all we think: every effort we can make to throw off our subjection, will serve but to demonstrate and confirm it. In words, a man may pretend to abjure their empire: but in reality, he will remain, subject to it all the while. The *principle of utility* recognises this subjection, and assumes it for the foundation of that system, the object of which is to rear the fabric of felicity by the hands of reason and of law. Systems which attempt to question it, deal in sounds instead of sense, in caprice instead of reason, in darkness instead of light.[6]

A few comments will have to suffice to put this introduction of one of the most important principles ever proposed in moral and legal philosophy into context. *Firstly*, it should be noted, as is not always done, that Bentham explicitly states, immediately after this introduction, that "enough of metaphor and declamation: it is not by such means that moral science is to be improved".[7] Even though the introduction is illustrative and pictures the principle of utility well, it may also be misleading if taken as a precise account of the new science Bentham aimed to develop.

Among Bentham's vast body of work, such metaphoric texts are rare. He sometimes admits that his writings are too detailed, dry and long to attain a large readership. However, sciences of morals and legislation deal with highly complex subject matters and must necessarily be detailed and complex themselves.[8]

---

5 Quoted from Francis Charles Montague, "Introduction", in Jeremy Bentham, *A Fragment of Government*, The Lawbook Exchange, Ltd., Clark, 2001, p. 14.

6 Jeremy Bentham, *An Introduction to the Principles of Morals and Legislation*, reprint of 1832 edition (see *supra* note 3), Clarendon Press, Oxford, 1876, pp. 1–2.

7 *Ibid.*, p. 2.

8 According to Bentham scholars, this might be one of the reasons for a seeming paradox: although Bentham became influential in his time and continues to be so, most of his texts remain

Secondly, in a note in the 1823 edition of *An Introduction to Principles of Morals and Legislation*, in which the introduction appears, Bentham indicates that the terminology might be improved. The 'principle of utility' should instead be named '*greatest happiness* or *greatest felicity* principle'. The principle states that "the greatest happiness of all those whose interest is in question" is "the right and proper, and only right and proper and universally desirable, end of human action: of human action in every situation, and in particular in that of a functionary or set of functionaries exercising the powers of Government. The word *utility* does not clearly point to the ideas of *pleasure* and *pain* as the words *happiness* and *felicity* do".[9] For some, Bentham contends, the use of the word utility had therefore made acceptance of the principle harder.

It then follows that Bentham would, for pedagogical reasons, prefer to refer to his main principle as the 'principle of happiness or felicity'. However, since in the history of philosophy, Bentham is perceived as a chief proponent of *utilitarianism* – which is derived from the word 'utility' – I will nevertheless stick to the terminology of the original version of the book.[10]

Thirdly, it should be noted that Bentham claims that the sovereign masters, pain and pleasure, both as a matter of fact, govern us in all we do, and as an ethical and legal foundational principle, *ought* to or *should* govern us in all we do. The principle both functions as a description of human nature – humans are creatures that minimize pain and maximize pleasure by their actions – and as a *prescription tool* on how each human being should act. Some have argued that Bentham in this way departs from David Hume, who in the third part of his *Treatise of Human Nature* (1739–1740) argues against moral rationalism by showing that transition from premises whose parts are linked only by "is" to conclusions whose parts are linked by "ought" are "altogether inconceivable".[11]

In explaining Bentham's position, the above-mentioned metaphorical character of the text should be kept in mind.[12] More important, however, is

---

unread. That may be because they often discuss, in much detail, the application of the principle of utility in different realms, and many of the controversies he engaged in are long forgotten. Many of his texts also went unpublished, or were published long after they were written. However, new and improved editions of some of his lesser known, but high-quality texts in the Collected Works of Jeremy Bentham may improve this situation. For more information on the Collected Works of Jeremy Bentham and the Bentham Project, see the web sites of Oxford University Press and the Bentham Project, University College of London, respectively.

9 Bentham, 1823, p. 1, see *supra* note 3.

10 It should also be noted that Bentham kept the original terminology in the revised version of the book, despite the difficulty in comprehension.

11 David Hume, *A Treatise of Human Nature*, Book III, Part I, Lewis Amherst Selby-Bigge (ed.), Clarendon Press, Oxford, 1888, p. 469.

12 See Steintrager, 2004, p. 17, see *supra* note 4.

Bentham's clarification of the epistemological status of the principle in his further explication. The principle is *not* susceptible to "any direct proof", he maintains, because any such proof must start somewhere. That which "is used to prove everything else, cannot itself be proved: a chain of proofs must have their commencement somewhere. To give such proof is as impossible as it is needles".[13]

Bentham holds that the principle nevertheless can be shown to "be a right principle to be governed by, and that in all cases, it follows from what has been just observed, that whatever principle differs from it in any case must necessarily be a wrong one".[14] One of the principles opposed to the principle of utility is the 'principle of asceticism'. Bentham's strategy is to show that this principle, as well as another opposing principle, the 'principle of sympathy and antipathy', is either impossible to apply consistently or "at bottom but the principle of utility misapplied". In contrast, the "principle of utility is capable of being consistently pursued; and it is but tautology to say, that the more consistently it is pursued, the better it must ever be for human-kind".[15]

The 'principle of sympathy and antipathy' is, according to Bentham, hardly a principle at all. It is rather "a term employed to signify the negation of all principle". It means approving or disapproving of "certain actions, not on account of their tending to augment the happiness, nor yet on account of their tending to diminish the happiness of the party whose interest is in question, but merely because a man finds himself disposed to approve or disapprove of them".[16] In criminal proceedings, this principle boils down to approval or disapproval by way of your feelings: "If you hate much, punish much: if you hate little, punish little: punish as you hate. If you hate not at all, punish not at all".[17]

Bentham admits, though, that sympathy or antipathy may be a motive or cause of an act. This must, however, be distinguished from the evaluation of the moral character of the act. Some acts which were motivated by sympathy may have bad effects, while acts committed based on antipathy may have good effects. Such sentiments can therefore never be a right ground of action.

Arguing thus, Bentham attempts to show that the "only right ground of action, that can possibly subsist, is, after all, the consideration of utility which,

---

13 Bentham, 1876, p. 4, see *supra* note 6.

14 *Ibid.*, p. 8.

15 *Ibid.*, p. 13.

16 *Ibid.*, p. 16.

17 *Ibid.*, p. 17.

if it is a right principle of action and of approbation [in] any one case, is so in every other".[18]

In conceding that there does not exist any direct proof from *psychological* to *moral* hedonism, Bentham respects Hume's argument that what 'ought' to be done cannot be deduced from what 'is' done. This lack of direct proof, is however, compatible with what John Stuart Mill later termed 'indirect proof'. Both Bentham and Mill, who was one of the main heirs of Bentham's utilitarianism, held that 'is' and 'ought' could be connected in a practical and psychological sense in the minds of humans.

In the words of another of the great architects of utilitarianism, Henry Sidgwick (1838–1900), "no cogent inference is possible from the psychological generalization to the ethical principle, but the mind has a natural tendency to pass from the one position to the other: if the actual ultimate springs of our volition are always our own pleasures and pains, it seems *prima facie* reasonable to be moved by them in proportion to their pleasantness and painfulness, and therefore to choose the greatest pleasure or the least pain on the whole".[19]

For Bentham, Hume's distinction between 'is' and 'ought' was important as an argument for the uncertainty of all knowledge. All statements can only admit of degrees of probability. There is no certainty in human knowledge, neither in jurisprudence nor in the natural sciences. This is an important point for Bentham. As H.L.A. Hart put it, Bentham "believed that, in general, tyranny and oppression in politics were possible only where claims to infallibility of judgment were presumptuously made and stupidly conceded. It was necessary to oppose to these arrogant claims the truth that all human judgment, 'opinion', or 'persuasion' is fallible".[20]

This view on the fallibility of all human knowledge became important in the further development of liberal thought. Mill in his famous book *On Liberty* (1859) maintained that because human judgments are fallible, freedom of thought and discussion are necessary to let the best arguments win. The view contains important incentives for democracy and rule of law, since it holds that any government who suppresses free thought and speech implicitly acts in contravention of the nature of human knowledge.

---

18 *Ibid.*, p. 23.

19 Henry Sidgwick, *The Methods of Ethics*, 7th ed., Macmillan and Company, Ltd., London, 1907, p. 42.

20 H.L.A. Hart, "Bentham: Lecture on a Master Mind", in Robert S. Summers (ed.), *More Essays in Legal Philosophy: General Assessments of Legal Philosophies*, Basil Blackwell Publishing, Oxford, 1971, p. 31. Hart, however, criticizes Bentham's position on why the claim to infallibility is always false, pointing to Bentham's limitations as a philosopher (pp. 31–32).

In sum, Bentham neither presented the principle of utility as *self-evident* nor *possible to prove*. His strategy was rather to show that competing principles failed, and that it was a reasonable principle given how humans are motivated to act. In any case, no principle or judgment are infallible, and to pretend so leads to tyranny and oppression.

This leads to my *fourth and final comment*, namely that Bentham explicitly explains that the principle of utility accounts for all kinds of actions, including "not only of every action of a private individual, but of every measure of government". It should be used both to "censure" existing legislation – to assess whether it tends to augment or diminish the happiness of affected parties – as well as to be applied by lawmakers to ensure that new legislation produces overall "benefit, advantage, pleasure, good, or happiness" (which are but a few of the words that Bentham used to describe his approved end goal).[21]

In Bentham's system of law, the civil code is of the greatest importance for maximizing happiness. This field of law is concerned with the distribution of rights and duties (or benefits and burdens), and should maximize the four subends of utility: subsistence, abundance, security, and equality.

To function well, however, civil law must be supported by a well promulgated and effective implementation of 'penal law'. The purpose of 'penal law', which can impose sanctions or punishment for certain acts which, because they tend to diminish happiness, are classified as offences, is to give effect to the civil law.

A state must also have a 'constitutional code', which is concerned with the powers, rights, and duties of public officials, and their modes of appointment and dismissal. Also, in this context, penal law plays an important role in giving effect to relevant parts of constitutional law. The penal, civil and constitutional law together form 'substantive law', which is again given effect by the 'adjective law', or the law of judicial procedure. There is also the 'law concerning the judicial establishment', which gives effect to the adjective law.

All these branches of law should, according to Bentham, be designed to augment happiness and diminish pain for all affected parties.

3.1.2. The Relevancy of Bentham's Philosophy

It might be apt, at this stage, to comment on the question of the relevancy of Bentham's thought to contemporary discussions of the foundational questions of international criminal law.

As a starting point, it should be noted that, for Bentham, there were no doubts about the relevance of the principle of utility and other utilitarian

[21] According to Hart, Bentham gave altogether 58 synonyms for 'pleasure', see *ibid.*, p. 24.

principles for assessing any legal system, including criminal law. To assess legislation in terms of its effects on society or for certain groups of society has become standard, not solely because of Bentham, although utilitarianism has certainly played its part in promoting the use of consequentialist criteria.

In contemporary discussions about the role and effect of international criminal law, utilitarian criteria are referred to such as in discussions about the effects of international or national prosecutions of core international crimes for the peace and/or the overall well-being of societies affected by the crimes as well as for categories of affected persons, such as victims, witnesses, suspects, and accused.

In many areas, Benthamite concerns have proved influential in the way societies perceive how legislation should be formed and applied. Relevant examples include:

1. Frequent use of utilitarian justifications of, and prescriptions on, the role of criminal law and punishment in terms of achieving positive effects for society;
2. Utilitarian-based demand for equality of everyone before the law, including women who are often provided less protection by the law, and government agents, who often remain above the law; and
3. Utilitarian-based arguments for the importance of clarity and simplification in legal language. For law and punishment to be successful in preventing crime, and thereby diminishing pain and augmenting happiness, the law has to be understood by ordinary people and punishment has to be meted out in proportion to the gravity of the crime in a comprehensible way.

A study of how Bentham reasoned about such topics may yet deepen our understanding of them, and strengthen our ability to argue in favour of sound principles. That is not to say, of course, that he should function as a moral arbiter or authority of what is good or bad in contemporary international criminal law and in the way international or national jurisdictions apply that branch of law.

A more constructive way of making use of Benthamite concerns would be to take inspiration from them to question the soundness of practices, values and ideas inherent in international criminal law. In providing answers to such questions, the foundations of international criminal law may be strengthened.

There are also other relevant aspects of Bentham's thinking, such as his criticism of the concept of 'natural rights' and his analysis of systemic corruption of the legal profession. He also presented a vision of an international legal order, including the establishment of a world court, to secure peace and co-operation among states.

Whole new fields of international law have come into existence since Bentham's times, such as international human rights law, international humanitarian law, and international criminal law. However, his reasoning on the law-like character of international law and its role in promoting overall happiness and preventing war might still be of relevance for contemporary debates about the status and role of international law.

Due to his own frustration with the English government and other governments that did not follow-up on reforms, Bentham also delved into strategic questions: how to promote reform ideas when faced with powerful groups that could lose benefits if reforms where enacted. His thinking on such issues may still have something to offer in a contemporary context.

Despite Bentham's frustrations over reluctant governments, he became increasingly influential in his own time and remains so in current times.[22] He inspired, *inter alia*, prominent political and legal philosophers such as Mill, Austin and Hart. Utilitarianism remains an important branch of contemporary ethical philosophy, and legal positivism remains among the main strands of contemporary legal philosophy. Both have borrowed heavily from Bentham's ideas.

There is certainly much to question and criticize in Bentham's thinking. I maintain, however, that there is also a lot to take note of and make use of in improving democratic institutions and legislation; both on the national and the international level.

In short, I find Bentham and Benthamite concerns especially relevant to modern discussions on the philosophical foundations of international criminal law in five aspects:

Firstly, he presented comprehensive ideas about the civilizing functions of law, including criminal law, and which conditions law must meet to fulfil such functions. He was very much aware of the *negative* aspects of laws – for instance in restricting human freedom and inflicting pain and suffering on those who were subject of lawful punishment. Based on such considerations, he contended that legislation had to be designed well and be based on sound principles to maximize overall happiness. Institutions had to be redesigned bearing these concerns in mind. Reforming and improving legislation and practice is an ongoing process, and will never end.

Secondly, his thinking and visions about international law as a tool to preventing wars and improving inter-state relations. His idea of codifying an international legal code also led him to see the need to establish an international court

[22] Like few other philosophers, Bentham experienced the forming of a 'sect' of followers, establishing their own magazine, *The Westminster Review*, founded in 1823; and the establishment of a university by inspiration of his ideas, the London University College, in 1826.

able to decide on disputes between states. He did not develop the foundations for international criminal law as such, but he clearly depicted needs for sanctioning violations of international norms by representatives and even heads of states. This means that some conditionality was inherent in Bentham's thinking when it comes to the sovereignty of states.

Thirdly, his thinking about creating conditions conducive of reforms and improvements of legislation may have valid points for contemporary efforts to build wider consensus on the practice of international criminal law. Politicization, corruption and other forms of failures of legal practice may weaken popular and state support for both the norms of international criminal law as well as their application. Bentham may provide useful ideas on how to overcome obstacles to reform and mobilize wider support of the norms.

Fourthly, Bentham may provide useful ideas for contemporary discussions on how to reform and develop further international criminal law to protect the most important values of humanity. He emphasized that reforming legislation should be based on a principled approach, evaluating the result or consequences of legislation in terms of protecting the well-being of the greatest number. It may be argued that, so far, international criminal law has mainly been developed as an *ad hoc* response to situations of massive crimes, and only a few states have been influential in forming it. As part of a systematic approach, more states should be invited to join discussions on how to further develop international criminal law, providing it with greater authority. An important part of the discussion should be to systematically identify the most important values of humankind to be protected by the law.

Fifthly, it is part of Bentham's strategy of influencing legislation that if he succeeded in one country, that country could serve as a model for legislation in other states. Transposed onto the role of contemporary international criminal law, the complementary principle of the Rome Statute may serve exactly that function. It may lead to reforms strengthening national jurisdictions because functioning states prefer to be able to prosecute crimes themselves and avoid interference by the ICC.[23]

In this way, the Rome Statute may serve as a model for national legislation and over time build capacity at the national level to prosecute core international crimes. This may even be the most important function of international criminal

[23] Articles 17 and Article 53(2)(b) of the Rome Statute of the International Criminal Court ('ICC Statute') define the principle of complementarity. The complementary nature of the ICC is stated in the Preamble of the ICC Statute, 17 July 1998 (https://www.legal-tools.org/doc/7b9af9/):

> The International Criminal Court established under this Statute shall be complementary to national criminal jurisdictions.

law and the ICC, since the beneficial influence on society of national prosecution of grave crimes tends to be larger than the influence of more distant international prosecution. Bentham may have applauded such an outcome, since for him the most important function of law is to influence society by producing maximum happiness and minimum pain. He would think that this could be done better domestically than internationally.

In this view, the ICC would be a successful institution if it were able to influence national jurisdictions effectively to genuinely prosecute international crimes, leaving few cases for the institution itself to deal with.

3.2. Bentham's Intellectual Profile

Bentham came from a family of lawyers. Both his father and grandfather were lawyers working in London. His father intended for him to follow and surpass them as practising lawyers. However, Bentham was not an impressive speaker, and he was not impressed himself by the state of English laws at the time. Rather than making money by practising law, he turned to a study of what the law might be or how it could be improved.

What was so frustrating with the English laws of his time? In his first book, *A Fragment on Government* (1776), Bentham distinguishes between the 'Expositor', who explains "to us what, as he supposes, the Law is", and the 'Censor', who observes "to us what he thinks it ought to be".[24] The book is a critique of Blackstone's *Commentaries on the Laws of England* (1765–1769). Bentham saw in Blackstone, who was a celebrated authority on English law at the time, a representative of a widespread and damaging attitude, namely, that the increasing crime rate in the country had nothing to do with the state of its laws.

There were other problems with Blackstone, according to Bentham, but the main point seems to be that in his exposition of England's laws, he did not see the need for reform. Bentham was, in the words of Bentham scholar James Steintrager, convinced that "the confusions, uncertainties and obscurity of the penal law and its enforcement were causing the increasing crime rate which he saw afflicting the country".[25]

Blackstone's commentary contained another important fallacy. Its constitutional theory was inspired by John Locke (1632–1704), and referred to fictitious entities such as 'state of nature', 'social contract' and 'natural rights'. According to Bentham, these were dangerous fictions, which could easily result in violent and anarchical revolutions.

---

24 Jeremy Bentham, in F.C. Montague (ed.), *A Fragment on Government*, The Lawbook Exchange, New Jersey, 2001 [1776], p. 98.

25 Steintrager, 2004, p. 15, see *supra* note 4.

England experienced at Bentham's time rapid social changes due to the industrial revolution and socio-economic upheaval. For many observers, these rapid changes were an important part of explaining the increasing crime rate.

For Bentham, however, the emphasis was not on social problems but on the lacking quality of England's penal laws. They were a wholly unsystematic mix of customs and (often badly) codified laws. In his own copy of *A Fragment on Government*, Bentham wrote that "this was the very first publication by which men at large were invited to break loose from the trammels of authority and ancestor-wisdom in the field of law".[26]

Bentham's recipe for solving the problems was first and foremost legal reform; and then, secondly, political reform. He grew up in an era in which the natural sciences were making rapid strides, both in theory and in their application. His vision was to remedy the problems and conflicts of his day, by imitating the methods of the natural sciences. Like Newton had succeeded by founding on "a single law a complete science of nature", Bentham thought he had found "an analogous principle capable of serving for the establishment of a synthetic science of the phenomena of moral and social life".[27]

He thought about himself as a reformer who was destined to introduce a new scientific approach to the reform of penal codes – both in England and in any other country. He was the Newton of the moral and social sciences. His reform ambitions were not confined to England: "That which is Law, is, in different countries, widely different: while that which ought to be, is in all countries to a great degree the same. The Expositor, therefore, is always the citizen of this or that particular country: the Censor is, or ought to be the citizen of the world".[28] His global ambitions are evidenced by his active promotion of reform proposals in a number of countries in Europe and America.

This self-asserting belief that by applying the principle of utility, he could reshape legislation in any country and thereby solve their main social and political problems, providing maximum happiness for the largest number, of course led to criticism. Even some of his followers, such as Mill, described him as 'one-eyed', lacking experience, and being overly rigid in his insistence on having discovered an Archimedean point.[29]

---

[26] Quoted from *ibid*., p. xi.

[27] Elie Halévy, *The Growth of Philosophic Radicalism*, trans. by Mary Morris, Beacon Press, Boston, 1955, p. 3.

[28] Bentham, 2001, p. 98, see *supra* note 24.

[29] John Stuart Mill, "'Bentham', Essays on Ethics, Religion and Society", in John M. Robson and F.E.L. Priestley (eds.), *The Collected Works of John Stuart Mill*, Vol. X, University of Toronto Press, 1969, p. 94 and pp. 77–115 in general.

However, there is much that points otherwise. From his inspiration from natural sciences, there is certainly a great deal of optimism. He realized, however, that morals and legislation are much more complex than natural sciences. He also knew, despite his programmatic declaration of psychological hedonism, that human nature is complex. He was aware of difficulties which stood in the way of his project, such as men not having a "clear view of their own interest". Religion, superstition and fictions could lead men astray from reason and their own best interest.

The science of calculating which legal norms or individual actions would provide maximum happiness and minimum pain is not an easy one. It can hardly be a quantitative science as indicated by such terms as 'felicity calculus'. It might be that Steintrager is close to the truth when he says that Bentham, above all, "found the principle of utility attractive because of its heuristic nature. The principle of utility was meant to generate a system, but it was intended to be an open system, one characterized by flexibility and development through the medium of rational discourse".[30]

Regardless of how Bentham is portrayed, the focus in our context should be on what is constructive and worth taking seriously today. His reaction to increasing crime rates in England at his time might have been one-sided. His optimism that he could achieve similar gains as Newton had done in natural science by applying the principle of utility may have been naïve. However, his insistence that legislation should serve the well-being of the many, not only of the rulers, or the lawyers, or other groups that benefitted from imperfect legislation, is a sound one.

3.2.1. The Misery of Bad Legislation and Its Healing

Bentham seems to have been convinced that there was more serious crime in England than in any other country in Europe.[31] The consequence of this situation was increasing unhappiness for an increasing number of victims, culprits, and for a large part of the population who suffered from an atmosphere of insecurity. For Bentham, this picture of his motherland was distressing because he believed that a lot of this unhappiness was unnecessary.

Even though extreme poverty and socio-economic upheaval was partly to be blamed for the high crime rate, weaknesses in legislation and juridical praxis was a more important factor. Legislation could be compared with medicine. It was, however, an art and science of healing on a grand scale, namely, of healing the whole body politic.

[30] Steintrager, 2004, p. 11, see *supra* note 4.

[31] I base the outline in this section on Steintrager's reading of Bentham, based on extensive consultation of unpublished manuscripts.

In England, Bentham contended, men often committed crimes because they did not know that their actions were criminal. Even if they did know, the penal sanctions anticipated were often too lenient to deter them or the application of sanctions was uncertain. Heinous crimes went unpunished or were only subject to minor sanctions while small illegal acts could be punished with severity. Acts which were rightly classified as crimes were punished without considering the nature of the crime or its circumstances.

There were several other problems, such as overly technical and unnecessarily complicated rules of evidence. The rules of procedures led to cases taking years to be finalized, while high fees and taxes prevented just treatment for many. Another problem was that the rights and duties of the citizens were not well defined, and the law was not properly promulgated. A systematic problem was that the access to judgments that functioned as precedents was often difficult. Such precedents were often collected in books written in Latin and therefore inaccessible to anyone except judges and lawyers.

There was therefore no way in which the public could know what the law was. The legal status of an act was unclear since precedents often were inconsistent with one another.

Bentham's vivid critical exposé of the state of England's legislation at his time may at some points resonate with the current state of legislation and legal practice in parts of the world. His proposals for how to remedy the deficiencies, may at several points remind of some of the steps proposed by current legal reform movements and human rights groups.

Some of the steps Bentham proposes are obvious – such as easing access to legislation, organize and systematize legislation in reasonable and understandable terms, improve rules of procedure and evidence so that cases can be decided within reasonable time, and so on – while others are subtler and sophisticated.

In this chapter, I will refer only to a few of his most important proposals and analyses. It is pertinent to mention, however, that even if Bentham thought of legislative reform – based on the principle of utility – as being of primary importance in remedying the dismal state of crime in England, he did not think that even the best legislation could completely solve the problems. Even though he was a rationalist in the sense that he believed humans apply reason in choosing to perform acts that promote their own best interests (happiness), he realized that there were plenty of passions and delusions that could lead humans astray.

He did, however, believe that crime could be reduced substantially by codifying law and systematically promulgating it. Law statutes should be made so anyone of ordinary intelligence could discover with relative ease which actions constituted crimes. He had high ambitions for the completeness possible for penal law, stating that it should contain "no *terra incognitae*, no blank spaces". It should be divided into sections so that individuals involved in certain activities can have access to a digest of relevant laws.

To succeed in reducing crime, Bentham argued that there was a need of a rational system of classifying offences. In the works of Blackstone and other legal authorities of his time there was no classificatory system to be found. The result was that their writings were as confused and complicated as the common law itself. Instead branches of law had to be divided into two parts and "then each of those parts into two others; and so on". In this way a detailed and accurate map of the law may be achieved.[32]

3.2.2. Bentham's Concept of Law

The misery of legislation had, however, a deeper cause in the way language function in legal texts. Scholars mostly agree that Bentham's theories about law and legal language is among his most original thought.[33]

His view on law is dependent on his understanding of the concept of 'human liberty', which is founded in the liberal tradition. According to this thinking, liberty is *absence of restraint and interference from society and rulers*. To the extent that one is not hindered by others, one has liberty and is free. There has never been a natural state of freedom, according to Bentham, and since people have always lived in society there is nothing like a 'social contract'. However, in society there is a distinction between *public* and *private* life. Liberty as non-interference by the society or the rulers is morally good since it is reflecting the greatest happiness principle.

Due to his view on liberty, Bentham followed Thomas Hobbes (1588–1679) in viewing law as 'negative'. Based on the principle of utility, liberty must be positive because it provides happiness, while law is negative since it restricts liberty. It follows that the control which the state exerts by legislation must be limited to maintain individual freedom.

Law is nevertheless necessary to social order, and good laws, promoting happiness and well-being to the greatest number, is essential to good

32 Readers of Bentham will recollect this model from his texts on legislation. Almost a third of the *Introduction to the Principles of Morals and Legislation* is devoted to a chapter on "Division of Offences", see *supra* note 6.

33 According to Hart, Bentham's theories on 'fictions' "anticipated by a century part of Bertrand Russell's doctrine on logical constructions and incomplete symbols. That doctrine, […] was looked upon by many English and American philosophers as the paradigm of philosophical method and the prime solvent of philosophical perplexities". See Hart, 1971, p. 19, *supra* note 20. Bentham also pioneered another important idea, namely that "sentences not words are the unit of meaning", which were later re-discovered by Gottlob Frege (1848–1925) and Ludwig Wittgenstein (1889–1959) in his *Tractatus Logico-Philosophicus* (prop. 3.3 and 3.3.4).

government. The problems that arises from bad legislation is therefore of the greatest importance to solve. Unlike many earlier thinkers, Bentham denied that there exists any 'natural law', which could be invoked to reject, amend or provide with authority existing law. Instead, his persuasion was that the principle of utility was the only sound basis for criticizing and improving legislation.

For Bentham, law is a phenomenon of large societies with a sovereign – a person or a group of persons with supreme power. Laws in such societies are a subset of the sovereign's commands: general orders that apply to classes of actions and people and are backed up by the threat of sanctions. This view was further developed by Austin and legal positivism. A consequence of the view is that law that contains morally questionable norms, or commands morally evil actions, or is not based on consent, is still law.

A popular misunderstanding is that legal positivism necessarily means that one must be *satisfied* with existing law. This is refuted by Bentham and other legal positivists. Understanding the phenomenon of law must be clearly distinguished from assessing or censuring (as Bentham would say) existing law. Large parts of Bentham's publications are devoted to criticizing legislation as well as juridical practice and to proposing better legislation. He also held that disobedience towards the law, stemming from considerations applying the principle of utility, was sometimes justified.

However, he was convinced that invoking *natural rights* or *natural law arguments* did not lead to increase in the overall happiness of the members of society. Rather it led to revolutions, anarchy and pain, as demonstrated by developments in France after the 1789 revolution and the proclamation of the *Declaration of the Rights of the Man and of the Citizen.*

There was also another possible unwanted result of insufficient understanding of law: oppression, legal corruption and barbarism, as exemplified by the state in England.

In criticizing both what he called the 'anarchical fallacies' resulting from declaring natural rights, as well as the unfortunate situation with English law, Bentham applied his theory on logical fictions.

Understanding law involves understanding concepts such as 'rights', 'obligations', 'contracts', 'property', 'immunity', 'privilege', and so on. This proves rather difficult. In the empiricist tradition, which Bentham adheres to, understanding is provided by *perception.* To allow for the understanding of things that are not directly perceived, Locke and Hume, the primary advocates of empiricism, distinguished between 'simple' and 'complex' ideas. A complex idea, such as that of a golden mountain, can be understood only because it can be analysed in terms of its simple constituents.

However, this technique does not work for legal terms. Bentham therefore invented an alternative way of giving meaning to such terms, called 'paraphrasis'. The idea is not to translate complex words into simpler words, but to translate the whole sentence of which it forms a part into another sentence. He called the legal terms in question 'fictional entities', and works out for several of them how sentences containing them can be translated to sentences that eventually only contains 'real entities'.

A much-used example is the term 'rights', which are explained by Bentham in terms of sentences about 'duties'. A right I have may be restated in terms of the imposition of duties on others who are obliged to fulfil my right. 'Duty' is of course also a 'fictional entity', never to be perceived directly, but a new paraphrasis may lead to something perceivable. Sentences about duties can be translated into sentences about the threat of moral disapproval or punishment. To have a duty is then to be under a threat of being sanctioned if the duty is not fulfilled. Finally, being under a threat of a sanction amounts to being under a threat of imposition of pain.

In this way, we reach what Bentham calls 'real entities'. A famous quote from *A Fragment on Government* reads: "*pain* and *pleasure* at least are words which a man has no need, we may hope, to go to a Lawyer to know the meaning of".[34] With such clarifiers, the law can become clear for lawyers and laymen alike.

The problem was that English common law terminology was full of fictions, and that judges, lawyers and laymen alike did not distinguish between them and real entities. There was a widespread belief that there were real objects which corresponded to the abstract words.

For Bentham, it was therefore not enough that common law was adequately codified, classified and promulgated as statutory law. The language of law should be transformed. He developed whole new sets of terms for a 'universal jurisprudence', with definitions consisting of simple ideas and which could replace the technical, ambiguous, obscure and fictitious language of English jurisprudence.

Even though he never presented his theory of fictions in full, it remains at the hearth of his explanations of why legal reform is necessary and how it can be done. For him, the project is not limited to refining and clarifying terminology. The task of legal philosophy, which Bentham in this context calls the "metaphysics of jurisprudence", is to clarify what is meant when we use certain words. Without such clarity, humans are destined to remain slaves to authority and the customs of barbaric times.

[34] Bentham, 1776, p. 121, see *supra* note 24.

3.2.3. Bentham's Attack on Natural Rights

No doubt, Bentham's criticism of the state of England's legislation at the time had many valid points. Some of the points he made may even be valid for contemporary legislation in many states. For any state to reduce crime and create a secure environment, the task of clarifying, simplifying, systematizing and making accessible its penal code remains a task of primary importance. The proposals on how what he calls 'legal fictions' may be translated into more readily understandable terms is also constructive, even though Bentham may have overstated the negative impact they have.

Also, Bentham's realizations of why his reform proposals were often not followed up on, have valid points.[35] He may have understood early on that reform was difficult, even though he later gave the impression that it took him a long time to fully realize how difficult it was. He realized that the people in power, adhering to the 'principle of self-preference' rather than the 'principle of utility', did not want reform. All his proposals were designed to improve the lot of the greater number, and thereby they could also threaten the interests of the few in power: the rulers and certain professional groups that benefitted from the situation, such as lawyers, judges, legislators, booksellers, and who gained financially from a confused legal situation.

He also realized that even those who would benefit the most from his proposals, people in general, in many cases were not ready to accept them because of fear of change and lack of understanding of complex matters.

Another striking feature of Bentham's reform proposals are their universal aspirations. In the same way that the laws of physics are the same everywhere, the principles of high-quality legislation and politics are valid everywhere. Of course, his main devotion was to improve the situation in England, but he made proposals for improved legislation in many other countries. In principle, Bentham was proposing a 'universal censorial jurisprudence', which criticizes law as it is considering what the law ought to be, and what ought to be transcends the boundaries of any given nation. It appeals to a universal standard – the 'principle of utility' – which is valid for all human's and societies.

Strikingly, Bentham's 'censorial jurisprudence' functions similar to the way international human rights function today. Human rights have become a universal standard from where domestic legislation and juridical practice may be *censored*. International human rights institutions provide model legislation and legal advice, like Bentham and his followers did. Similar frustrations as

[35] An overview of Bentham's reflections on the obstacles to reform is provided in Steintrager, 2004, Chapter 2, see *supra* note 4.

Bentham experienced also exist. National authorities often disregard or cheat in their following-up on the advices.

The analogy could even be extended to the codification of international criminal law in the Rome Statute. It is hard to imagine that Bentham would have been anything but positive towards such an endeavour that in his terms would clarify the law and serve as a model for domestic legislation.

Equally striking, however, is Bentham's attack on predecessors of the modern human rights movement, namely, thinkers that referred to the natural rights of all human beings in political declarations. For any contemporary reading, his denouncing of the 1789 French *Declaration of the Rights of the Man and of the Citizen* seems overblown. A comment by Hart may enlighten an important point:

> It seems to me that Bentham really was afraid not merely of intemperate invocations of the doctrine of Natural Rights in opposition to established laws, but sensed that the idea of rights would always excite a peculiarly strong suspicion that the doctrine of utility was not an adequate expression of men's moral ideas and political ideals. There is, I think, something strident or even feverish in Bentham's treatment of rights which betrays this nervousness.[36]

Bentham's view on fictional entities – such as legal rights – was that they needed to be translated and established on firmer foundations. Legal rights, however, had an important place in legislation and political life, and should not be disposed of.

Natural rights, however, were not fictional but *fabulous* entities and 'contradictions in terms'. Legal rights could be analysed in terms of the corresponding duties and the threat made by law of sanctions against those who did not fulfil their duties. This was not possible for natural rights since they were not part of any law at all. They were more akin to poetry, than to legal language. Unfortunately, the language of law had been infested with such entities.

> The purpose of the legislator requires that both the composer and the reader be as much as possible in their sober senses that they may be able (the one for the purpose of determining what he shall command, the other for that of knowing what he is to obey) to distinguish every object as perfectly as possible from all other with which it is in danger of being confounded. No kind of enthusiasm ought either the Legislator or the Judge to have about them, not even the enthusiasm of humanity.[37]

36 Hart, 1971, p. 33, see *supra* note 20.

37 Steintrager, 2004, p. 9, see *supra* note 4. The quotation is from University College London, Bentham Manuscript, Box 27, p. 123.

Bentham invented a whole range of expressions to describe that natural rights are non-existing, such as calling them 'counterfeit rights', 'nonsense on stilts' and so on. More constructive, however, is his suggestions that the reference to natural rights is a way of arguing or stating a strong wish about which *legal* rights there ought to be. He would then add that this must be done with care in order not to create expectations and enthusiasm that could lead to anarchical consequences.

Supposing that natural rights exist is wrong for another reason as well, because it indicates that these rights would be the same for all time. According to Bentham, only those systems of rights that produce utility should be upheld. Over time, different conditions may mean that we must restate rights or change them altogether. It is therefore a mistake to think that any rights are unalterable.

In the utilitarian view on rights, they are reduced to tools to promote the principle of utility. In this author's view, important features of rights are then lost, such as their defence of the dignity, autonomy, privacy and personal freedom; in particular of persons belonging to vulnerable groups of society.[38]

According to Hart, Bentham failed to see that 'rights' have a different time direction than the principle of utility, which always points to the future consequences of actions to assess whether they are acceptable. Reasons for ascription of moral rights "must refer to the present properties or past actions of the individuals who are said to have moral rights as in themselves sufficient grounds for treating them in a certain way independently of the beneficial consequences to society of doing so".[39]

The point is that rights do not depend on an analysis of future consequences, but on whether a person has done something that make her or him *deserve* certain treatment. The claim of natural and human rights is that if only a person is born as human being she or he qualifies to certain basic rights. Even if treating someone according to human rights has neutral or negative consequences for the overall well-being of affected persons, the rights should be respected.

In many cases, there would not be a conflict between the results of applying the principle of utility and applying human rights. However, it is easy to find examples where there are. For instance, should the law permit applying torture if you by torturing a person could obtain information that could save innocent

---

[38] See Hugo Adam Bedau, "'Anarchical Fallacies': Bentham's Attack on Human Rights", in *Human Rights Quarterly*, 2000, vol. 22, no. 1, pp. 261–79. Bedau argues that Bentham's restrictive utilitarian view misses the key points of human rights, and that they should instead be derived from "recognition of our common nature as rational, autonomous, moral agents for whom liberty, privacy and other goods are paramount, rather than from any collective or aggregative fact about net social welfare or the general happiness" (p. 278).

[39] Hart, 1971, pp. 38 ff., see *supra* note 20.

civilians from a terrorist attack? Utilitarian and human rights consideration would provide opposite answers. In human rights, the prohibition of torture is an absolute one, resulting in a certain inflexibility that Bentham would oppose.[40]

3.2.4. Punishment and Criminal Responsibility

The philosophical foundation of any criminal law – which imposes forms of punishment on those who are found guilty of breaching the law – must entail a theoretical justification for punishment as such. Traditionally, such justifications have been either 'consequentialist' or 'deontological'.

In general, the practice of punishment could be justified by reference either to 'forward-looking' or to 'backward-looking' considerations. If the former prevails, then the theory is likely to be 'consequentialist' and likely some version of utilitarianism. According to this view, the point of the practice of punishment is to increase overall net social welfare by reducing or ideally, preventing crime.

If the latter prevail, the theory is 'deontological'. In this approach, punishment is seen either as a good in itself or as a practice required by justice. A 'deontological' justification of punishment is likely to be a 'retributive' justification.

There is also a third alternative, providing justifications in hybrid combinations of these two independent alternatives.[41]

The consequentialist views punishment as justified to the extent that its practice achieves (or is believed to achieve) an end-state such as "happiness for the greatest number", general welfare or another specified common good. Most philosophers today would modify this view by introducing various constraints on punishment, such as those following from human rights or other humanistic considerations. Whether these constraints can in turn be justified by their consequences is not a necessary condition. An important part of the theory of punishment is thus a careful articulation of the norms that provide these constraints on the practice and their rationale.

As we have seen, the assessing of the future consequences of individual actions, application of legal norms and implementation of government decrees is at the centre of Bentham's normative approach. His justification of punishment follows the same logic.

---

[40] For the sake of the argument, I disregard considerations about the effectiveness of torture in getting reliable information. Much modern research indicates that coercive interrogation methods are not to be relied on. See, for example, Norwegian researcher Asbjørn Rachlew, "From Interrogating to Interviewing Suspects of Terror: Towards a New Mindset", in *Penal Reform International*, 14 March 2017.

[41] Hugo Adam Bedau and Erin Kelly, "Punishment", in *Stanford Encyclopaedia of Philosophy*, 31 July 2015.

The proper aim and justification for punishment is to produce pleasure and prevent or reduce pain. However, punishment is painful. The only viable justification of it is therefore to prove that the pain inflicted on the person who is punished, is outbalanced by the reduction in pain or increase of pleasure it causes for all affected persons.

If the threat of punishment is deterring people from doing things which would produce more pain – such as rape, theft, murder or committing international crimes – then punishment is justified. A consequence of the theory is also that the amount of pain which is inflicted must be less than the reduction of pain or the happiness it produces. In other words, there must be a valuation of the likely pains produced by future offences, which can be averted by setting out a meted punishment.

This way of reasoning does not implicate that the punishment should be similar to the offence. If punishment is, however, justified as a *deliberate form of revenge*, such ideas of mimicking the offence come to the fore. For Bentham, this is an example of applying the principle of 'sympathy and antipathy', whereby you punish according to your feelings, "if you hate much, punish much: if you hate little, punish little: punish as you hate".[42] Instead, punishment should be a tool to improve society by deterring future offences and rehabilitating criminals.

Currently, there may be six prevailing standard justifications of punishment. According to these views, we punish criminals because it:

1. serves justice by giving criminals the hard treatment they deserve ('retributivism');
2. deters everyone from committing crimes ('deterrence');
3. helps to morally educate both the criminal and society at large ('moral education');
4. allows society to express its moral values ('expressivism');
5. helps restore the victims along with their friends and families ('restitutivism'); and, finally
6. provides a controlled, peaceful outlet for socially disruptive emotions ('social safety valve theory').

Even though each of these justifications may carry different weight, I think they are all part of what we today would come up with if pressed to justify punishing criminals. "Each of the traditional theories helps illuminate what we stand to gain from an effective institution of punishment", in the words of Christopher

[42] Bentham, 1876, p. 17, see *supra* note 6.

H. Wellman. I also agree with him, that of the six, the second might be the most important.[43]

In Nordic countries, the so-called 'general' and 'individual' prevention of crimes is at the centre of the foundations of penal legislation. Such considerations also have a prominent place in many other countries and in international jurisdictions.

It is thus hard to question that Benthamite views have prevailed. However, different from his exclusionist approach of treating justifications, the utilitarian justifications have prevailed in concert with others. Depending on circumstances, as of today, many would be willing to refer to all six justifications mentioned above as valid, however, granting Bentham that deterrence and moral education should be viewed as most important.

In thinking about criminal responsibility, Bentham's view is restrictive, based on a narrow understanding of what can legitimately constitute a 'reason for action'. According to Hart, the restrictive view has its origin in Bentham's denial that the past actions of an individual who is said to have moral rights could serve as "sufficient ground for treating them in a certain way independently of the beneficial consequences to society of doing so".[44] To invoke past achievements as a reason to grant someone special treatment today is, in Bentham's eyes, "a form of bad faith which uses the language of reason to express personal 'antipathy or sympathy', mere irrational sentiment".[45]

Few of Bentham's passages are more revealing of his way of thinking than the following:

> It is the principle of antipathy which leads us to speak of offences as *deserving* punishment. It is the corresponding principle of sympathy which leads us to speak of certain actions as *meriting* reward. This word *merit* can only lead to passion and error. It is *effects* good or bad which we ought alone to consider.[46]

In line with this restrictive line of thought about what can be a reason for rewarding or punishing someone, Bentham also has diverging views on how to justify mental conditions of criminal responsibility. In any civilized legal system, if a person was insane, a young child, under duress, or could not control himself

43 Christopher Heath Wellman, "Piercing Sovereignty: A Rationale for International Jurisdiction Over Crimes That Do Not Cross International Borders", in R.A. Duff and Stuart Green (eds.), *Philosophical Foundations of Criminal Law*, Oxford University Press, 2013, p. 461.

44 Hart, 1971, p. 38, see *supra* note 20.

45 *Ibid.*

46 Jeremy Bentham, *Theory of Legislation*, 2nd ed., Trübner & Co., London, 1871, p. 76.

when committing a crime, he or she should not be liable to punishment or blame.[47]

Even if Bentham accepts this doctrine, he turns "its face to the future away from the past. We are to observe such restrictions on the use of punishment not because there is any intrinsic objection to punishing a man who at the time of the crime lacked 'a vicious will' or lacked the 'free use of his will but because his punishment will be 'inefficacious'".[48]

This approach is, in my view, counter-intuitive. However, Bentham's challenging of traditional justifications of punishment and criminal responsibility – and a range of other concepts – still has some bearing. Even if we do not accept that future consequences are the *only* relevant concerns when justifying punishment or determining the limits of criminal responsibility, they should be part of the consideration.

His approach also has the beneficial effect of bringing to the discussion on the foundations of punishment, questions on how to strengthen the component of rehabilitation and moral education.

3.2.5. Extending the Principle of Utility to International Law

Bentham did not write extensively on international law. He did nevertheless play a crucial role by re-naming the field and providing a vision for international law's role in securing world peace and happiness for all nations. He was of the view that international law should play a similar role in the society of states as national law played in the society of individuals. It should be shaped to provide happiness for the greatest number of states.

He coined the English word 'international' in the last chapter of his book *An Introduction to the Principles of Morals and Legislation*, to replace the term 'law of nations'. The term 'law of nations' is a misnomer, according to Bentham and "were it not for the force of custom, it would seem rather to refer to internal jurisprudence" of nations.

In discussing how jurisprudence may be classified, Bentham suggests that it can be divided in terms of "the political quality of the persons whose conduct is the subject of the law". He states that persons "may [...] be considered either as members of the same state, or as members of different states; in the first case, the law may be referred to the head of *internal*, in the second case, to that of international jurisprudence".[49]

---

[47] The doctrine of *mens rea* as a necessary condition of criminal responsibility and liability for punishment is prescribed in Articles 30 and 31 of the ICC Statute, see *supra* note 23.

[48] Hart, 1971, p. 40, see *supra* note 20. See also Bentham, 1876, Chapter XV, *supra* note 6.

[49] *Ibid.*, p. 326.

In putting Bentham's view on international law in context, he had a rather Eurocentric view on the globalization taking place at his time, while also acknowledging the important role of the United States as a model of representative democracy, and arguing for de-colonization. It was, in his view, primarily the European states that civilized the world, although there were many deficiencies in their legislation and political life.

Accordingly, he promoted his first book, *A Fragment on Government*, as the product of a global moment in British and human history because it was published just after James Cook's return from his second voyage around the world in 1775. In the preface, he notes that "[t]he age we live in is a busy age; in which knowledge is rapidly advancing towards perfection. In the natural world, in particular, everything teems with discovery and with improvement. The most distant and recondite regions of the earth traversed and explored [...] are striking evidences, were all others wanting, of this pleasing truth".[50]

The context of Bentham's thinking about international matters and the regulation that international law may provide thus seems to be the expanding British and European empires. This was, however, somewhat balanced by his application of the principle of utility, which defined its subjects to have equal status.

In framing the concept of international law, his starting point was his critical appraisal of Blackstone's exposition on the law of nations. *A Fragment of Government* may have been inspired by global expansion of the British Empire, but it was first and foremost a critique of Blackstone's account of municipal law. *A Comment on the Commentaries*, which Bentham drafted between 1774 and 1776, and which the *Fragment* was based on, remained incomplete and was never published by Bentham. It is in this work; however, that he explains what he thinks is wrong with Blackstone's account of the law of nations.[51]

Not surprisingly, among Bentham's chief concerns was that Blackstone included the law of nature in the concept of the law of nations, as well as mutual compacts, treaties, leagues and agreements, which were of doubtful legal content. It might be that Bentham did not treat Blackstone's account fairly;[52] however, the direction of his criticism was clearly in line with his thoughts about how to improve international legislation presented 13 years later, in *An Introduction to the Principles of Morals and Legislation*.

[50] Jeremy Bentham, *A Fragment on Government*, printed for T. Paine, P. Elmsly and E. Brooke, London, 1776, p. i.

[51] See M.W. Janis, "Jeremy Bentham and the Fashioning of International Law", in *American Journal of International Law*, 1984, vol. 78, no. 2, pp. 405–418. *The Comment on the Commentaries* was first published in 1928. It is currently available in *The Collected Works of Jeremy Bentham*, Oxford University Press, 2008.

[52] See Janis, 1984, p. 408, *supra* note 51.

In an oft-quoted footnote to his introduction of the term 'international jurisprudence',[53] he explains that "the word *international*, it must be acknowledged, is a new one; though, it is hoped, sufficiently analogous and intelligible. It is calculated to express, in a more significant way, the branch of the law which goes commonly under the name of the *law of nations*".

It is clear from Bentham's further explanations of international law, that it deals exclusively with the rights and obligations of states between themselves and not about rights and obligations of individuals. He also assumed that foreign transactions before municipal courts were decided by internal, not international, rules. In effect, without ever mentioning that he realized to have done so, Bentham "excluded from the domain of his 'international law' all of those rules mentioned by Blackstone that concerned individual rights and obligations. [...] More or less inadvertently, Bentham changed the boundaries of the field he sought to define".[54]

There are several other important aspects of Bentham's view on the status and scope of international law. His disciple, John Austin is well-known for his conclusion that international law lacks law-like qualities. He viewed it as rules established merely by general opinion, such as laws of honour or law set by fashion.[55] According to Austin, law-like qualities included that legal provisions should be based on a command of the sovereign and those violating it should face sanctions.

Since there was no international sovereign and because the sanctions for violating international law were only moral, Austin rejected the claim that international law really was law at all. Bentham may have expressed similar views; however, his main line of thought was quite different. In a manuscript called *Of Laws in General*,[56] he elaborates further on necessary qualities of laws. He contended that "concessions of sovereign are not laws" and that "a treaty made by one sovereign with another is not itself a law". He also held that the enforcement of the treaties depended only on moral and religious sanctions.

He nevertheless pointed out that national sovereigns *could* make international law, and that *real* law could be enforced only with a religious or a moral sanction. It seems then that we "have strong suggestions that Bentham, for

[53] Bentham, 1871, see *supra* note 46.

[54] Janis, 1984, p. 410, see *supra* note 51.

[55] John Austin, *The Province of Jurisprudence Determined*, Weidenfeld & Nicholson, London, 1954, p. 201.

[56] *Of Laws in General* was not part of the 1843 John Bowring edition of Bentham's collected works, but was only discovered in 1939. It was published in 1945 under the title *The Limits of Jurisprudence Defined*. Hart edited the manuscript and published it in 1970, under the title *Of Laws in General*.

himself, was at least sometimes satisfied that there was enough to international law that was lawlike to let one call it law".[57] In this, he was later followed by Hart, who famously argued in the *Concept of Law* (1961) that "no other social rules are so close to municipal law as those of international law".[58]

More important than Bentham's discussions on the status of international law at his time, is his four essays with proposals of principles of international law.[59] It is the first, *Objects of International Law*, and the fourth, *A Plan for a Universal and Perpetual Peace*, which identify most clearly Bentham's aims for international law.

As to be expected, Bentham's method in the essays is to apply the principle of utility to international law, as he did to municipal law. Overall, he has an optimistic view of what international law might accomplish. The beginning of *Objects of International Law* sets the tone: "If a citizen of the world had to prepare a universal international code, what would he propose to himself as his object? It would be the common and equal utility of all nations: this would be his inclination and his duty".[60]

Bentham questions whether a legislator, being a citizen of one nation, could at the same time be trusted to develop laws for the whole world. He attempts to resolve the dilemma by arguing in favour of surrendering national self-interest: "But ought the sovereign of a state to sacrifice the interests of his subjects for the advantage of foreigners? Why not? – provided it be in a case, if there be such a one, in which it would have been praiseworthy in his subjects to make the sacrifice themselves".[61] His point of departure is clearly the principle of utility.

> [...] the end that a disinterested legislator upon international law would propose to himself, would therefore be the greatest happiness of all nations taken together [...] he would follow the same route which he would follow with regard to internal laws. He

[57] Janis, 1984, p. 412, see *supra* note 51.

[58] H.L.A. Hart, in Joseph Raz and Penelope A. Bulloch (eds.), *The Concept of Law*, 3rd ed., Oxford University Press, 2012, p. 237.

[59] Bentham did not make it easy for the scholar to detect his full meaning as to the proposals. In the latter half of the 1780s, he drafted a series of proposals under the general headings of "Law Inter National 1786" and "Pacification and Emancipation". These remained incomplete and in manuscript form until they were translated from French to English, edited and published as four essays in 1843, under the title *Principles of International Law*. They appeared in the second volume of Bowring's edition of Bentham's collected works. The essays are sketchy and reflect the editor's choice as to what to include.

[60] Jeremy Bentham, in John Bowring (ed.), *Principles of International Law*, Vol. 2, William Tait, Edinburgh, 1838–1843, p. 536.

[61] *Ibid.*, p. 537.

> would set himself to prevent positive international offences – to encourage the practice of positively useful actions.
>
> He would regard as a positive crime every proceeding – every arrangement, by which the given nation should do more evil to foreign nations taken together, whose interests might be affected, than it should do good to itself. [...]
>
> In the same manner, he would regard as a negative offence every determination, by which the given nation should refuse to render positive services to a foreign nation, when the rendering of them would produce more good to the last-mentioned nation, than it would produce evil to itself.[62]

Bentham views war as a type of procedure by which nations endeavours "to enforce its rights at the expense of another nation". He named the laws of peace the "substantive laws of the international code", while the laws of war were the "adjective laws of the same code". He proposes several ways to prevent war:

> 1. Homologation [codification] of unwritten laws which are considered as established by custom;
> 2. New international laws to be made upon all points which remain unascertained; upon the greater number of points in which the interests of two states are capable of collision; and
> 3. Perfecting the style of the laws of all kinds, whether internal or international. How many wars have there been, which have had for their principal, or even their only cause, no more noble origin than the negligence or inability of a lawyer or a geometrician![63]

Bentham thought that wars could be prevented by dealing more methodically with the various causes of a conflict, by elaborating new international rules where no such rules exist, and by making unwritten customs explicit. And as he believed internal peace and reduction of crime could be achieved domestically by systematic reforms based on the utility principle, he believed international peace was in sight if international law was improved in similar ways.

The central theme of his *Plan for a Universal and Perpetual Peace,* the fourth of the essays on international law, is that to establish world peace nations should sacrifice national self-interest. He addresses proposals to all nations, especially to England and France, which include giving up of colonies, establishing free trade, reducing the navies to what is necessary to protect against pirates and the mutual reduction of the size of armies.

Bentham realized, however, that even if these reforms were to be adopted, there could still be conflicts between nations. He suggests therefore that to

[62] *Ibid.*, p. 539.

[63] *Ibid.*, p. 540.

prevent disputes nations should agree to establish an international court of arbitration, "a common court of judicature for the decision of differences between the several nations, although such court were not to be armed with any coercive powers".[64]

As envisioned by Bentham, the international court would work by establishing gradual responses. The first would be the mere reporting of the court's opinion. The second would be the circulation of the opinion in each nation to stimulate a favourable public reaction. The third would be "putting the refractory state under the ban of Europe". And the fourth, last resort, would be that participating states would contribute and deploy armed contingents to enforce the court's decisions.

In a manuscript written in the 1820s, Bentham proposed a legislative alliance among "all civilised nations", each to be represented by an envoy at a congress with both judicial and legislative authority. He criticized Emmerich de Vattel (1714–1767) for providing inadequate foundations for a new international order. He argued that only an international order "grounded on the greatest happiness principle, […] would, if the plan and execution be more moral and intellectual than Vattel's, possess a probability of superseding it, and being referred to in preference".[65]

In sum, Bentham introduced the English term 'international law' to replace the term 'law of nations', which he had found and criticized in Blackstone. He, however, narrowed the scope somewhat, restricting international law to only those rules which concern sovereign states among or between themselves. That was Bentham's original meaning in crafting the term 'inter-national'.

Blackstone's 'law of nations' includes laws characterized by their sources, which are non-municipal. It includes rules provided in multistate agreements or practice or other non-municipal sources. It is more inclusive than Bentham's definition, and according to some commentators it includes much of what had been traditionally thought of as within the realm of the law of nations.[66]

Bentham was called during his lifetime "legislator of the world".[67] That was not because he succeeded in codifying international law. He did not. What he did, however, to earn such a title was to propose a term – 'international law' – that became a success even in his own time.

---

[64] *Ibid.*, p. 547.

[65] Quoted from Carolina Kenny, "Jeremy Bentham, Principles of International Law (1786–1789/1843)", in *Classics of Strategy and Diplomacy*, 20 August 2015.

[66] Janis, 1984, p. 41, see *supra* note 51.

[67] José del Valle, a Guatemalan politician, wrote in a letter to Bentham: "Your works give you the glorious title of legislator of the world". See Kenny, 2015, endnote 45, *supra* note 65.

There was, however, more to it. Bentham was a visionary well ahead of his time, believing that a codified international law, thoroughly based on the principle of utility, could change the world for the better. In the words of Janis, "[i]t should be no surprise that Bentham brought his reformatory zeal, albeit briefly, to international, as well as to municipal, law. Realist and idealist – Bentham displayed both the scepticism and the romanticism that still invests the discipline he named".[68]

Bentham also included a proposal for a world institution – a world court – that could decide on contentious issues between the states. In other words, by strengthening the law-like character of international law – by proposing an international institution that could legitimately impose sanctions on states that violated the law – he thought he could prevent war and build a peaceful world.

Finally, Bentham's central concern during the 1810s and 1820s was to promote codification of the municipal law of "nations professing liberal opinions". He argued that a code of law should be based on a rigorous logical analysis of the categories of human action, and that each enactment should be followed by the reasons which justified it. Such a comprehensive approach would signal a new era in legislation.

His idea was that, once one state had adopted such a code, other states would be obliged to follow its example. He attempted to persuade legislative authorities in the United States, Russia, Spain, Portugal, Greece, South and Central America, and elsewhere, to invite him to draft a code of law for them.[69]

Bentham's concept of universal jurisprudence and his belief in rational model legislation, including all branches of law, is an important part of his legacy. Such international legislation as the Rome Statute of the ICC could be seen as such model legislation. The fact that states – if international core crimes take place on their territory or if their nationals are victims or offenders – must ascertain that they are willing and able to prosecute the crimes, build a strong case for them to copy the Rome Statute's definitions of the crimes. In effect, many countries have already incorporated or otherwise given the treaty's definitions effect in their national legal systems.

Bentham would, however, criticize the *ad hoc* manner in which international criminal law has been developed. He would favour a systematic approach, defining the most serious crimes that demanded a global legal response. It is an important part of his legacy not to merely accept the law as it is. One should

[68] Janis, 1984, p. 415, see *supra* note 51.

[69] Bentham's correspondence with, and proposals to, authorities in these countries is published in: "Legislator of the World: Writings on Codification, Law, and Education", in Philip Schofield and Jonathan Harris (eds.), *The Collected Works of Jeremy Bentham*, Clarendon Press, Oxford, 1998.

quest for a better law, drafted by applying rational and systematic methods to achieve the set goal of global well-being.

3.3. Utilitarianism Refined

Bentham did not invent the 'principle of utility'. His achievement was to apply it in reform proposals to improve legislation in any state with liberal opinions. By doing so, he developed a range of distinctions of types of pains and pleasures, categorized and mapped types of offences, defined secondary ends such as subsistence, abundance, security, and equality, and developed other concepts to make utilitarianism work. He explained 14 types of pleasures, 12 types of pains, and defined four sources of them: the 'physical', the 'political', the 'moral' and the 'religious'.[70]

In making his case for utilitarianism, he also developed aiding principles and proposals for mechanisms to ensure that those in charge of institutions would see it in their interest to apply the principle of utility. He had a realistic view about how the selfishness of persons in power could lead them to detract from the road to happiness for the largest number. The so-called 'duty-and-interest-juncture-principle' should be applied for instance in the poor house or in prisons to ensure that managers looked after those in their care. For instance, the salary of a governor should be reduced for every woman who died in childbirth. A prison director's salary should vary with the number of juvenile inmates who survived from year to year. According to Bentham, this should be so because:

> Every system of management which has disinterestedness pretended or real for its foundation is rotten at the root, susceptible of a momentary prosperity at the outset but sure to perish in the long run. That principle of action is most to be depended upon how's influence is most powerful, most constant, most uniform, most lasting and most general among mankind. Personal interest is that principle and a system of economy built on any other foundations is built upon a quicksand.[71]

Another important feature of Bentham's account of utilitarianism is that it is based on equality in two directions: (1) any individual's pleasure and pain should count equally with the pleasure and pain of any other individual in the felicity calculus ("everybody to count for one, nobody for more than one"), which is shorthand for the utilitarian principle of justice; and (2) there is no distinction between the worth of the different forms of pleasure or pain. Intensity,

[70] These themes are outlined in Chapters III and V of *An Introduction to the Principles of Morals and Legislation*: see Bentham, 1876, *supra* note 6. Chapter XVI, 'Division of Offenses', also includes a detailed outline of all categories of conceivable crimes and their subdivisions.

[71] Quoted from H.L.A. Hart, "Bentham", in Bhikhu Parekh (ed.), *Jeremy Bentham: Ten Critical Essays*, Frank Cass and Company Ltd., 1974, p. 76.

duration or extent of pleasure or pain are though important factors legislators should take into consideration.

Even though Bentham can be criticized for not leaving some groups of society much chance of integrating utilitarian sentiments in their motivations, in principle, he developed a refined system of evaluating actions on the individual level open for everyone to adopt.[72] For this author, however, his insistence that *legislation* should adhere to the 'principle of utility' may be of even higher importance. He consequently therefore adhered to a view that while the foundation of law may be the *command of the sovereign*, it is its consequences for society that must be assessed to find out whether it should be reformed.

3.3.1. John Stuart Mill

Mill played a crucial role in refining and making utilitarianism as an ethical doctrine accessible to the wider public. It could also be said that the most important question he dealt with – the balance between personal freedom and state control – was an inheritance from Bentham. Based on inspiration from Bentham and Adam Smith (1723–1790), Mill wrote pivotal texts for the liberal democratic tradition in Western political thinking.

The main idea of this tradition is that even a democratically elected government is no guarantee of real liberty. The ruling elite may become a class removed from the people, and a popularly elected government may still oppress minority groups of society, leading to the 'tyranny of the majority'. In a democratic society, the vital question is therefore where to put the balance between the need for social control, and the freedom of the individual to think and act as he or she wish. Humans are by nature intolerant, and therefore must be disciplined by policies and laws that protect them against each other. This leads to Mill's famous principle for ensuring freedom:

> The only purpose for which power can be rightfully exercised over any member of a civilised community, against his will, is to prevent harm to others. His own good, either physical or moral, is not a sufficient warrant. He cannot rightfully be compelled to do or forbear because it will be better for him to do so because it will make him happier, because, in the opinions of others, to do so would be wise, or even right.[73]

Mill defined Bentham's qualities in terms of an "essentially practical mind. It was by practical abuses that his mind was first turned to speculation – by the abuses of the profession which was chosen for him, that of the law". According

[72] For a criticism of Bentham along these lines, see Bhikhu Parekh, "Introduction", in *ibid.*

[73] John Stuart Mill, *On Liberty*, John W. Parker and Son, West Strand, London, 1859, p. 22.

to Mill, Bentham was shocked to learn for the first time that English lawyers demanded a client "to pay for three attendances" when only one was given.[74]

Unlike Bentham, Mill argued that pleasures differ in quality, and that pleasures that are rooted in one's higher faculties should be weighted more heavily than baser pleasures. He held that people's achievements of goals and ends, such as virtuous living, should be counted as part of their happiness. He explained that the sentiment of justice is based on utility, and that rights exist only because they are necessary for human happiness.

In his essay on utilitarianism, Mill discusses some of the criticisms of the doctrine – that it does not provide adequate protection for individual rights, that not everything can be measured by the same standard, and that happiness is more complex than reflected by the theory.[75] In proposing solutions, he refines and develops the theory.

Like Bentham, Mill argued that the fact that a law would maximize well-being or minimize suffering is an obvious reason to adopt it. He did not, however, develop detailed assessments and proposals for reforms of laws as Bentham did. His main contribution related to the philosophy of law may have been in prescribing the limits of law, the need for legal protection of minority and individual rights in democratic societies, and definitions of liberty and freedom that explicitly and implicitly criticized definitions of state power and ideologies that could lead to tyranny, oppression – and international crimes.

3.3.2. John Austin

While Mill's achievements included refining the ethical doctrine of utilitarianism, Austin's *The Province of Jurisprudence Determined* (1832) is a classic in English jurisprudence, and exerted considerable influence on the development of legal philosophy. Austin also developed an ethical doctrine; however, in doing so, he departed from Bentham in arguing for divine law being the basis of ethical doctrines. His ideas on divine law were similar to the so-called 'theological Utilitarians', including Archdeacon William Paley, a highly influential British theologian of the late eighteenth century.

Largely through Bentham's influence, Austin was appointed professor of jurisprudence at the newly founded University of London in 1826. He resigned in 1834 and did not experience notable success in his lifetime. His book on

[74] John Stuart Mill, "Bentham (1838)", in John Stuart Mill, *Essays on Ethics, Religion and Society*, University of Toronto Press, Routledge, and Kegan Press, London, 1985, p. 80.

[75] John Stuart Mill, in George Sher (ed.), *Utilitarianism*, 2nd ed., Hackett Publishing Company, Inc., Indianapolis, 2001. The essay first appeared as a series of three articles published in Fraser's Magazine in 1861. The articles were collected and reprinted as a single book in 1863.

jurisprudence became influential only after his death when his wife published a second edition in 1861.

Austin's goal was like Bentham's, to transform law into utilitarian science. To do this, he thought it was necessary to purge the law of all moralistic notions and to define key legal concepts in strictly empirical terms. Law, according to Austin, is a social fact and reflects relations of power and obedience. According to this view, known as legal positivism, (1) law and morality are separate, and (2) all positive laws can be traced back to human lawmakers.

Drawing heavily on the thought of Bentham (although without having access to many of Bentham's unpublished manuscripts at the time), including his criticism of natural rights and natural law, Austin was the first legal thinker to work out a completely positivistic theory of law.

Austin argues that laws are general commands issued by a sovereign to members of an independent political society. They are backed up by credible threats of punishment or other adverse consequences ('sanctions') if they are not complied with.

A command is a declared wish that something should be done or is prohibited to do. Only general commands are laws, that is, commands that refer to a course of conduct or class of actions, not specific actions. Such commands give rise to legal duties to obey. All the key concepts in this account ('law', 'sovereign', 'command', 'sanction', 'duty') are defined in terms of empirically verifiable social facts. No moral judgment, according to Austin, is ever necessary to determine what the law is – though, of course, morality must be consulted in determining what the law should be. As a utilitarian, Austin believed that laws should promote the greatest happiness of society.

An important part of Austin's account of law, was his discussion of sovereignty in the last chapter of his book. Every independent political society not only has, but *must have*, a sovereign. This might be either a single person, or an aggregate of persons. The criteria for identifying the sovereign is that it receives habitual obedience from the bulk of the population, but does not habitually obey any other determinate human superior. In every society "somewhat advanced in civilization", the identity of the sovereign is clear. It is also clear that supreme power, the sovereign, may not be limited by positive law. Such a view is a contradiction in terms, since a person cannot legislate on his own behaviour.

In federal states, such as the United States, there is an extraordinary and ulterior legislature, according to Austin. The sovereign in this case consists of the states' governments "as forming one aggregate body", and their ratification of the Constitution establishes its legal validity. They also have a power to amend it, by three-quarter majority.

Austin held that international law was not "law properly so called". His map of human law was then considerable narrower than Bentham's. He divided human laws (namely, laws set down by men for men) into positive laws or laws 'strictly so called' (laws laid down by a sovereign) and laws laid down by men who were not political superiors or not in pursuance of legal rights. Laws 'improperly so called' are firstly laws by analogy, that is, laws of fashion, constitutional, and international law. Secondly, there are also laws by metaphor, such as the law of gravity.

According to Austin, public international law cannot be deemed to be law, since no specific sovereign can be identified as the author of the rules. There are neither proper sanctions against states that disregard its requirements.

3.3.3. H.L.A. Hart

When reading Bentham, Austin or Mill, you soon encounter formulations and references that remind you that these thinkers lived in another time. H.L.A. Hart's texts differ. They belong to our own post-war era. Many of his ideas and terminology is part of contemporary views of what constitutes law and legal systems. His most famous book, *The Concept of Law* (1961) is still read as an introduction to the theoretic study of law. He and Hans Kelsen (1881–1973) are probably the most influential twentieth-century philosophers of law.

Hart served in British intelligence during World War II, and was well informed about crimes that had taken place, including the fact that German laws permitted many of those crimes.

There are important links between Hart, Bentham, Mill and Austin. Hart wrote about the previous thinkers, and acknowledged his intellectual debt to them. He shared their positivist approach to law, while also criticizing and refining their theories on several accounts. During his later years, he wrote much about Bentham and edited new versions of some of his works. In his 1963 publication, *Law, Liberty, and Morality*, he wrote in the liberal tradition of Mill, applying Mill's 'harm principle' in arguing that homosexual intercourse between consenting adults should not be legally proscribed since it did not cause harm to somebody other than the participants.[76]

In *The Concept of Law,* Hart presents law as a social construction, a historically contingent feature of certain societies.[77] Law emerges as one of several systematic forms of *social control*, administered by institutions. It both rests on and supersedes custom, providing a system of 'primary rules' that direct and

[76] H.L.A Hart, *Law, Liberty, and Morality*, Stanford University Press, 1963.

[77] There are several editions of the book available. For this study, I consulted Hart, 2012, see *supra* note 58.

appraise conduct. In advanced, legal societies, law also entails 'secondary rules' about how to identify, enforce and change the primary rules.

There is an important distinction between the 'internal' and 'external' points of view or aspects of rules. If law is constructed of social rules, rules are made up of practice. And this practice has both an external and an internal aspect. The external aspect of a rule is its forming of *behavioural uniformity*: people act in a common way. Its internal aspect involves a complex attitude Hart calls 'acceptance': a willingness to use the uniformity as a standard to guide and assess behaviour. Acceptance is though not necessarily a reflection of approval. The acceptance may also be due to a wish of pleasing others, fear or conformism.[78]

Among the secondary rules, the ultimate 'rule of recognition' has special importance.[79] It provides criteria of *legal validity* by determining which acts create law, and is based on the practice of those whose role it is to apply primary rules. It means that the foundation of a legal system is not constituted by moral justifications or logical presuppositions. Rather it is based on a customary social rule created by "a complex [...] practice of the courts, officials, and private persons in identifying the law by reference to certain criteria. Its existence is a matter of fact".[80]

Hart criticizes Austin's concept of law – or a simplified version of it – as commands or orders of a sovereign backed by threats. Hart agrees that there is significant conflict and disagreement about law; not merely consensus and agreement. There are many situations in which laws are not simply applied by courts to settle cases, but where judges settle arguable cases and thereby create law. He would, however, argue that *consensus* at other points are necessary to make law function. The 'rule of recognition', at least, needs to rest on agreement about which activities make law.

In advanced societies, however, it may be that only *officials* accept and use "the system's criteria of validity". In such societies, "the acceptance of rules as common standards for the group may be split off from the relatively passive matter of the ordinary individual acquiescing in the rules by obeying them for his part alone".[81] The point is that while custom and social morality are immune to deliberate change and evolve only gradually, large and complex societies need mechanisms of social control that enable customs and other norms to be publicly

[78] *Ibid.*, pp. 56–57.

[79] Other secondary rules are the rule of change, that is, the rule by which existing rules might be created, altered or deleted, and the rule of adjudication, that is, the rule by which society might determine when a rule has been violated and prescribe a remedy.

[80] Hart, 2012, p. 110, see *supra* note 58. Hart suggests that the rule of recognition in the United Kingdom is something like "whatever the Queen in Parliament enacts is law".

[81] *Ibid.*, p. 117.

ascertained and to be changeable. This is made possible by the emergence of institutions with power to identify, alter and enforce the rules.

According to Hart, the result of this division of 'normative labour'[82] between the officials and ordinary people brings both benefits and costs: "The gains are those of adaptability to change, certainty, and efficiency [...] the cost is the risk that the centrally organized power may well be used for the oppression of numbers with whose support it can dispense, in a way that the simpler regime of primary rules could not".[83]

So even if Austin's view is simplified and crude, there are ample examples of legal systems which do not express the values of its community, but rather the interests of the few. There is always a risk that law becomes legalistic or morally fallible. One of the strengths of Hart's exposure of the concept of law is that he shows that laws may fail not by accident, but because of their nature as social institutions.

So, law can be beneficial, but always at a price. It poses special risks of injustice, for instance, against members of minorities, and of alienating its subjects from important norms that govern their lives. In the words of Leslie Green, Hart's view is that "[a] typical society under law depends less on broad social consensus than it does on a narrow official consensus. What the existence of law requires of the population in general is little more than acquiescence with respect to the mandatory norms of the system".[84]

One must therefore be cautious; law is not always a reason for celebration. A critical approach to law is also needed because it sometimes pretends to an objectivity it does not have. Judges may say different things, but in fact they wield serious power to create law.

Law and adjudication are inherently political. In understanding law, a theory of law therefore needs the help of resources from social theory and philosophic inquiry. It is thus neither the sole preserve, nor even the natural habitat, of lawyers or law professors. It is but one part of a more general political theory.

A concept of law in terms of social constructions, constituted solely of social facts, is very different from a concept of law in terms of eternal natural norms. Perhaps the classic formulation of natural law, is Cicero's summary of a Stoic doctrine: "True law is right reason in agreement with Nature; it is of universal application, unchanging and everlasting [...] [T]here will not be different

[82] I am using a term from Leslie Green's "Introduction", in Raz and Bulloch (eds.), 2012, p. xxix, see *supra* note 58.

[83] H.L.A. Hart, in Raz and Bulloch (eds.), 2012, p. 202, see *supra* note 58.

[84] *Ibid.*, p. xxix.

laws at Rome and at Athens, or different laws now and in the future, but one eternal and unchangeable law will be valid for all nations and for all times".[85]

Modern proponents of natural law doctrines seldom subscribe to all elements of this classical account of the doctrine. However, after the World War II, natural rights theories experienced a renaissance in Western jurisprudence, especially in Germany. The idea was that the Nazis had violated norms that were above and beyond the enacted laws in Germany; they had violated human rights and fundamental freedoms and could be prosecuted for crimes against humanity. A law that permitted such crimes was not to be considered a valid law.[86]

Also in the Anglo-American world, natural rights theories have strong proponents, such as John Finnis (1940–) and Ronald Dworkin (1931–2013).[87] Both developed their theories in response to Hart's version of legal positivism, and their arguments became the starting points for comprehensive academic debate.

Dworkin maintained that "law includes not only norms found in treaties, customs, constitutions, statutes, and cases, but also moral principles that provide the best justification for the norms found there. While the things justified by moral principles are socially constructed, the justifications are not".[88] These justifications are the same everywhere and at all times.

Hart's concept of law denies that law includes such eternal moral principles. Law consists only of rules or principles which have been put there by humans. All rules have a pedigree, and they can all be changed. This denial, however, does not imply that Hart denies that there are *relations* between law and morality. There are several. Both law and morality are system of norms that say something about how we should live.

Another connection is related to the question of law's purpose. Law is made for purposes such as guiding conduct, promoting the common good, for doing justice, or licensing coercion. Hart argues (in Chapter IX of *The Concept of Law*) that (1) human survival is morally good, and that (2) a law which does not aim at it would not be a law. Such a constitutive aim of law, does not, however, mean that it must succeed to remain law. A legal system failing to do what laws should do may remain a legal system.[89]

---

[85] Cicero, *De Re Publica*, III.xii.33, trans. by Clinton W. Keyes, Harvard University Press, Loeb Classical Library, Cambridge, 1943, p. 211.

[86] For classification of natural law theories and an account of the German post-war debates, see Henrich Henkel, *Einführung in die Rechtsphilosophie*, C.H. Beck Verlag, Munich, 1977.

[87] John Finnis, *Natural Law and Natural Rights*, 2nd ed., Oxford University Press, 2011; Ronald Dworkin, *Taking Rights Seriously*, Harvard University Press, Cambridge, 1978; Ronald Dworkin, *Law's Empire*, Harvard University Press, Cambridge, 1986.

[88] Green, 2012, p. xvii, see *supra* note 82.

[89] It remains an open question whether Hart withdrew this view, see *ibid*., p. xxxv.

Moral principles may also be authorized to become part of law by a legitimate source of law. In this way, Hart interprets the constructivist doctrine in favour of what is called 'inclusive legal positivism'.

According to Hart, the value of legal theory lies not in helping advice clients or deciding cases. It rather contributes to understanding our culture and institutions and in underpinning any moral assessment of them. That assessment must be sensitive to the nature of law, and to morality, which comprises plural and conflicting values.

For this study, which aims at applying utilitarianism and legal positivism in the tradition of Bentham, Mill, Austin and Hart, on foundational issues of contemporary international criminal law, Hart's view on international law and its status as law proper is of especial relevance. Hart presents his concept of law as "a union of primary and secondary rules [...] as a mean between juristic extremes. For legal theory has sought the key to the understanding of law sometimes in the simple idea of an order backed by threats and sometimes in the complex idea of morality".[90]

According to Hart, the reason why we should not "attempt to narrow the class of valid laws by the extrusion of what was morally iniquitous" is that to do this does not "advance or clarify either theoretical inquiries or moral deliberation". The broader concept of law proved, in his analysis, to be consistent with "so much usage" and "on examination to be adequate".[91]

3.3.4. Hart's Concept of International Law

The case of international law is "converse", according to Hart. Here the problem is not that laws are morally iniquitous, but "the absence of an international legislature, courts with compulsory jurisdiction, and centrally organized sanctions".[92] In Hart's view, international law lacks secondary rules – such as rules of recognition, change and adjudication – and therefore cannot be categorized as a developed legal system.

However, as Hart underlines, the union of primary and secondary rules should not be thought of as a necessary (or sufficient) condition for a system of law to be categorized as a 'legal system'. In his view, it is more important to ask whether "the usage that speaks of 'international law' is likely to obstruct any practical or theoretical aim".[93]

[90] Hart, 2012, p. 213, see *supra* note 58.

[91] *Ibid.*, p. 213.

[92] *Ibid.*

[93] *Ibid.*, p. 214.

To be sure, the issue is not about the proper use of words, Hart contends. The issue is about whether a general term should be applied to a set of international norms despite serious doubts that have been raised, such as concerning the sources of international law and concerning states as subjects.

An important part of his argument for international law to be categorized as law is to show that 'voluntarist' theories or theories of 'auto-limitation' fail. These theories attempt to "reconcile the (absolute) sovereignty of states with the existence of binding rules of international law, by treating all international obligations as self-imposed like the obligation which arises from a promise. Such theories are in fact the counterpart in international law of the social contract theories of political science".[94]

Hart's point is that states *are* bound by international law obligations, not by deciding to be so but as members of international society. The 'voluntarist' approach fails because it is unable to explain how it is known that states are only bound by self-imposed obligations. Hart also points to the underlying rule which must exist that a state which takes upon itself certain obligations is "bound to do whatever it undertakes by appropriate words to do".[95] A state may promise to perform a specific action, however, for that promise to become an obligation there must be a rule that promises create obligations. This rule is binding independently of the choice of the party bound by it.

Hart's third argument refers to certain facts, such as the case of a new state. According to Hart, it has never "been doubted that when a new, independent state emerges into existence, [...] it is bound by the general obligations of international law, among others, the rule that give binding force to treaties".[96]

It is true, he contends, that international law resembles regimes that only contain primary rules, even though its rules are very different from rules in primitive societies. Many of its concepts, methods, and techniques are the same as those of modern municipal law.

An argument exists that since international law does not contain secondary rules, it must be a form of 'morality'. This view is mistaken, according to Hart, and is often associated with "the old dogmatism" stemming from Austin's concept of law as "orders backed by threats". Although it is possible to construe a concept of morality in this way, as denominating all systems of rules which are not backed by threats, it would not serve any practical or theoretical purpose. It would comprise systems which are very different in form and social function, and represent an overly crude classification.

[94] *Ibid.*, p. 224.

[95] *Ibid.*, p. 225.

[96] *Ibid.*, p. 226.

There are several reasons for not classifying international law as a form of morality, such as the fact that states in arguments against other states that they think violate rules of international law refer to "precedents, treaties, and juristic writings; often no mention is made of moral rights or wrong, good or bad".[97] It is true that states sometimes adhere to moral arguments in denouncing the conduct of other states, but that happens also in case of violations of municipal law. Many rules of international law are also morally indifferent; such as rules that provide for the functioning of inter-state relations.

A typical function of law, unlike morality, is to introduce detailed distinctions, formalities and procedures that serve the purpose of maximizing "certainty and predictability and to facilitate the proof or assessments of claims". This 'formalism' or 'legalism' is found in international law, clearly distinguishing it from 'morality'. That does not mean that all rules of international law must be of such moral neutral, formal character. "The point is only that legal rules *can* and moral rules *cannot* be of this kind."[98]

The fact that there is no international legislature, which by applying certain procedures can change the rules of international law, like rules of morality cannot be changed by any legislature, is "a defect one day to be repaired", according to Hart. It is true that states may abide by rules of international law based on moral considerations. But the foundation of international law lay in wide adherence to its rules, which may be motivated rather by "calculations of long-term interest, or by the wish to continue a tradition or by disinterested concern for others", than by a sense of moral obligation.

Hart's conclusion is that, because international law lacks a legislature, courts with compulsory jurisdiction and officially organized sanctions, it resembles in form though not in content "a simple regime of primary or customary law". In content, however, it resembles advanced municipal law, and this makes it possible for lawyers to freely transfer from the one to the other.

In his time, Bentham concluded that international law was "sufficiently analogues" to municipal law to be called 'law'. Hart refines this conclusion by stating that "the analogy is one of content not of form; secondly, that, in this analogy of content, no other social rules are so close to municipal law as those of international law".[99]

I hold this conclusion as still valid. However, for contemporary discussions his observations on how international law could become a developed system of law, may be of even greater importance. True to his descriptive approach, he

[97] *Ibid.*, p. 228.

[98] *Ibid.*, p. 229.

[99] *Ibid.*, p. 237.

does not argue that international law *should* become a developed system of law. But he states how that could happen, and an unspoken wish in that direction may perhaps be sensed.

It is true, he contends, that important relations between states are regulated by multilateral treaties, and sometimes arguments are made that these treaties also may be binding on other states that are not parties:

> If this were generally recognized, such treaties would in fact be legislative enactments and international law would have distinct criteria of validity for its rules. A basic rule of recognition could then be formulated which would represent an actual feature of the system and would be more than an empty restatement of the fact that a set of rules are in fact observed by states. Perhaps international law is at present in a stage of transition towards acceptance of this and other forms which would bring it nearer in structure to a municipal system.[100]

It should be noted that, since Hart wrote these words in the early 1960s, international law has indeed developed in directions which could further the transition. International courts have been established with binding jurisdiction over a subset of states, such as the European Court of Human Rights, the *ad hoc* tribunals for Rwanda and the Former Yugoslavia, and the ICC. Some of these jurisdictions have been imposed on a group of states by decisions of the United Nations Security Council, while others exist based on states' self-imposition. The ICC is, in this respect, a hybrid, since it can exercise jurisdiction over citizens of non-States Parties which commit ICC crimes within its jurisdiction on the territory of States Parties.

The existence of such courts leads to judicial decisions ascertaining which rules, based on treaty or customary law, could be binding upon all states, irrespective of treaty obligations. However, it seems a way to go for states to reach consensus on so-called *jus cogens* norms.[101]

According to legal literature, the following international crimes may be characterized as *jus cogens*: aggression, genocide, crimes against humanity, war crimes, piracy, slavery, slave-related practices, and torture. The legal basis for this claim consists of:

100 *Ibid.*, p. 236.

101 The term '*jus cogens*' means 'the compelling law' and, as such, a *jus cogens* norm holds the highest hierarchical position among all other norms and principles. Because of that standing, *jus cogens* norms are deemed to be 'peremptory' and non-derogable, see M. Cherif Bassiouni, "International Crimes: *Jus Cogens* and Obligation *Erga Omnes*", in *Law and Contemporary Problems*, 1996, vol. 59, no. 4, p. 67.

1. international pronouncements recognizing that these crimes are part of general customary law;
2. language in preambles or other provisions of treaties indicating that these crimes have a higher status in international law;
3. the large number of states which have ratified treaties related to these crimes; and
4. international investigations and prosecutions of perpetrators of these crimes.[102]

Further arguments for including specific crimes in the *jus cogens* category are that they "affect the interests of the world community as a whole because they threaten the peace and security of humankind and because they shock the conscience of humanity".[103]

In 1996, Professor M. Cherif Bassiouni stated that:

> It is still uncertain in ICL whether the inclusion of a crime in the category of *jus cogens* creates rights or, as stated above, non-derogable duties *erga omnes*. The establishment of a permanent international criminal court having inherent jurisdiction over these crimes would be a convincing argument for the proposition that crimes such as genocide, crimes against humanity, and war crimes are part of *jus cogens* and that obligations *erga omnes* to prosecute or extradite flow from them.[104]

The problem remains, however, that the Rome Statute of the ICC as it was adopted in 1998 does not provide for the ICC to have 'inherent jurisdiction', which is a doctrine of the English common law that a superior court has the jurisdiction to hear any matter that comes before it, unless a statute or rule limits that authority or grants exclusive jurisdiction to some other court or tribunal. Even so – the ICC only having limited temporary and territorial jurisdiction – it could be argued that it represents a further step in the direction of establishing rules binding upon all states.

States disobeying such rules, by committing international crimes, weaken the system, but do not destroy it. Municipal law is frequently violated without its status as law being questioned. However, it may be true that international law, and especially international criminal law, is more vulnerable.

The four points mentioned above constituting a legal basis for the claims of *jus cogens* crimes may be a rule of recognition in the making. However, it is not functioning as such yet. Obviously, it is also a rather complicated rule.

---

[102] *Ibid.*, p. 68.

[103] *Ibid.*, p. 69.

[104] *Ibid.*, p. 74.

3.4. Benthamite Perspectives on International Law

Bentham's formative years took place in the context of eighteenth-century Enlightenment. He engaged in a battle against both tradition and authoritarianism, as well as against anarchical fallacies and revolutions. He devoted a lifetime of developing a third way, namely, gradual reforms in legislation and policies based on the principle of utility. The end goal was for governments and legislators to ensure happiness for the greatest number of people. These were radical ideas at his time, but over time they became influential.

In 1871, 29 years after Bentham's death, one of his translators, R. Hildreth concluded that "whatever may be thought of the principle of utility, when considered as the foundation of morals, no one now-a-days will undertake to deny that it is the only safe rule of legislation".[105]

It was mainly due to Bentham and a small group of followers that the principle achieved such a status. Bentham's science of applying the principle has had a lasting effect on jurisprudence, legal theorizing and in informing legislators up to the present. It is therefore pertinent to ask what can be learnt from him in discussing the foundations of international criminal law.

There can be no doubt that the 'principle of utility' is providing foundation for a branch of law that deals with heinous crimes, such as genocide, crimes against humanity and war crimes, which inflict unbearable pain and unhappiness on large numbers of human beings. These are crimes that in their very nature attack the well-being and even the existence of collectives of people. The crimes also have the potential of leading to further pain and unhappiness for the world community, leading to escalation of conflicts, wider security risks, humanitarian crisis, and so on.

Based on utilitarian premises, there is therefore wide space for inflicting pain in the form of prosecution and punishment of those bearing the responsibility for or performing such crimes. The main motivation would be to prevent such crimes from being committed again in the future; the end goal being ultimately to eliminate such crimes completely.

Challenged whether law is effective in preventing or eliminating such crimes to occur, Bentham offers a wide range of arguments and viewpoints. He presents convincing ideas about the civilizing functions of law, including criminal law. However, he cautions that there are a set of necessary conditions law must meet to fulfil such functions. Legislation must be designed well and be based on sound principles to maximize overall happiness, and institutions must be redesigned bearing these concerns in mind, not the least taking into consideration that mechanisms must be in place to counter corruption and other

[105] R. Hildreth, "Preface", in Bentham, 1871, p. iii, see *supra* note 46.

negative practices to take root. Investigations and trials must be conducted effectively to avoid delays and high expenses.

Reforming and improving legislation and practice is an ongoing process. Reform efforts often lead to interest-based resistance by narrow groups who have something to lose from them, as Bentham experienced himself. Strategic thinking about how to create conditions conducive of reforms and improvements of legislation is therefore of primary importance.

Bentham would insist to give priority to arguments that demonstrate how criminal law may benefit the overall well-being and positive development of society. As mentioned, this may have led him to embrace the complementarity principle of the Rome Statute. He would point to local trials having greater beneficial effects than more distant international trials or to the importance of international trials taking place in the proximity of crime affected societies whenever feasible.

The prospect of the ICC exerting jurisdiction if national jurisdictions were unable to do so, could lead to national legal reform. States prefer to be able to prosecute crimes themselves and avoid interference by the ICC, and in this way, the Rome Statute could serve as a model for national legislation and over time build capacity at the national level to prosecute core international crimes.

The consequentialist challenge stemming from Bentham's approach also have other aspects. International courts are often criticized by civil society organizations for conducting poor outreach or for creating expectations in affected communities, which they are unable to fulfil. Thinking justice in consequentialist terms would lead to international courts stepping up efforts to explain how justice works not only to those involved in trials but to the wider society.

The ICC might represent some progress in this regard from previous international criminal courts. There may, however, be more to be done. In pointing to the future beneficial consequences of prosecutions as their main *raison d'être* (deterrence of similar crimes), Bentham would ask for well-thought-out and well-resourced strategies of outreach being part of any international legal intervention into situations where core international crimes had taken place.

Bentham's justification for punishment was based on its overall tendency to produce more happiness than pain for affected persons. Only a well-organized state with rational and accessible laws, where legislators were elected by the people to apply the principle of utility in their legislative work, could succeed in achieving that. He had in mind that successful states in this regard, could serve as models for other states. He, however, also realized that even democratic and peaceful states could end up in conflicts that would need international intervention to avoid violent wars to break out.

Consequently, he argued for international law to be reformed so it could become an effective tool in preventing wars and improving inter-state relations. His idea of codifying an international legal code also led him to see the need for establishing an international court able to decide on disputes between states. He did not develop foundations for international criminal law as such, but he clearly depicted needs for sanctioning violations of international norms by representatives and even heads of states. This means that some conditionality was inherent in Bentham's thinking about the sovereignty of states. I think he would have supported international criminal law as a way of ensuring utility-based punishment of the most serious crimes in cases where national states were unable or unwilling to do so.

He would, however, have wanted to introduce a systematic approach to reforming and developing further international criminal law. His method would be to ask which crimes are most detrimental to overall happiness among the greatest number of people. He would not erase the already existing crimes from the law book – aggression, crimes against humanity, genocide, and war crimes – but he would question whether other serious pain-inflicting crimes should be included, as discussed in *Philosophical Foundations of International Criminal Law: Legally Protected Interests* (2022).[106] Central to reform of international criminal law would be to ensure that the gravest crimes – with the largest negative consequences for specific societies, and ultimately to humankind – were included, and that they were expressed in language that could be understood by legal experts, governments as well as by ordinary people.

Were he alive today, Bentham would of course come up with his own reform proposals. But he would also have liked to see experts and representatives from as many countries as possible being involved in discussions about the proper scope of international criminal law. His vision was an alliance of states with liberal opinions perfecting legislation.

He would also have noticed the existence of a branch of international law named human rights law. He would have been worried by the fact that the declarations of human rights he criticized so vehemently had been followed up by the enactment by a large majority of states of the Universal Declaration of Human Rights and a range of international legal documents protecting human rights, giving them status as legal rights.

---

[106] This is the third volume in the Centre for International Law Research and Policy's Symposium on Philosophical Foundations of International Criminal Law. Morten Bergsmo, Emiliano J. Buis and Song Tianying (eds.), *Philosophical Foundations of International Criminal Law: Legally-Protected Interests*, Torkel Opsahl Academic EPublisher, Brussels, 2022 (https://www.toaep.org/ps-pdf/36-bergsmo-buis-song/).

Maybe he, in the end, would accept that as Newton's law on gravity later was shown by Albert Einstein to be incorrect and only valid in certain circumstances, his principle of utility also was valid only as a special case of a more all-encompassing theory. He would have to see that states with liberal opinions, fully respecting individual and minority human rights, are the only states in which the principle of utility could be applied without modifications. In other states, human rights concerns should in some cases override utilitarian conclusions to protect minorities' and individuals' rights from being sacrificed for the greater good of the majority.

3.5. Philosophical Foundations of International Criminal Law

Philosophical foundations of international criminal law may take diverse forms. Its inherent values, norms, rules and concepts may be supported by reference to existing religious or philosophical principles and views. International criminal law – being both in theory and in practice, "a marriage between criminal justice and human rights activism"[107] – may be especially attractive for adherents of religious or philosophical schools that want to strengthen protection of core human values.

For the international human rights movement, however, international criminal law is not merely about seeing wrongdoers punished and thereby having some basic values confirmed. Its most important function may be to help end a global climate of impunity and lack of accountability in which grave abuses of human rights so regularly occur.

Bentham and the way of thinking he inspired come with a similar approach. He would see the most important function of international criminal law not in the fact that it gives legal effect to protection of natural rights (which do not exist, according to him), or protection of human dignity or any other preconceived highest value. Its most important function would be to promote the largest happiness of the greatest number by educating people and deterring crimes. He believed that the law could civilize and improve human societies even at moments when civilization has broken down.

This approach also puts a test in front of international criminal law jurisdictions: do they contribute effectively to achieving these aims? If not: which reforms are needed to improve them?

In other words, the foundation given is conditional upon success. Bentham would, however, address failure not by revolutionary measures but by reforms.

[107] See Wellman, 2013, p. 477, *supra* note 43.

4

Sir Thomas More and Integrity in Justice*

Beati quorum via integra est: qui ambulant in lege Domini[1]

Integrity issues in international organizations have gained wide attention in recent years due to extensive media coverage of problematic practices and non-compliance with codes of ethics by actors within such organizations. Particularly shocking were revelations by eight international media organizations of the European Investigative Collaborations in 2017 that undermined the credibility of the International Criminal Court ('ICC').

The revelations included serious allegations that members of the ICC Office of the Prosecutor had helped the first Prosecutor of the ICC, Luis Moreno-Ocampo, to make money by assisting persons suspected of having aided ICC crimes in Libya. There were also issues connected with situations under ICC investigations in Côte d'Ivoire and Kenya as well as some broader issues linked to the heritage of the first Prosecutor.[2]

In the following, I engage in finding out what Sir Thomas More (1478–1535) may offer in terms of principles and strategies on how to strengthen personal and institutional integrity within international justice institutions. His image is on the cover of the book *Integrity in International Justice*, and I have had

---

* This chapter was first published as Chapter 4 of Morten Bergsmo and Viviane E. Dittrich (eds.), *Integrity in International Justice*, Torkel Opsahl Academic EPublisher, Brussels, 2020 (https://www.toaep.org/nas-pdf/4-bergsmo-dittrich/), and has not been updated since. The author extends his gratitude to Berit Lindeman for input to Section 4.1.1. on election observation and Section 4.1.2. on corruption in the Parliamentary Assembly of the Council of Europe.

[1] "Blessed are the undefiled in the way, who walk in the law of the Lord". Book of Psalms 119:1, King James Version. An alternative translation from the New International Version reads as follows: "Blessed are those whose ways are blameless, who walk according to the law of the Lord".

[2] For a short account of the issues, see Pierre Hassan, "Scandals rocks international criminal court", *Justiceinfo*, 8 October 2017. For the broader issues, see Morten Bergsmo, Wolfgang Kaleck, Sam Muller and William H. Wiley, "A Prosecutor Falls, Time for the Court to Rise", FICHL Policy Brief Series No. 86 (2017), Torkel Opsahl Academic EPublisher, Brussels, 2017 (https://www.toaep.org/pbs-pdf/86-four-directors/). At the heart of many of the issues related to the ICC Office of the Prosecutor may be Mr. Moreno-Ocampo's unwillingness to follow-up on the ground-breaking work of the ICC preparatory team, see Morten Bergsmo, Klaus Rackwitz and Song Tianying (eds.), *Historical Origins of International Criminal Law: Volume 5*, Torkel Opsahl Academic EPublisher, Brussels, 2017 (https://www.toaep.org/ps-pdf/24-bergsmo-rackwitz-song/).

the honour of writing the chapter on him. What can an outstanding representative of so-called 'Northern Humanism', a friend and ally of Erasmus of Rotterdam (1466–1536), and a statesman serving in the highest positions during large parts of King Henry VIII's reign (1509–1547) offer to contemporary debates about integrity issues, in particular in international justice institutions?

It is well-known that More, despite his long and outstanding service, was unjustly executed by the King. What is less well known is the reason More offered so as not to give in to the immense pressure to condone the King and Parliament abolishing the independence of the Church of England and making the King its head. More dealt with the issue of integrity in many of his works, including his famous *Utopia* (1516)[3] and *The History of King Richard the Third* (1557).[4] An underlying question for much of his political writings was how a wise man with integrity ("a first citizen")[5] could serve a King or prince with tyrannical inclinations. (The references to the 'King' and 'Kings' throughout this chapter should be understood as a legacy of More's times and for consistency, not a deliberate exclusion.)

Central to More's thinking on how to develop and preserve integrity was to train yourself to be faithful to your conscience. He also frequently referred to respect for the law, which in his view justly limited the power of the King and protected the right to dissent. Leaders should serve the people, not their own narrow interests.

Among the reasons to include More in contemporary discussions on integrity is also that he was the first English writer to use the word 'integrity', being well aware of the concept's both classical and biblical roots.[6] For him, integrity signifies consistency in thought, word and action, based on conscience and comprehensive understanding. It is the fruit of a successful struggle to be just *one* person, rather than to be several. It is "what makes a person a unity rather than a duplicity. Integrity makes a particular life resemble a good poem rather than a dubious collection of fragments, with doubtful authorship".[7]

---

3 *Utopia* is available in several editions. I consulted the following: Thomas More, *Utopia*, Cambridge University Press, 2016 [1516].

4 Thomas More, *The History of King Richard the Third*, in Richard S. Sylvester (ed.), *The Complete Works of St. Thomas More*, Vol. 2, Yale University Press, New Haven, 1963.

5 Thomas More, epigram 111, in *Utopia*, see *supra* note 3.

6 "Conscience and Integrity", in Gerard B. Wegemer and Stephen W. Smith (eds.), *A Thomas More Sourcebook*, Catholic University of America Press, Washington, D.C., 2004, pp. 212–214.

7 Stephen W. Smith, "Thomas More: Patron Saint of Leading Citizens", in Travis Curtright (ed.), *Thomas More: Why Patron of Statesmen?*, Lexington Books, New York, 2015, p. 145.

This chapter deals with the arguments and stance of Thomas More, situating them in a context of modern integrity. The first section deals with integrity issues recently faced by international organizations, such as biased election observation, lack of quality control and transparent procedures in both the Council of Europe and the International Criminal Police Organization ('INTERPOL'), acquittals in the international tribunals, as well as misconduct by members of the ICC Office of the Prosecutor (Section 4.1.). To ground the discussion of More's relevancy for current integrity discussions, I provide a typography of these problems, focusing on individual versus institutional integrity, politicization or instrumentalization of institutions, and the specificities of *professional* integrity (Section 4.2.). These challenges to integrity form the basis upon which we turn to More for guidance, which is the subject of the following sections. The chapter progresses with a discussion on More's thoughts on tyranny and how to confront it (Section 4.3), before turning to More as a statesman and his views on heresy (Section 4.4.). Finally, the chapter turns briefly to More's conflict with Henry VIII (Section 4.5.), before concluding with More's lessons as well.as returning to the topic of integrity in justice (Sections 4.6. and 4.7.).

4.1. Integrity Failures in International Political Institutions

My organization, the Norwegian Helsinki Committee, has a history of addressing integrity issues publicly, rather than only raising them discretely behind the scenes. Maybe it is part of a wider Nordic tradition that to demonstrate your support for an institution, you do not shy away from publicly criticizing it and appeal for effective measures to address failings.

Part of this tradition is a perception that for criticism to be effective, it must be *constructive*. Only denouncing practices, without pointing to remedies and good examples that could help improve them, is not enough. External inquiries into institutional misbehaviour, which is widely used in the Nordic countries, is expected to produce recommendations on remedies as well as to clarify and evaluate the facts.

I will point to a few examples of integrity issues in international organizations at the time when this chapter was first published. These examples are telling in themselves but also help to characterize *main types* of contemporary integrity issues. Such a typology, as further developed in Section 4.2., may make it easier to answer questions about the relevance of More's approach to developing and preserving integrity.

4.1.1. Biased Election Observation

During the 1990s, election observation as a distinct form of human rights monitoring developed rapidly. In post-conflict situations and in societies in transition from communist dictatorship to democratic rule, Western states, the United

Nations ('UN'), the Council of Europe, the Conference on Security and Co-operation in Europe ('CSCE', renamed the 'OSCE' on 1 January 1995)[8] and some other international organizations put great emphasis on promoting free and fair elections as necessary steps towards democratic rule.

A telling expression of this view is to be found in the landmark 1990 CSCE Copenhagen Document, where all 35 participating states at the time declared that "the will of the people, freely and fairly expressed through periodic and genuine elections, is the basis of the authority and legitimacy of all government".[9]

The CSCE-OSCE Office of Democratic Institutions and Human Rights ('ODIHR') played an important role – as did several academic institutions and non-governmental organizations – in developing a methodology to ensure that findings reflected both election day performance of elections as well as contextual factors.[10]

In some of the transitional countries, hopes for democratic developments were soon to be replaced by the reality of 'managed' democracy. States like the Russian Federation, Belarus, Azerbaijan and the Central Asian states do perform elections, but they adhere to systems where the 'elected' government weakens and/or controls the judiciary, the media, the parliament, and other state institutions to such an extent that there are little, if any, checks and balances. Furthermore, no effective opposition in the parliament exists.

In some of the countries, widespread cheating on election day does take place. However, the states increasingly adhere to more sophisticated ways of controlling the election results.[11]

Even if these states centralize power and are intolerant of criticism, they make efforts to retain an institutional set-up that mimics democratic governance. Among former communist countries, the Russian Federation has often played the role of pioneering the development of methods of 'controlling' and 'faking' democracy.

---

[8] Budapest Summit Declaration, "Towards a genuine partnership in a new era", 21 December 2004, para. 3.

[9] CSCE, Document of the Copenhagen Meeting of the Conference on the Human Dimension of the CSCE, 29 June 1990, para. 6 (https://www.legal-tools.org/doc/f85146).

[10] ODIHR, *Election Observation Handbook*, 6th ed., OSCE-ODIHR, Warsaw, 2010. An extensive library of election related guidelines and tools are available in the OSCE's web site.

[11] For a compelling account of the main methods used to 'control' democracy, see Andrew Wilson, *Virtual Politics: Faking Democracy in the Post-Soviet World*, Yale University Press, 2005. He argues that the post-Bolshevik culture of 'political technology' is the main obstacle to better governance in the region. There is no real popular participation in public affairs, and no systematic modernization of the political economy.

It is precisely because these states do not adhere to principles of separation of power and rule of law, and do not tolerate free media and independent civil society, that arranging elections is of crucial importance to strengthen legitimacy and present themselves as adhering to democratic principles.

Sometimes leaders of the states recognize that the governance model is not democratic in the full sense. President Vladimir Putin refers to 'managed' or 'controlled' democracy,[12] while Prime Minister Viktor Orbán became infamous for characterizing the European Union ('EU') Member State Hungary as an 'illiberal state'.[13] Other leaders resorted to terms like 'transitional democracy', indicating that the state might not be fully democratic yet, but is *en route* towards that end goal.[14]

Faced with increasingly professional independent election observation, which is able to detect election fraud not only on election day, but also pre- and post-election day measures that were initiated to produce the desired election results, the regimes set out to tackle this challenge as well. They organized, *inter alia*, *alternative* election observation missions, which stated that elections were free and fair even if they were not.

A group of parliamentarians from Western countries constituted a special problem. Being members of respected international election observation missions, they breached codes of conduct, made positive statements on Election Day, and tried to influence mission statements to become more positive than justified. These problems were in particular linked to elections in Azerbaijan, and the Parliamentary Assembly of the Council of Europe ('PACE') eventually initiated an investigation into alleged corruption among its members.[15]

---

[12] This term may be inspired by the concept of 'guided democracy', coined by the American journalist Walter Lippmann in his influential book *Public Opinion* from 1922. In such a system, a formal democratic government function as a de facto autocracy. For an early criticism of Putin's managed democracy, see Masha Lipman and Michael McFaul, "Managed democracy in Russia", in *Harvard International Journal of Press/Politics*, 2001, vol. 6, no. 3, pp. 116–127.

[13] Prime Minister Orbán proclaimed Hungary as an illiberal democratic state in a speech at the Tusványos Summer University and Student Camp on 26 July 2014. "Proclamation of the Illiberal Hungarian State", *The Orange Files*, 1 August 2014.

[14] Freedom House has, since 1995, run a project called "Nations in Transit", which according to a certain methodology survey democratic reforms in 29 former communist countries. The report covering developments in 2018 registered the most score declines in the project's 23-year history: 19 of the 29 countries had declines in their overall Democracy Scores. For the second year in a row, there were more Consolidated Authoritarian Regimes than Consolidated Democracies (Freedom House, "Nations in Transit 2018" (available on its web site)).

[15] Council of Europe, "Report of the Independent Investigation Body of the allegations of corruption within the Parliamentary Assembly", 15 April 2018. For extensive coverage of the so-

To respond to biased election observation, a coalition of non-governmental organizations, the European Platform for Democratic Elections ('EPDE'),[16] initiated several studies of threats to the integrity of election observation in 2016.[17]

According to the EPDE, the main integrity issues were:

- "a growing tendency among authoritarian regimes in the OSCE region to orchestrate benevolent election observation in order to give legitimacy to fraudulent elections";[18]
- "a series of cases where European parliamentarians *individually* make public assessments of elections abroad, giving an impression to represent the position of their parliament also while their activity is not endorsed by their parliament or their faction, and when they are not member of any official Election Observation Mission. By that, they discredit not only the parliament and the faction they represent but election observation as such";[19]
- "there are European parliaments which did not sufficiently elaborate effective internal control mechanisms (i.e. Codes of Conduct) to discourage their members from participating in biased international election observation missions";[20]
- "an increasing number of GONGOs (governmental organized NGOs) publish assessments on election processes which are not based on any methodological election observation, while often being purely politically motivated";[21]
- "election administrations in some countries of the OSCE region deliberately deny accreditation to independent international Election Observation Missions adhering to international standards as the ODIHR methodology";[22]

---

called 'caviar diplomacy' in PACE, see European Stability Initiative's ('ESI') thematic web site on corruption problems in the PACE.

16 Members of the coalition include Helsinki Citizens' Assembly Vanadzor, Election Monitoring and Democracy Studies Centre, Belarusian Helsinki Committee, International Society for Fair Elections and Democracy, European Exchange, International Elections Study Centre, Promo-LEX Association, the Norwegian Helsinki Committee, Stefan Batory Foundation, Golos, Swedish International Liberal Centre, and Committee of Voters of Ukraine.

17 EPDE, "Politically biased election observation – A threat to the integrity of international institutions", 13 July 2018.

18 *Ibid.*, p. 8.

19 *Ibid.*

20 *Ibid.*

21 *Ibid.*, p. 9.

22 *Ibid.*

- several parliamentary assemblies send election observation missions that "do not operate on the basis of a transparent and clearly defined election observation methodology for the assessment of the election process".[23]

4.1.2. Corruption in the Parliamentary Assembly of the Council of Europe

An enabling factor for these unfortunate developments was a lack of quality control mechanisms. There were, *inter alia*, no established mechanisms to monitor the conduct of parliamentarians participating in observation missions of PACE, the OSCE Parliamentary Assembly, or the European Parliament. Nor were there procedures to establish the basis for reaching conclusions that significantly differed from those of the long-term professional missions of the OSCE's specialized agency for conducting election observation, ODIHR.

Lack of quality control and transparent procedures may also have been at the core of the integrity issues connected with the so-called 'caviar diplomacy' in PACE. In short, this diplomacy may have started as early as in 2001 and consisted in bribing members of PACE with money and gifts to influence their voting in favour of Azerbaijan and possibly some other Council of Europe Member States.[24]

The conclusion of the external review of the allegations was as follows:

> The key deficiency in the organisation of work and political processes in PACE was found to relate to the manner in which the decisions on appointments to different functions were made. This in particular concerned the lack of transparency and sufficient regulation of the procedures for such appointments, especially the appointments of members of the Monitoring Committee and the Rules Committee, as well as the appointments of rapporteurs in general. An issue of lack of transparency and an absence of safeguards against abuse was also found to arise with regard to the voting processes in the committees, which might affect the voting results and open the door to the possibility of exertion of improper influence, including that of a financial nature.
>
> As to the functioning of PACE in matters concerning Azerbaijan, the Investigation Body established that there was a group of persons working in PACE in favour of Azerbaijan. A certain level of cohesion in their various activities existed, although the Investigation Body found it difficult to establish with a sufficient degree of certainty that they all formed part of a single orchestrated

[23] *Ibid.*

[24] For a short description of the problems, see Organized Crime and Corruption Reporting Project, "Council of Europe Expels 13 in Azerbaijan Bribe Case", 3 July 2018.

> structure. In this context, the Investigation Body found that, in their activities concerning Azerbaijan, several members and former members of PACE had acted contrary to the PACE ethical standards.[25]

The review also found that,

> the Guidelines on the observation of elections by the Parliamentary Assembly required to be further strengthened and clarified and that PACE should consider including in the ethical framework a specific part dedicated to election observation, in order to ensure that members of PACE participating in that type of missions complied with those guidelines.[26]

The conclusions on corrupt behaviour of former and present members of PACE were also fairly clear, namely,

> that a number of former PACE MPs who had performed … [lobbying activities on behalf of Azerbaijan] had acted contrary to the PACE Code of Conduct. As to the corruptive activities in favour of Azerbaijan, the Investigation Body established that there was a strong suspicion that certain current and former members of PACE had engaged in activity of a corruptive nature.[27]

The review was, however, limited in time and resources, and therefore also concluded that there was a need for further investigations, *inter alia*, to elucidate whether countries other than Azerbaijan had been involved in corruption as well as more detailed questions about the extent and planned nature of the corruption schemes.

A trial in Milan, which started 10 December 2018, was the only follow-up to hold anyone criminally responsible for the biggest scandal in the history of the Council of Europe, by the time this chapter was first published. In this case, three former members of PACE were charged with corruption, namely Luca Volonte (Italian member, 2008–2013), Elkhan Suleymanov (Azerbaijani member, 2011–2018), and Muslum Mammadov (Azerbajani member, 2016–2018).[28]

The facts of the case were not disputed: in the period 2012–2014 the two Azerbaijanis transferred large sums of money to the Italian, who as a leader of the biggest political group in PACE, the European People's Party, had considerable influence on voting results in the Assembly.

Among the evidence in the case were e-mail communications between the three PACE members. One of them, from 1 February 2013, is especially telling

---

[25] Council of Europe, 15 April 2018, p. x, see *supra* note 15.

[26] *Ibid.*, pp. x-xi.

[27] *Ibid.*, p. xi.

[28] ESI, "Human Rights with Teeth (I) – Battle of Europe", *ESI Newsletter*, 2018, no. 9, p. 2.

of their relationship. It was written after a vote on a resolution on political prisoners that Azerbaijan's government wanted to see defeated and which to the surprise of both members of PACE and external observers was rejected by a large majority. In the e-mail, Volonte addressed Mammadov with the following words: "Your wish is my command, so I think that we should discuss the new version [of a motion] during the next meeting in Baku with Elkhan [Suleymanov] and Pushkov", the then powerful leader of the Russian delegation to PACE.[29]

4.1.3. Integrity Issues in International Police and Judicial Institutions

Over time, documentation has been presented on abuse by a range of authoritarian states of the INTERPOL's 'wanted person' alerts in politicized criminal cases. The background is an extensive increase in the use of INTERPOL Red Notices and Diffusions, which has heightened the risk of misuse. For example, the number of Red Notices issued each year increased from 1,418 in 2001 to 13,048 in 2017 and to 13,516 in 2018. There were, at the time this chapter was first published, approximately 58,000 valid Red Notices, of which some 7,000 are public.[30]

The high numbers of alerts increase demands on resources for control. According to its Constitution, INTERPOL's main goal is "to ensure and promote the widest possible mutual assistance between all criminal police authorities within the limits of the laws existing in the different countries and in the spirit of the 'Universal Declaration of Human Rights'".[31]

In other words, a constitutional requirement exists that the mutual assistance provided by INTERPOL and the cases presented by national police authorities to its platforms should be based on investigative or other activities that respect international human rights. This is further underlined by Article 3 of the Constitution, which states that "it is strictly forbidden for the Organization to undertake any intervention or activities of a political, military, religious or racial character".[32]

Fair Trials, a United Kingdom-based non-governmental organization that works for fair trials according to international standards of justice, has

[29] *Ibid.*

[30] Amy Mackinnon, "The Scourge of the Red Notice: How some countries go after dissidents and debtors", *Foreign Affairs*, 3 December 2018. See also, David Satter, "Russia's abuse of Interpol", *Russia Studies Centre Policy Paper*, 2015, no. 6, The Henry Jackson Society, July 2015. The figures were taken from Interpol's web site.

[31] Constitution of the International Criminal Police Organization-INTERPOL, 1956 (2017), Article 1 (https://www.legal-tools.org/doc/07a066).

[32] *Ibid.*, Article 3

documented such abuse since 2013.[33] According to the organization, INTERPOL has started to make reforms to strengthen control, but there are still major problems with "transparency, missing statistics and a simple lack of resources".[34] The solution, according to Fair Trials, is not to exclude any of the 194 Member States of INTERPOL: "We need strong international organisations to tackle international crime and keep the world safe. We don't want countries like Russia and Turkey to become safe havens for criminals by excluding them from Interpol altogether".[35]

To strengthen the integrity of the organization, there is rather a need to speed up implementation of its reform programme. The programme is designed to make it harder to abuse its systems as a vehicle of political repression. The Council of Europe and other international organizations may play important roles in monitoring how well INTERPOL implements the programme.[36]

Part of the programme is to 'clean up' its databases to identify and delete alerts that were circulated without proper review. INTERPOL may also restrict certain countries' access to databases if they believe that they are repeatedly and systemically violating its rules.

Similar to the 'caviar diplomacy' scandal in PACE, at the core of INTERPOL's problems are actions of Member States that undermine the integrity of the institution. The problem is then aggravated by the institution's lack of proper safeguards and capacity to detect and prevent the misuse of its systems.[37]

---

33 Fair Trials International, *Strengthening respect for human rights: Strengthening Interpol*, 2013. The report documented abuse in specific cases and recommended measures to detect and prevent such abuse. It also referred to resolutions and statements by international organizations since 2010 about the need to strengthen control mechanisms within the organization.

34 Fair Trials, "How to end the abuse of INTERPOL: insights from America and Europe", 18 December 2018. On measures to strengthening safeguards against abuse, see INTERPOL: "New measures approved to strengthen INTERPOL information sharing system", 9 November 2016.

35 Fair Trials, 18 December 2018, see *supra* note 34.

36 PACE, "Abusive use of the INTERPOL system: the need for more stringent legal safeguards", Doc. 14277, 29 March 2017. It should be noted that even if PACE has had serious integrity issues of its own to deal with, it often played strong and beneficial external roles in promoting and securing adherence to human rights, democracy, and integrity norms.

37 Commission of Security and Co-operation in Europe, "Helsinki Commission leaders introduce translational repression accountability and prevention (TRAP) act", 12 September 2019. Recognizing the extent of the problem, the leaders of the United States Helsinki Commission on 12 September 2019 introduced the Transnational Repression Accountability and Prevention (TRAP) Act in the House of Representatives. The Act declares that it is the policy of the United States to pursue specific reforms within INTERPOL and use its diplomatic clout internationally to protect the rights of victims and denounce abusers. The bill requires the Departments of Justice, Homeland Security, and State, in consultation with other relevant agencies, to provide

In PACE, an additional problem was that several members from democratic countries by corruptive influence were willing to compromise the integrity of the organization. There were both an institutional integrity problem – among others, lack of safeguards which enabled corrupt members to change the course of the institution – as well as individual integrity issues.

As a result, well-intended Member States may not rely on INTERPOL alerts without conducting thorough investigations into the background of persons that have been put into the system. Several persons have been repeatedly arrested or questioned by police based on politicized INTERPOL alerts. The result is often that their freedom of movement becomes severely restricted.[38]

In an exposé of international integrity failures, acquittals in 2012–2013 by the Appeals Chamber of the International Criminal Tribunal for the Former Yugoslavia ('ICTY'), and media revelations about a deep split among its judges should also be mentioned. The acquitted included high-ranking Croat and Serb officials, such as Ante Gotovina, Mladen Markač, Momčilo Perišić, Jovica Stanišić and Franko Simatović, and generated concerns about the quality of the legacy of the ICTY. Much of the criticism focused on the role of the then ICTY President Theodor Meron, thus challenging his impartiality and alleging that he sought to unduly influence other Tribunal judges. According to diplomatic cables released by WikiLeaks, he was close to the United States government, being characterized by United States diplomatic personnel as a pre-eminent supporter of specific government interests. The criticism extended to the International Criminal Tribunal for Rwanda ('ICTR') which shared its Appeals Chamber with the ICTY.[39] The acquittals did not come as a result of new evidence, but rather

---

Congress with an assessment of autocratic abuse of INTERPOL, what the United States is doing to counteract it, and how to adapt United States policy to this evolving autocratic practice. The State Department would also be required to publicly report on the abuse of INTERPOL in its annual Country Reports on Human Rights to create a transparent, public record of these violations of the rule of law.

[38] A telling example is former hedge fund investor in Russia, William Browder, who since 2009 has led an international human rights campaign, "Justice for Sergei Magnitsky". He has been placed on INTERPOL's red alert list seven times by Russia, which wants him extradited for alleged tax evasion. See "Russia asks Interpol to arrest Kremlin critic Bill Browder: letter", *Reuters*, 9 April 2018. For Browder's best-selling auto-biographical book see William Browder, *Red Notice: How I became Putin's No. 1 Enemy*, Transworld Publishers Ltd., London, 2015.

[39] See Chapter 6 of this book, "ICTY Shifts Have Made Its Credibility Quake". See also Julija Bogoeva, "International Judges and Government Interests: The Case of President Meron", FICHL Policy Brief Series 48 (2016), Torkel Opsahl Academic EPublisher, Brussels, 2016 (https://www.toaep.org/pbs-pdf/48-bogoeva/); and Frederik Harhoff, "Mystery Lane: A Note on Independence and Impartiality in International Criminal Trials", FICHL Policy Brief Series 47 (2016), Torkel Opsahl Academic EPublisher, Brussels, 2016 (https://www.toaep.org/pbs-pdf/47-harhoff/).

as a consequence of changes in judicial interpretation at a late stage in the life of the ICTY affecting the ability of the Tribunal to hold leaders accountable. Combined with revelations of an apparent power struggle between the then American Tribunal President and the Danish judge Frederik Harhoff, leading to the exclusion of the latter, this not only revealed serious disunity among the judges, but at the time reduced trust in the Tribunal in ways that disoriented victims, their families, and the wider struggle against impunity. According to Judge Harhoff, his main concern was undue influence by "the military establishments in countries involved in armed conflicts in other parts of the world, such as the United States and Israel – and […] Russia, France, the UK and others".[40]

My own conclusion at the time was that there existed a,

> persistent reason to doubt the impartiality of President Meron. Regrettably, this doubt has a cancerous staying power. We are so-called 'informed observers', a part of the community of actors that has helped make and protect the ICTY for more than 20 years. If such 'informed observers' perceive bias on the part of an ICTY Judge and MICT President, and have the courage to say so publicly, that has immediate relevancy under the ICTY's law. Losing trust among the informed part of the public is detrimental for a judge of an institution whose authority depends on being – and being perceived as – impartial.[41]

My final example is the media revelations in 2017 about possible misconduct by members of the ICC Office of the Prosecutor and the first ICC Prosecutor, Luis Moreno-Ocampo. Even if there have been serious integrity issues in other international institutions – as shown by the far from exhaustive exposé presented above – there was something particularly disturbing about these revelations. A former high official of the ICC, its first Prosecutor, who had been elected based on legal requirements of "high moral character" in addition to professional skills (being "highly competent in and […] [having] extensive practical experience in the prosecution or trial of criminal cases"),[42] had allegedly been making money by assisting a potential suspect in the Libya situation under ICC investigation.

[40] Harhoff, 2016, p. 2, see *supra* note 39.

[41] See Chapter 6 of this book, Section 6.5., first published as Gunnar M. Ekeløve-Slydal, "ICTY Shifts Have Made Its Credibility Quake", FICHL Policy Brief Series No. 49 (2016), Torkel Opsahl Academic EPublisher, Brussels, 2016 (https://www.toaep.org/pbs-pdf/49-slydal/).

[42] Rome Statute of the International Criminal Court, 17 July 1997, Article 42(3) ('ICC statute') (https://www.legal-tools.org/doc/7b9af9/).

It is not infrequent that prosecutors become private lawyers or legal advisors after their tenure (and after a regulated quarantine period ends), but one part of the revelations was far from acceptable: the first prosecutor relied on ICC staff members sharing information with him.

In addition, there were a range of broader issues resulting from a culture institutionalized by the first Prosecutor which weakened quality control, removed open internal discussions, and resulted in a "sense of fear" and "intimidation" among staff members.[43] Within a few years, 22 top staff members had left his office. These internal problems were known by several government officials and leaders of non-governmental organizations since late 2003.[44]

A further aggravating fact was that the ICC's achievements in terms of convictions of major war criminals have been very disappointing. There have been only three convictions, by the time when this chapter was first published, and cases against 12 persons have collapsed.[45]

Two other factors were also at play. When created, the ICC received widespread support from large parts of the international community, even though some influential states showed reservation and sometimes acted in a hostile manner to the institution.[46] For the human rights community, the adoption of the Rome Statute and its rapid ratification by the required number of states created widespread optimism that the ICC would help create an effective system to fight impunity for core international crimes. In general, institutions do create expectations and provide implicit promises. The establishment of the ICC had created high expectations, some of them perhaps unrealistic.

The second factor is linked to the concept of 'professional integrity'. As a physician is not evaluated only based on his or her personal integrity – being a morally solid and consistent person – but as a person who honours profession-specific requirements, the same goes for prosecutors in international justice. During his time as ICC Prosecutor, Moreno-Ocampo was often hailed in popular culture as a hero in the fight against unspeakable crimes and criminal leaders. His fall due to his failure to uphold professional and integrity requirements

43 Morten Bergsmo, "Institutional History, Behaviour and Development", in Bergsmo, Rackwitz and Song (eds.), 2017, p. 24, see *supra* note 2.

44 Bergsmo, Kaleck, Muller and Wiley, 2017, p. 2, see *supra* note 2.

45 Morten Bergsmo, «La CPI, l'affaire Gbagbo et le rôle de la France», *Le Monde*, 18 January 2019 (https://www.legal-tools.org/doc/d499f6 and https://www.legal-tools.org/en/doc/693bee (English version)).

46 For an overview and evaluation of United States relations with the ICC since 2002, see William Pace, "The Hague Invasion Act remains dangerous", *Diplomat Magazine*, February 9, 2019.

consequently created great disappointment, along with the collapse of the cases he had initiated.[47]

In a letter to Fatou Bensouda, the ICC Prosecutor since 2012, the Norwegian Helsinki Committee raised these issues and asked her to use her "full authority over the management and administration of the Office" to conduct credible and transparent reviews of the legacy of the first Prosecutor in order to establish relevant facts of professional and ethical misconduct".[48]

In her 22 May 2018 reply, Bensouda concluded that,

> my staff and I have made every effort to learn from past experience, improve the culture of the Office of the Prosecutor to encourage openness and critical thinking, and transform our working methods to achieve success. We have endeavoured to be transparent. We uphold ethical standards of the highest order. Should credible allegations of misconduct arise, they are dealt with appropriately and according to a fair process. As such, I am of the respectful view that the sort of broad inquiry you call for is unnecessary considering the steps the Office itself has taken, what we are already accomplishing and have put in place.[49]

In her letter, Bensouda failed to address the most serious allegations referred to in our letter, which implicated the first Prosecutor as well as his *Chef de cabinet* at the time. There were, however, indications in her letter that could be interpreted in the direction that "further measures" could be taken that included "fact-finding concerning the first Prosecutor and former staff members".[50]

---

47 For portraits of Mr. Ocampo that build the hero-narrative, see for instance the films: Edet Belzberg, Kerry Propper, Amelia Green-Dove and Taylor Krauss (Producers) and Edet Belzberg (Director), "Watchers of the sky", motion picture, 2014, United States, Propeller Films; and Paco de Onis (Producer) and Pamela Yates (Director), "The reckoning: the battle for the International Criminal Court", motion picture, 2009, United States, Skylight Pictures.

48 Norwegian Helsinki Committee, "Letter to Mrs. Fatou Bensouda, Prosecutor of the ICC", 12 March 2018 (https://www.legal-tools.org/doc/b745e4/).

49 Fatou Bensouda, "Letter to Messr Engesland and Ekelove-Slydal", 22 May 2018 (available on the Norwegian Helsinki Committee's web site).

50 Norwegian Helsinki Committee, "Letter to Mrs. Fatou Bensouda, Prosecutor of the ICC", 8 June 2018 (available on the Norwegian Helsinki Committee's web site). Also Women's Initiatives for Gender Justice argued for "external review of the practices relevant to the allegations", see Women's Initiatives for Gender Justice, "A critical time for the ICC's credibility", 18 November 2017 (https://www.legal-tools.org/doc/e2fbc7/). The ICC Bar Association ('ICCBA'), urged in a statement, "States Parties and the ASP to initiate a thorough, effective and independent investigation into the serious allegations raised in these recent public reports", see ICCBA, "ICCBA Statement on Allegations Against Former ICC Prosecutor", 29 November 2017 (https://www.legal-tools.org/doc/a8cdcb/).

4.2. Typology of Integrity Issues

There may exist several motives for criticizing integrity failures of institutions and high officials. Most of them fall into two categories: either one wants to *undermine the credibility of the institutions or the officials*, or one wants to *improve, modify and eventually strengthen them.* While critics falling into the first category may wish for the institution to become irrelevant or closed down, those falling into the second category may wish for the opposite. Their vision is a renewed and strengthened institution that plays a stronger beneficial role in its mandated field.

A third category may include critics with motives that are less definite, simply wanting to place failures and problems into the open to initiate debates that may lead in different directions.

To act on any of these motives may, due to circumstances, be quite risky. Consequences of public criticism and debates are difficult to predict. It might be next to impossible to carry out the *utilitarian test* with any degree of certainty, that is, to answer the question whether consequences of a critical engagement will be more beneficial than harmful for the overall goal of advancing the mandate of the institution in question. Is the criticism doing more good than harm?

Such questions were not alien to Thomas More. Regardless of views on whether he was right in his conflict with the King and the legal establishment of his time, it cannot be denied that he was exceptionally skilful in the way he navigated impossible waters. He was in no way seeking martyrdom, but he held steadfastly to viewpoints and strategies he though would lead to the best results.

In his writings, he publicly criticized the Kings that ruled in England and other European states. Sometimes he did so in very direct ways, using strong language to depict the wretchedness of the character of the person he denounced.

At the same time, he eventually decided to serve at high positions in the developing state bureaucracy of England under King Henry VIII (1491–1547). His intention was never to undermine the authority of the King and to instigate a revolt against him. On the contrary, he wanted to improve and thereby strengthen the legitimacy of his rule. Overall, it seems that his main goal was to promote peace and improve the lot of ordinary people.

One of his best-known books, *The History of King Richard the Third*, is a sharply formulated Christian humanist attack on tyrannical rule and a King that personalized excesses connected with ruthless power-struggle and disregard for the well-being of his people.[51]

---

[51] More probably, he started to write the book in 1513 and did never finish it. He wrote two versions simultaneously, one in English and one in Latin for a wider European audience. It was published only after More's death, in 1557. A modernized and easy to read version of the book

More's world-famous *Utopia* (1516) criticizes the state of European politics and exemplifies how politics governed by reason may function by way of describing the state of affairs at a fictive island state.[52] Interestingly, it also includes discussions on whether a wise person should separate himself from politics, or rather serve leaders who are less than ideal and at least contribute to moderating their evils and mistakes.

According to More, a good leader has a duty to "take more care of his people's welfare than of his own, just as it is the duty of a shepherd who cares about his job to feed the sheep rather than himself".[53] If a King departs from his duty, his servant should do what he or she could to minimize the negative consequences of such departure.

More presented strong arguments against the execution of or other harsh penalties imposed on thieves. He was behind legal reforms that would ease access of the poor to justice. Stealing was the only way of surviving for many poor people. Executing them would not contribute to solving any problems, More argued. Part of his progressive agenda was also arguments that leaders should accept free speech, and that Parliament should have a decisive say on legislation.

Even if realities were far from these ideals, More decided eventually to serve for many years under one of the Kings he had both hailed and criticized, Henry VIII. First serving in high legal positions in the city of London, he had accepted prominent positions offered by the King from 1518. He was Chancellor of England from 1529 to 1532.

When entering the King's Council in 1518, More was well aware of the conflicting demands such service would entail. What he did not know, of course, was that Henry VIII would develop into a tyrant, killing wives, high officials that had served him, among many others. He could not foresee that he himself would eventually be killed by the King because of a conflict about fundamental principles concerning the relationship between state and church. In 1535, More was beheaded after a show trial, on the order of the King, for refusing to accept Henry VIII as head of the Church of England. His vision was an internationally unified and independent church.

More has been recognized as a saint by the Roman Catholic Church (1935). Even more important in the context of integrity discussions, he has been

has been made available online by The Centre for Thomas More studies: Thomas More, *The History of King Richard the Third*, Mary Gottschalk (ed.), 2012 [c. 1513]. This version is based on the 1557-edition that inspired William Shakespeare (1564–1616) to write his play 'Richard III'. Whether More's negative account of King Richard was wholly justified, is another question, which I do not intend to discuss here.

52 More, *Utopia*, see *supra* note 3.

53 *Ibid.*, p. 33

proclaimed as a Patron Saint of Statesmen (2000).[54] His example of integrity is not only recognized by the Catholic Church, but by people belonging to different religions and beliefs.

His example remains to a certain degree controversial. The critics claim that he was a fanatic responsible for the execution of heretics during his tenure. It is undisputed that he was responsible for such executions, and it is therefore mandatory in discussions about his enduring legacy to identify exactly what to keep and what to disregard from his thought and practice. Before discussing further More's relevancy for current integrity discussions, though, I will return to the above examples of such issues within international institutions, providing a categorization of the problems.

4.2.1. Politicization or Instrumentalization of Institutions

The examples include issues related to integrity both on institutional as well as individual levels. There were issues related to both current and former officials within the institutions, which enjoyed certain 'privileges' which they reportedly abused (that is, former members of PACE lobbying for Azerbaijan and the first Prosecutor of the ICC).

By institutional integrity, I mean upholding institutional activities and views in line with reasonable interpretations of the institution's mandate. The mandate of the Council of Europe, for instance, is to promote and protect human rights, democracy and the rule of law in its Member States.[55] Mandates of institutions of international justice are typically to "exercise [...] jurisdiction over persons for the most serious crimes of international concern".[56] The institutions may have different rules concerning that jurisdiction, but the core purpose remains the same: to hold persons (at high places) accountable for international crimes they conducted, were responsible for, or failed to prevent.

If institutions fail to fulfil their mandates in specific cases or situations because of *corruption*, *giving in to political pressure*, or *neglect*, these may amount to instances of institutional integrity failures. In international justice institutions, the ICTY's 2012–2013 acquittals may be a case at hand. The point here is that failures to uphold integrity at a personal level may translate into *institutional failure*.

---

[54] Pope John Paul II, Apostolic Letter Issued Moto Proprio, *Proclaiming Saint Thomas More Patron of Statesmen and Politicians*, 31 October 2000.

[55] Statute of the Council of Europe, 5 May 1949 (https://www.legal-tools.org/doc/7rqhpflx/). For an updated presentation of the organization's aim and prioritized areas of activity, see the Council of Europe's official web site.

[56] ICC Statute, Article 1, see *supra* note 42.

Justice institutions are particularly vulnerable to such failure, since the number of people taking binding decisions is limited. The example of PACE's failure to adopt a resolution on political prisoners in Azerbaijan mentioned above indicate that also in bodies where decision-making includes hundreds of persons (PACE has 324 members), this risk is still present.

4.2.1.1. Establishing Fake Institutions

As we have seen, one way of undermining genuine international institutions is to establish *alternative* institutions with a similar mandate, but which applies the mandate in a politicized or biased way.

The purpose may be to undermine the views of genuine institutions in front of the international community or at domestic levels. By presenting alternative views as if they were based on systematic and methodologically sound research, the institutions serve to disorient public opinion and undermine trust in genuine institutions.

The primary example given above was biased election observation. There might, however, also be discussions about whether specific justice institutions should be placed in this category. It is hardly controversial to place highly politicized courts and prosecutorial services in authoritarian states in this category. Such institutions 'mimic' independent courts and prosecutorial services, but in reality, they often function as tools of the highest political authorities or other powerful circles to further their interests.[57]

More controversial – and in my view misleading – would be to place internationalized or international jurisdictions in this category, due to claims that they were one-sided, applied double standards, or professed other mandate restrictions preventing them from applying a strict criteria-based approach to case selection.

The main challenges to their legitimacy centred around the way they were created or their assertion of jurisdiction over heads of states.[58] Another important issue is related to the application of double standards. Double standards in international criminal law raises important and difficult questions about the legitimacy and credibility of the project of ensuring accountability for core

[57] See among others, Maria Popova, *Politicized Justice in Emerging Democracies: A Study of Courts in Russia and Ukraine*, Cambridge University Press, 2012. In particular, Chapter 6 gives an instructive overview of how the integrity of the courts are jeopardized by so-called informal practices of influence, such as 'ex parte communication' between judges and litigants and 'telephone justice' between politicians (or other important players) and judges.

[58] For examples of how high-profile defendants have challenged the legitimacy of the international(ized) courts they were brought for, see Michael A. Newton, "The Iraqi High Criminal Court: Controversy and Contributions", in *International Review of the Red Cross*, 2006, vol. 88, no. 862, p. 405.

international crimes since there is not yet equality before the law. However, this is a different problem from justice institutions that are created to 'mimic' justice, while serving only or mainly political purposes, and which are continuously unduly influenced.[59]

As the ICTY example shows, there reportedly were instances of undue political influence on high officials of international justice institutions, but not of such a systematic and massive scale as to question the genuine character of the institutions as such.

In my view, the main remedy against the fake institution threat to integrity is principled and fact-based criticism exposing the failure of the institutions to uphold agreed standards and professional implementation of their mandate.

4.2.1.2. Undermining Integrity of Genuine Institutions

Concepts of personal integrity mainly fall into two categories: those that underline "formal relations one has to oneself, or between parts or aspects of one's self" and those that see integrity as an "important way to acting morally, in other words, [that] there are some substantive or normative constraints on what it is to act with integrity".[60]

In the first category fall conceptions of persons with "a harmonious, intact whole";[61] persons that are able to keep "the self intact and uncorrupted".[62] Other important characteristics are wholeheartedness and being steadfastly true to one's commitments, especially commitments that are most important for the person's self-respect.

A step further, inspired by existentialist and Kantian thoughts on categorical imperatives, is a view that underlines integrity as 'self-constitution'. The point here is that in addition to coherence, there is an act of rational endorsement of the principles by which a person decides his or her projects. The way to make yourself into a particular person, who can interact well with yourself and others, "is to be consistent and unified and whole – to have integrity".[63]

The second category includes views that point to integrity as a social virtue, which is defined by a person's relations with others. Persons with integrity stand for something, but not in the same way as fanatics do because they respect the deliberations of others. This might be one of the more difficult questions related

---

59 For a description and discussion of the problem of double standards in international justice, see Wolfgang Kaleck, *Double Standards: International Criminal Law and the West*, Torkel Opsahl Academic EPublisher, Brussels, 2015 (https://www.toaep.org/ps-pdf/26-kaleck/).

60 "Integrity", in *Stanford Encyclopedia of Philosophy*, 9 April 2001.

61 *Ibid.*

62 *Ibid.*

63 *Ibid.*

to integrity: what does it mean to respect other's views, when you in the end are willing to sacrifice even your life, as was the case with More, to stand by your own view?

More, like Socrates (470–399 BC) and several other exemplary figures of integrity, stood by their judgment in the face of enormous pressure to recant. There is a strong argument that it is exactly from such examples we may detect the essence of integrity. These are persons who hold to their views despite pressure, efforts to help them escape, efforts to bribe them, or blaming them for letting down their family, friends and social obligations because of their perceived stubbornness.

In the case of More, it is clear that he thought the judges in the trial against him to be both morally and legally wrong in convicting him to death for treason. He had remained silent about his views, and the law protected silence in a case like his. At the same time, he did not denounce his judges, some of whom were his long-term friends. One way of interpreting this seemingly paradoxical situation might be to conclude that as he thought the judges to be wrong, he still respected their right to be wrong in the way they were. He knew, and the judges knew, that to oppose the will of the King equalled endangering your life.[64]

More fought for the unity and integrity of the Catholic Church. While England's bishops (except Bishop John Fisher (1469–1535)), universities and other institutions had given in to the demands of the King to be the head of the Church of England, he would not. He fought for something he believed in very deeply. To give in would be to betray his own convictions, but also to fail in upholding the integrity of a unified church and the future of Christendom.

He fought both to uphold his own integrity and the integrity of an institution he deemed to be of unique importance to upholding the material and spiritual existence of human beings. Dividing the church and placing it under the leadership of Kings would weaken it, lead to violent conflict, and eventually undermine the standing of the Christian states, which at his time was under considerable pressure from the Ottoman Empire as well as from internal conflicts in the Christian world.[65]

The examples presented above primarily illustrated weakening of the integrity of genuine institutions. While INTERPOL's problem was the lack of sufficient institutional safeguards to detect and prevent politicized alerts from its Member States, the other examples showed how institutional integrity was

[64] See Gerard B. Wegemer, "The Trial of Thomas More: July 1, 1535", in *Portrait of Courage*, Scepter, Cleveland, 1995, pp. 210–217.

[65] For a vivid description of the challenging times of More for Britain and, in particular, for Europe, see Robert Tombs, *The English and Their History*, Penguin Books, London, 2015, pp. 157–160.

undermined by individual actors within the institutions or by external actors with a privileged access to the institutions. The methods were, among others, *bribing*, *exertion of pressure*, and *abuse of personal relationships*.

Corruption of high officials may be both internally and externally directed. It may be facilitated by clearly illegitimate methods, but there is also a vast area of less clear but still *integrity-sensitive* ways of changing institutional policies or even outcomes of trials in justice institutions. Such methods may include *forceful argumentation* towards persons in lower positions, reference to *perceived interests of important allies of the institution*, or *gradual undermining of a culture of quality control*.

The examples illustrate the close nexus between professionalism and integrity: if you are weak in the practice of your profession, you may be easy prey for someone who wants to instrumentalize your professional role in ways that weaken institutional integrity.

To counter the threats to institutional integrity, the main methods are institutional safeguards, transparency in appointments and elections of high officials, adherence to codes of conduct, and proper oversight mechanisms. But even an institution that is well set up and protected against corrupt practices may fail.

A culture of individual adherence to norms of professional integrity is vital. In particular, leaders of institutions play an important role in this regard. They may set examples and nourish cultures of integrity. Or they may fail to do so with detrimental consequences for the institution.[66]

In my view, More is especially relevant in this regard. His foremost contribution may be his insight into the importance of leaders exemplifying and talking convincingly about integrity.

4.2.2. Professional Integrity

Each profession creates its own framework of integrity. The reason we trust our health to physicians we do not personally know, is that they represent competence and a wider practice that we confide in. The same goes for justice professionals. We respect and adhere to court decisions because we confide in the wider practice of courts and the professional competence and integrity of the key actors taking decisions.

[66] For a powerful account of the important role of leaders adhering to democratic norms and functioning as gatekeepers to uphold democratic rule, see Steven Levitsky and Daniel Ziblatt, *How Democracies Die*, Broadway Books, New York, 2018. While their analysis mainly deals with the question of how to uphold democratic *political* institutions, their insistence on the important role of leaders or gatekeepers is also highly relevant for discussions on how to uphold and strengthen integrity of justice institutions.

There are several reasons to conceptualize *professional* integrity as a distinct virtue, and not as 'ordinary' integrity placed in a specialized context. Firstly, any profession has specific ends, such as health for medical personnel and justice for prosecutors, defence lawyers and judges. Loyalty to such profession-specific ends may be perceived as an integrity factor *sui generis*. It is precisely because we expect this form of integrity that we entrust important aspects of our lives to professionals.[67]

Secondly, we expect role holders within specialized institutions to put professional standards above self-interest. When issues of corruption or conflict of interests are brought up, professional integrity is seen as the virtue of honouring norms of the profession more than any personal interest. A judge that gives in to political pressure or accepts bribes to decide in favour of one of the parties is not living up to the assurances or promises of her or his profession.

Professionals should not be like people who constantly question their own decisions or backslide in the face of social pressure. Professionals trust their own convictions. They may change their views, but only in light of compelling reasons.

Upholding professional standards may at times be hard, not because of pressures or temptations, but because issues are hard to solve. Such hard cases demand a certain degree of interpretive skills, deliberative capacity and competence and ability to balance different views and concerns. In these situations, professional competence is not only about finding a solution but to be able to *demonstrate* why this is the preferred solution in terms of professional standards and practice.

In this view, professional integrity is characterized by a mode of reasoning that calls for the role holder to engage critically and creatively with the varied and sometimes conflicting demands of practice. The 'fundamental normative relation' that governs the situation is a promissory relation: the profession has given its word to the public, and role holders are given the task of keeping the promises. In keeping the promises, they must both honour professional standards and have a wider understanding of the practice they fulfil.[68]

---

[67] Andreas Eriksen, "What is Professional Integrity?", in *Nordic Journal of Applied Ethics*, 2015, vol. 9, no. 2, pp. 3–17.

[68] *Ibid.*, p. 10. Eriksen uses Ronald Dworkin's figure of a 'chain novelist' to illustrate this interpretive view of professional integrity. The task of judges is like the task of authors engaged in a 'chain novel'. This novel is written one chapter at a time. Each finished chapter is passed along to a new author, who writes the next one. The task of each author is to make this the best novel it can be. According to Dworkin, the good judge views earlier decisions "as part of a long story he must interpret and then continue, according to his own judgment of how to make the developing story as good as it can be".

In important aspects, this view balances the responsibility of the role holder with the practice of the profession. The judge remains responsible because he or she has to interpret with a view to deciding the case according to his or her best reading of practice. The responsibility is nevertheless shared with the practice of the profession, which is regarded as a justifiable social institution.

Ordinary or personal integrity is about consistency in upholding the moral values one has chosen to be guided by – in words and deeds. Professionals, in addition, have to honour the standards and practice of their profession. But not in a careless and automatic way. They have to give their own contribution by interpreting previous practice and decide on new cases based on the best reading of that practice. Sometimes they have to depart from previous judgments, but only if they can base that departure on a justifiable reading of previous practice.

4.2.2.1. Disregard of Professional Norms and Interpretive Requirements

Seen from this view on integrity, it appears that many current integrity issues stem from the failure of leaders of the institutions to uphold their own professional integrity, to uphold a culture of integrity within the institution, as well as weak oversight mechanisms. They fail to honour the inherent promises, the standards and practices of their profession.

Pedro Agramunt, a Spanish conservative politician, resigned as President of PACE after conducting a visit to Syria's president Bashar al-Assad in March 2017, together with Russian Duma members. Although he underlined that he undertook the visit only in his capacity as Spanish Senator, the Bureau of PACE stated that he was no longer "authorized to undertake any official visits, attend meetings, or make public statements on behalf of the Assembly in his capacity as president".[69] His resignation, however, had a wider context. Already as PACE Rapporteur on political prisoners in Azerbaijan, he became controversial by human rights groups for not reporting accurately on the problems in the country. This criticism continued and was strengthened during his tenure as PACE President, 2016–2017. Several others of the members that were involved in the so-called 'caviar diplomacy', also had leading roles. Luka Volonté was heading the European People's Party in PACE.

[69] Rikard Jozwiak, "PACE President Stripped of Powers After Meeting Syria's Assad", *Radio Free Europe*, 28 April 2017. A Motion for dismissal was tabled by Ingjerd Schou, a Norwegian member of the PACE, on 30 June 2017, see PACE, "Dismissal of Mr Pedro Agramunt, President of the Parliamentary Assembly", Doc. 4383, 30 June 2017. The Motion reads: "We, the undersigned, consider that the President of the Parliamentary Assembly no longer enjoys the confidence of the Assembly, on the grounds that his behaviour seriously harms the reputation of the Parliamentary Assembly and tarnishes its image". Agramunt, however, resigned on 6 October 2017 before the Motion was scheduled to be decided on, see PACE, "Pedro Agramunt resigns as PACE President", 6 October 2017.

Members of the ICC Office of the Prosecutor continued to stay in close contact with the first Prosecutor, reportedly based on personal relationships. In the example of the ICTY given above, the situation was complex: the ICTY President may have felt pressure from military establishments to change judicial interpretation. He then himself may have exerted undue pressure on some of his colleagues.

From these examples, four main categories of breaches with professional integrity may be detected:

1. Integrity failures may result from giving in to *external political* or *undue internal collegial pressure*. The colleague exerting undue pressure often has a superior role, but this may not necessarily be the case.
   a. A subcategory, not exemplified above, is the famous Soviet and Russian use of '*Kompromat*' or 'compromising material' to blackmail, for instance, judges to receive certain outcomes of criminal or other cases before a court. In these cases, the pressure was based on exerting fear of a ruined career or reputation.
   b. The position of power necessary for exerting effective pressure to undermine the integrity of professionals may vary, from being able to obstruct promotions, making sure the person loses her or his job, or more serious consequences, as the one faced by Thomas More: risking losing his life.
   c. The position of power may also be of such a nature that not only the fate of the professional but the survival of the institution she or he serves is at stake. In such situations, professionals may feel obliged to give in to undue pressure to save the institution while losing out on integrity.
2. Giving up integrity may result from giving in to *material temptations*, such as bribes, luxury travels or other forms of material gains, such as reportedly was the case in the PACE 'caviar diplomacy' scandal. Bribery can come from both colleagues and from external actors. The effect of the bribes may be augmented by the development of a personal relationship, which places the person who bribes and the person who receives bribes in a relationship of mutual loyalty.
3. A third category comprises *personal relationships as such*. This factor may often remain neglected in dealing with integrity issues. However, in any institution personal bounds may play an important role in weakening scrutiny of decisions and decision-making processes. An important part of creating a culture of integrity is to uphold norms of quality control, professionalism and internal oversight not only in situations of *difficult* personal relations between staff members but also in situations of *strong reciprocal*

sympathies. Such sympathies may weaken the willingness to challenge decisions that violate professional integrity.

4. A fourth category comprises *lack of professional and moral convictions*. Stories of professionals who give in to pressure or material temptations may not only be diagnosed as lack of will-power, but also as lack of basic identification with the profession's ends and means. Such identification may develop over time from education and experiences in the profession, but it may also be weakened by cynicism and pessimism about the achievements of the profession and institutions. The idealism of the newly educated staff member may over time be taken over by cynicism and lack of identification with the practice of the profession.

4.2.2.2. Failure by External Actors to Hold Institutions to Account

Finally, the role of external actors should be mentioned. There are several differences in the accounts of integrity issues in PACE and in the ICC given above. One of the most striking is that the call for external review was successful in the case of PACE, while the Prosecutor of the ICC did not initiate such review. One of the likely explanations for this may be the lack of consistent public pressure on the ICC from 'informed observers' and watchdogs to do so.

In the case of PACE, a large number of non-governmental organizations, think-tanks as well as members of PACE were alerted of the situation and strongly requested such review.

Justice institutions are obviously different from political bodies in several aspects. There are fewer persons involved in decision-making and, for external supportive actors, the concern of upholding and respecting the independence of prosecutors and judges may lead to more muted criticism than warranted by the seriousness of their failures.

The important role of external guardians of integrity for justice institution should not be understated. Independent media, professionalized civil society organizations, academics and other informed observers are vital parts of a necessary structure to uphold institutional integrity. Without such a structure, consistently challenging the institution on professional and integrity issues, it becomes increasingly vulnerable to under-performing.

4.2.3. The Role of Exemplary Stories and Personalities

As described above, international institutions face a range of integrity challenges. These are the basis for the questions we ask More for guidance on in the following.

There are questions related to 'professionalism', in particular for legal personnel, who are tasked to take decisions based on legal rather than on purely political grounds. There is an inherent requirement not to adhere to 'horse-trading' to get support from important states or other powerful actors.

There are questions related to upholding institutional consistency and being in line with the mandate and aim of the institution. 'Independence', 'incorruptness' and 'not giving in to political pressure' are among the key words in this context, as well as 'professional competence'.

Given the difficult political environment of international justice, 'integrity' may play a crucial role in upholding the authority of an institution. Arguably, a culture of professional integrity is decisive to ensure that international justice institutions live up to expectations, create public trust, and withstand unfounded criticism.

There are large integrity deficits in justice institutions at the national level in many states, and international jurisdictions are therefore needed as integrity models.[70] The complementarity principle of the ICC Statute implies that the ICC may prosecute only when national jurisdictions fail to uphold justice, including because of integrity deficits. That puts an additional pressure on the ICC to be exemplary on integrity.

Studying personalities and stories of the past to get guidance on current integrity issues obviously carries a risk of misrepresenting them to extract relevant messages. Nevertheless, integrity issues being inherent in personal and professional relationships of all times, there are remarkable similarities between the contemporary issues and the issues inherent in the writings and life of More and other heroes of integrity of the past.

In the story about More's conflict with King Henry VIII, and central to his thinking on political issues, all four challenges to upholding integrity as described above are to be found. He reflected on and exemplified how to withstand strong *pressure* from both the political leadership of his time, headed by King Henry VIII and his chief minister, Thomas Cromwell (1480–1540), his colleagues, many of whom had been his personal friends for a long time, and even his own family.

During his service both for the city of London and for King Henry VIII he was well known for his uncorrupted and efficient dealing with public affairs under his responsibility. Based on Christian beliefs, he seemed to endorse a

[70] As an indicator of possible lack of integrity in national jurisdictions, I take low scores on civil and criminal justice in the World Justice Project Rule of Law Index. A further indication of issues of integrity being widespread at the national level, is the renewed focus by the United Nations Office on Drugs and Crime on integrity issues in the criminal justice system. See also *supra* note 57.

simple lifestyle, although he ran a big family estate with frequent guests, and sometimes provided meals for the poor.[71]

When it comes to integrity being weakened by personal relationships and lack of personal or professional convictions, More stands out as particularly serious about his role as a lawyer, high official and a leading citizen.

In his twenties, he may seriously have doubted whether to become part of public affairs. He was attracted to a life secluded from the temporal world, living in or next to the London Charterhouse from around 1500–1503, a Carthusian Monastery at the time.[72] There he tested his vocation for the priesthood, although without withdrawing completely from the world. He continued to teach his students and gave public lectures on St. Augustine's *City of God* during this period.

In the end, he decided to seek political engagement. This was not based on naïve or utterly idealistic ideas that he could drastically change things for the better. But he had ideas of legal and political reform, the need to balance executive power with adherence to reasonable laws, and about developing amicable relations with foreign states. He realized that the best way to improve society was not to stay in a cloister, but to become an active citizen of a Christian commonwealth in line with the humanist thinking of his day.[73]

In seeking political engagement, he knew that abuse of power was frequent. Among his lasting contributions as a political thinker is his discussions on how to confront tyranny.

[71] The literature on Thomas More's life and thinking is vast. For general introductions, I consulted John Guy, *Thomas More: A Very Brief History*, Society for Promotion of Christian Knowledge, London, 2017; Richard Marius, *Thomas More: A Biography*, Alfred A. Knopf, New York, 1984; Raymond Wilson Chambers, *Thomas More*, Endeavor Press, London, 2017 (first published 1935); George M. Logan (ed.), *The Cambridge Companion to Thomas More*, Cambridge University Press, 2011; and Peter Berglar, *Thomas More: A Lonely Voice Against the Power of the State*, Scepter Publishers, Cleveland, 2009 (first published in German, 1999).

[72] The London Charterhouse was a Carthusian Priory 1371–1537, when it was dissolved by Henry VIII. The Carthusian order, also called the Order of Saint Bruno, is a Catholic religious order of enclosed monastics. It was founded by Bruno of Cologne in 1084 and includes both monks and nuns. The order has its own Rule, called the *Statutes*, rather than the Rule of Saint Benedict, and combines eremitical and coenobitic monasticism. The motto of the Carthusians is *Stat crux dum volvitur orbis*, Latin for "The Cross is steady while the world is turning"; Wikiwand, "London Charterhouse" (available on its web site).

[73] For a short discussion of More's motivations to seek political engagement, see John Guy, "Shaping a mind", in *Thomas More: A Very Brief History*, Society for Promotion of Christian Knowledge, London, 2017, pp. 1–8.

4.3. Civilizing Politics

Abuse of power may be as old as power itself. Since power-relations are part of any human society – and human beings per definition are political creatures, living in more or less stable societies – such abuse and how to stem it constitutes fundamental issues of political and moral philosophy.

In his thinking on such issues, More applied concepts and doctrines framed by Greek philosophers such as Plato (427–347 BC) and Aristotle (384–322 BC). He belonged to a small group of English intellectuals who were influenced by Italian Renaissance philosophers' re-reading and translations of original Greek philosophical texts, in particular Plato's and Aristotle's texts on governance and the best ways to organize society.

Renaissance humanism did not form a coherent ideology or school of philosophy. Rather, it provided new readings of some of the same antique texts that Medieval philosophy was based on. In its Northern version, humanism also relied heavily on the foundational texts of Christian antiquity, notably those of the New Testament and the Church Fathers.[74] It represented a break with Medieval metaphysical system-building and speculation, scholastic culture, arts of disputation and dialectic and a renewed focus on reforms of church and society to improve the situation of its members. Its educational programmes, designed to enable active citizens to cope with the needs of the day, "carried an inherent moral purpose in the furtherance of the common good, so that another component was moral philosophy, especially directed to the obligations of the ruler and the citizen".[75]

In More's thinking, a shift took place with ancient Greek values of *equality* and *justice*, breaking with the Roman influenced values prevailing in his society of *glory*, *honour*, *ambition* and *private property*.[76] The humanist emphasis on moral and political philosophy may also have made it easier for More to combine his extensive humanist studies with his study of law, which his father John More (1450/1453–1530), a highly respected lawyer and judge, favoured. The proper role of law in society, being binding on both rulers and citizens, was at the core of the humanist reform agenda. The impulses from Italy seem first to

[74] James McComica, "Thomas More as Humanist", in George M. Lugan (ed.), *The Cambridge Companion to Thomas More*, Cambridge University Press, 2011, p. 22.

[75] *Ibid.*, p. 23.

[76] *Ibid.* Several of More's friends and teachers were prominent scholars and linguists who had travelled to Florence and Rome to study Greek language and philosophy, such as William Grocyn (1446–1519), Thomas Linacre (1460–1524), John Colet (1467–1519), and William Lily (1468–1522).

have made its way to court circles and to the legal world of the Inns court, where More learnt law from 1494.[77]

It may seem paradoxical that Plato was among the foundational thinkers of this paradigm shift in Western philosophy. He is primarily known for his belief in a world of invisible *forms* or *ideas*, which he held to be the *real* world, and for abstract speculation. However, the larger parts of his works – such as *The Republic* and *The Laws*, but also many of the Socratic dialogues – focus on how to improve the less than perfect material and political world.[78]

A central point for Plato, resonated in the writings of Cicero (106–43 BC), one of the few Roman thinkers that More held in high esteem, was that humans are not born for themselves alone, "but our country claims a share of our being, and our friends a share".[79] In developing this perception of humans as socially inter-connected, More warned against misconstrued views on *human liberty.*

False expectations of life arise from such views, namely that *a free person is the one that can do whatever he wants.* Rather, inherent in liberty are to be guided by constraints such as the high commandments of God, the laws made by humans to rule society, and the commands of those with legitimate power. Given human nature, persons may easily fall prey to enslavement by obsessions, sins, or by society and rulers. One part of society often enslaves another.

An antidote to such enslavement is to connect liberty with law, as advocated by Cicero and further developed by More.[80] In his early works, More underlined that liberty without law, even if you are a rich person, is tantamount to bondage. In particular, he points to the importance of 'skilled princeps', 'leading citizens' respecting the law. These are leaders that have the virtues, training and ingenuity needed to secure the safety of the people and provide justice. Their integrity is of utmost importance for society.

Leaders who do not respect law and liberty, develop into tyrants. The quality of a ruler is made clear only by the actual liberty, prosperity, peace, and joy of his people.[81]

---

77 *Ibid.*, p. 26.

78 See "Plato", in *Stanford Encyclopedia of Philosophy*, 20 March 2004.

79 Marcus Tullius Cicero, *De Officiis*, trans. by Walter Miller, Harvard University Press, Cambridge, 1913 [44 BC].

80 More was shortly after his death called "the Christian English Cicero", see Nicholas Harpfield, *Life and Death of Sir Thomas More*, Early English Text Society, London, 1932, p. 217.

81 Gerard Wegemer, "Thomas More on Liberty, Law, and Good Rule", in Curtright (ed.), 2015, pp. 5–13, see *supra* note 7.

4.3.1. The Ever-Present Danger of Tyranny

There is a strong continuity in More's thinking about the duties of leaders, from his first literary works until his last works written during his 14 and a half months of imprisonment before he was beheaded. A main theme is that true leading citizens have a duty to ensure that justice is done. To neglect to do what the duty of his office requires is "like a cowardly ship's captain who [...] deserts the helm, hides away covering in some cranny, and abandons the ship to the waves".[82]

Even though More was a Christian thinker and statesman, many of his ideas have resonated well beyond Christian circles. This is no surprise since More's humanist writings conveyed arguments and views which were based on philosophical ideas. He held the view that reason and practical wisdom led to conclusions that would not be contradicted but rather further enlightened by Christian revelation.

More's example has appealed to Christians, persons with other faiths, as well as to non-believers. This is an important part of the reasoning behind pope John Paul II's proclamation of More as "Patron of Statesmen and Politicians". In the apostolic letter making the proclamation, the pope referred to support from "different political, cultural, and religious allegiances", indicating a "deep and widespread interest in the thought and activity of this outstanding statesman".[83]

A fundamental issue for More and the tradition of thought he belonged to, was how a leading citizen, a statesman or a philosopher should respond to tyranny. Rulers developing into tyrants was seen as an ever-present danger, given the temptations of power and the lack of strong institutional set-ups that could temper the ruler's tyrannical inclinations. More certainly realized that serving King Henry VIII could become precariously difficult, given the Kings propensity to pass from mild rule into repressive and arbitrary rule. In general, More favoured republican and consultative government over that of a single ruler to avoid abuse of power.[84]

More also favoured that members of Parliament should be given freedom of expression, so that the King would know what they really felt about his propositions. In April 1523, he was chosen as speaker of the House of Commons, and in a speech there he made the first recorded petition for the exercise of

[82] Thomas More, *De Tristita Cristi*, in *The Complete Works of St. Thomas More*, 15 vols., Yale University Press, New Haven, 1963–97, vol. 14, p. 265.

[83] John Paul II, *Apostolic Letter Issued Motu Proprio: Proclaiming Saint Thomas More Patron of Statesmen and Politicians*, Section 1, see *supra* note 54.

[84] Cathy Curtis, "More's public life", in Logan (ed.), 2011, p. 74, see *supra* note 71.

freedom of speech in parliament. Effective governance depended on parliamentarians' freedom to speak their mind without fear of reprisals, he argued.[85] He also practised free speech in Parliament himself, by speaking against Henry VII's and later against Henry VIII's proposals for funding of wars or other purposes by increasing taxation. He was influential in convincing Parliament to reduce the demanded amounts, much to the Kings' displeasure.

These views and practices were part of a well-thought-out strategy that More in his humanist works advised to confront and minimize the consequences of tyranny or abusive rule. They were based on a realistic view that to influence rule by a tyrant so it at least to some extent benefitted the people, and not only the ruler, killing the tyrant or rebelling against him would not lead to the desired results. More's theorizing on tyranny and how to confront it, is an important key to understanding him as a statesman and his motivation for serving King Henry VIII at the highest levels, despite his knowledge of the Kings tyrannical inclinations.

More elaborated his view in *Declamation* in response to Lucian's *The Tyrannicide*, a text More translated from Greek into Latin in 1506.[86] Lucian of Samosata (120–after 180 AD) was a Greek rhetorician, pamphleteer and satirist who wielded considerable influence on both More and Erasmus. His writings embody a sophisticated and often embittered critique of the shams and follies of the literature, philosophy, and intellectual life of his day.

The Tyrannicide presents a fictional court speech in which a citizen claims to deserve the city's reward, provided for by law, for having killed the tyrant, although indirectly. He had actually only managed to kill the tyrant's son, but when the tyrant found his son killed, he committed suicide. The speaker nonetheless presents himself as a tyrannicide and the city's saviour.

More's *Declamation* presents a court speech of a fellow citizen who challenges the tyrannicide's right to the legal reward. In effect, the *Declamation* provides a diagnosis of tyranny and an account of how best to confront it.[87]

There are several noteworthy points in More's account. Firstly, he shows how tyranny represents an ever-present danger. Even benevolent rulers may decay into tyrants. True, the tyrant is a disturbed individual, caring for his own interests only despite being a leader with a duty to care for the interests of his

85 *Ibid.*, p. 77.

86 More's *Declamation* is available in: *The Complete Works of St. Thomas More*, vol. 3, part 1, see *supra* note 82. In 1505–1506, More and Erasmus translated some of Lucian's writing into Latin. More translated the *Cynicus, Minippus, Philopseudes* and *Tyrannicide*, and both he and Erasmus wrote declamations replying to the latter work.

87 For a detailed account of the *Declamation*, see Carson Holloway, "Statesmanship, Tyranny, and Piety", in Curtright (ed.), 2015, pp. 17–36, see *supra* note 7.

people. He is, however, not so different from other people as we like to think. As More showed in his history of *Richard III*[88] and in the first book of *Utopia*,[89] European rulers of his own time were prepared to use several measures associated with tyranny, such as aggressive wars, killing their opponents, and manipulating currency and law to serve their interests.[90]

Secondly, since tyranny is an ever-present danger, those with influence and political authority must make efforts to learn how to respond to it intelligently and efficiently. Killing the tyrant (or his son) is not to produce sustainable results. We need to think as a physician, who knows that to cure a disease you must know its cause as well as which treatments are best suited to cure it.

In understanding tyranny, More refers to Plato (*The Republic*) and Aristotle (*Politics*), who define a tyrant as a solitary ruler.[91] However, not all solitary rulers are tyrants. For Aristotle, the difference is that a King rules for the good of his subjects, while a tyrant rules only with a view to his own advantage. For More, the solitary status of the tyrant is a consequence of the disorder of his soul. He has an unrestrained desire that respects no limitations. He cannot have a partner; not even his son.

In analysing the tyrant's desire, More follows Plato and Cicero in perceiving the human soul as composed of three parts, each with its own object of desire. *Reason* desires truth and the good of the whole individual, the *spirit* is preoccupied with honour and competitive values, while *appetite* has the traditional low tastes for food, drink and sex.

Because the soul is complex, an erroneous calculation is not the only way it can go wrong. The three parts pull in different directions, and the low element in a soul in which it is overdeveloped, can win out. It follows that a good condition of the soul requires more than just cognitive excellence. The healthy or just soul has harmony in which its three parts all functions properly. Reason understands the Good, while spirit and appetite desire what is good for them to desire, being guided by reason.

The soul of the tyrant has departed from this order. He is, according to Plato, ruled not by his reason but by his appetite, which craves for satisfaction without boundaries. He is driven by lust for money, food and sex.[92] More agrees with Plato on the distorted order of the tyrant's soul. Tyranny involves the rule

---

88 More, 1513, see *supra* note 4.

89 More, 1516, see *supra* note 3.

90 Holloway, 2015, p. 19, see *supra* note 87.

91 Plato, *The Republic*, trans. by Allan Bloom, Basic Books, New York, 1991 [376 BC], Book 9; and Aristotle, *Politics*, trans. by Carnes Lord, University of Chicago Press, 1984, Book 3, Chapter 7.

92 Plato, 1991, 572d–575d, see *supra* note 91.

in the soul of the lower parts. But he lays the emphasis on the role of *spiritedness*, the desire for honour and a unique position in society, rather than on the bodily desires. A tyrant is dominated by ambition, lust of power, greed and thirst for fame. He wants to elevate himself above other human beings by becoming the supreme power in the city or the realm.[93]

In arguing for this position, More points that beasts that are driven by bodily desires such as hunger, can only show certain elements of a tyrannical nature. Human beings go further in succumbing more completely to tyranny. Appetite or bodily desires are not in themselves enough to bring tyranny into being.[94]

If satisfying bodily desires was the main desires of tyranny, becoming a wealthy businessman would probably give better results. A tyrant, in contrast, lives under threat of violent death at the hands of oppressed and desperate subjects. His ability to enjoy bodily pleasures would be limited.

Because the tyrant is driven by spirited desires, he cannot share power with anyone. If the beast does not tolerate partners in the hunt due to their hunger (appetite), how can we "imagine that a human tyrant, puffed up by pride, driven by the lust of power, impelled by greed, provoked by the thirst for fame, can share his tyranny with anyone?".[95]

Thirdly, even if the tyrant is driven by spirited desires, he also lacks restraint in relation to bodily desires, resulting in him resorting to murder, rape and robbery. This is so because he may use objects of bodily desires to ascertain his total dominance over his realm. To keep public order and rule moderately, would not satisfy his lust for complete dominance. He cannot accept any kind of equality between his subjects and himself. He murders, robs and rapes to manifest his supremacy and humiliate those he rules over.

There is also an important impunity factor, explaining the tyrant's excessive abuses. Since he is placed totally above the law, he is free to fulfil any bodily desire. In his soul, the worst parts dominate the best (reason), and this results in him being unhappy and "full of confusion and regret".[96] He is therefore constantly seeking distractions by fulfilling his bodily desires.

Fourthly, the resulting characteristics of tyrannical rule may be summarized as a lawless form of rule in contrast to legitimate authority, that governs by laws and obeys laws. The tyrant may call his directives 'laws', but they hardly deserve the name since he can change them at any time. A law is a settled rule superior to any single man's will, and the tyrant therefore cannot accept it.

93 Holloway, 2015, pp. 22–23, see *supra* note 87.

94 *Ibid.*

95 More, *Declamation*, p. 101, see *supra* note 86.

96 Plato, 1991, 577e, see *supra* note 91.

His rule becomes unpredictable, spreading fear and distress among his subjects.[97]

Tyranny is also a regime devoid of any freedom. All of the tyrant's subjects evidently lack freedom, living at the mercy of the tyrant. However, the tyrant himself also lacks genuine freedom. He cannot choose what is good for human beings, namely to be governed by reason and laws. He does not know real friendship; he reduces other human beings to become tools of his own desires. His freedom is therefore empty and illusory. He is enslaved by his own desires, dominated by forces within his own distorted soul.

More's teaching on tyranny is a dark tale. Not the least because of his insistence that it is rooted in human nature and its strong desires. It is extreme and evil, but it is not as rare as we would like to think. It tends to develop from the normal functioning of the human soul, which is often not properly regulated. When the man who killed the tyrant's son claims to have eradicated tyranny and demand to be rewarded, it is another example of the spirited desire for public recognition beyond what is truly reasonable.

That means that the impulses – the inflated desire for honour and public praise – that led to tyranny is also present in the attempted destruction of tyranny. In addition, there is a question about the motives: was the attack on the tyrant based on a genuine will to eradicate tyranny or was it done "in revenge or retaliation for some private injury done to you"?[98] Those acting against the tyrant may include decent men who suffered under brutal oppression, but it could also include selfish men who resented the fact that the tyranny operated against their own benefit. There might even be men included who want to replace the tyrant, while upholding tyranny.

According to More, in any society there is a part of the population that must be categorized as wicked. Even if they form just a small part, their views might influence the deliberations of the society if they are not refuted. The recognition that wickedness is always part of politics, also in non-tyrannical regimes, must make us realize that any regime carries the seeds of tyranny.[99]

In More's own words, even "legitimate authorities, not only governing by laws but also obeying laws, and so very much milder than a tyranny, are nevertheless so dominated by the desire for power that they spare not the lives of intimate friends rather than allow them to share their rule".[100]

[97] More, *Declamation*, p. 101, see *supra* note 86; Holloway, 2015, p. 24, see *supra* note 87.

[98] More, *Declamation*, p. 107, see *supra* note 86.

[99] Holloway, 2015, p. 27, see *supra* note 87.

[100] More, *Declamation*, p. 101, see *supra* note 86.

More's conclusion is that it is naïve to think about the tyrant as an exceptional person, a monster or a psychopath, and that lawful rulers could not become tyrants. The same spirited motives that result in tyranny – love of power and fame – are present even in legitimate rulers. The difference is that they are present in more restrained forms.

Finally, it must not be forgotten that, even if the tyrant does not tolerate co-rulers, there are plenty of enablers, supporters and henchmen. You may succeed in killing the tyrant, but utterly fail in eradicating tyranny which is brought forward by those who willingly benefited from his rule, were protected by it and themselves committed outrageous crimes.

4.3.2. The Fundamental Question of Integrity

We have now reached the point in discussing tyranny where what could be called the fundamental question of integrity should be asked: *How to confront tyranny in such a way that you don't sow the seeds of further tyranny, neither in your own soul nor in society?*

According to More, the answer is that you should rebalance your soul and leave the level of spiritedness. Reason should become the guide of your actions, not motives of being recognized for courage, becoming famous and publicly praised. Since the cause of tyranny is the domination of spirited desires, actions based on these desires cannot be the solution.

It does not mean, however, that there is no need for courage and other spirited desires in confronting tyranny. The problem arises, however, when desires of fame, honour and power remain uncontrolled. What is needed are courageous actions under the direction of reason.

The fundamental question could thus be rephrased as: *How to ensure that reason remain in control of spirit and appetite in confronting tyranny*?

More makes this point clear by comparing the tyrannicide with a doctor. The criteria by which to judge the professional quality of a doctor is whether he heals or improves the condition of a patient, not how strongly he *wants* or *tries* to do so. If he pretends to know how to heal me, without being competent, he deserves only "condemnation for rashly meddling, to my danger, in this matter in which he was unskilled".[101]

In a similar way, what the law seeks in rewarding killing of the tyrant and eradicating tyranny, is a "resourceful man, one not only stronghanded but (much more) strong-hearted; able in stratagem rather than in force; one who knows how to lay plots, hide his traps, make the most of his opportunities".[102]

---

[101] *Ibid.*, p. 109.

[102] *Ibid.*

Confronting tyranny effectively requires intelligence and skill. An incompetent doctor may leave the patient in a worse condition than before his intervention. Likewise, confronting tyranny without proper strategies and skills may strengthen it and increase the suffering of ordinary people who now may be targeted innocently by an enraged tyrant.

Even if Lucian's character, claiming that he should be rewarded for tyrannicide, had succeeded in killing the tyrant himself, the forces that had enabled tyranny would still be operational. There would be men who had been privileged by his rule, stealing from and suppressing their fellow citizens, and who would be eager to find a successor to the tyrant. Even if they failed, there would be civil war or uprisings, people would die and the goal of establishing a legitimate free public order would be hard to attain.

More returns to the question of how a leading citizen or a statesman could confront tyranny or milder forms of corrupted politics in the first book of *Utopia*, which was written about 10 years later than the *Declamation* (in 1515–1516).[103] Here the focus is on the problem of ensuring that rulers receive – and take – appropriate advice. Given the corrupted nature of politics, from the point of view of a prospective councillor, the question is if he should commit himself to public affairs at all. The discussion between the philosopher-traveller, Raphael Hythloday (who in the second part recounts his experiences from Utopia, an island state based on socialist, tolerant and equality principles), Peter Giles (a humanist official, based on a real person), and Thomas More (the author, but not necessarily always presenting the author's views) on this issue is revealing:

> 'My dear Raphael', he said, 'I'm surprised that you don't enter some King's service; for I don't know of a single prince who wouldn't be very glad to have you. Your learning and your knowledge of various countries and peoples would entertain him while your advice and supply of examples would be helpful at the counsel board. Thus you might admirably advance your own interests and be of great use at the same time to all your relatives and friends.'
>
> 'About my relatives and friends', he replied, 'I'm not much concerned, because I consider I've already done my duty by them tolerably well. While still young and healthy, I distributed among my relatives and friends the possessions that most men do not part with till they're old and sick (and then only reluctantly, when they can no longer keep them). I think they should be content with this gift of mine, and not insist, or even expect, that for their sake I should enslave myself to any King whatever.'

[103] More, 1516, see *supra* note 3.

'Well said', Peter replied; 'but I do not mean that you should be in servitude to any King, only in his service.'

'The difference is only a matter of one syllable', said Raphael.

'All right', said Peter, 'but whatever you call it, I do not see any other way in which you can be so useful to your friends or to the general public, in addition to making yourself happier.'

'Happier indeed!' said Raphael. 'Would a way of life so absolutely repellent to my spirit make my life happier? As it is now, I live as I please, and I fancy very few courtiers, however splendid, can say that. As a matter of fact, there are so many men soliciting favours from the powerful that you need not think it will be a great loss if they have to do without me and a couple of others like me.'

Then I [More] said, 'It is clear, my dear Raphael, that you seek neither wealth nor power, and indeed I prize and revere a man of your disposition no less than I do the mightiest persons in the world. Yet I think if you could bring yourself to devote your intelligence and energy to public affairs, you would be doing something worthy of your noble and truly philosophical nature, even if you did not much like it. You could best perform such a service by joining the council of some great prince and inciting him to just and noble actions (as I'm sure you would): for a people's welfare or misery flows in a stream from their prince as from a never-failing spring. Your learning is so full, even if it weren't combined with experience, and your experience is so great, even apart from your learning, that you would be an extraordinary counsellor to any King in the world.'

'You are twice mistaken, my dear More', he said, 'first in me and then in the situation itself. I don't have the capacity you ascribe to me, and if I had it in the highest degree, the public would still not be any better off if I exchanged my contemplative leisure for active endeavour. In the first place, most princes apply themselves to the arts of war, in which I have neither ability nor interest, instead of to the good arts of peace. They are generally more set on acquiring new Kingdoms by hook or crook than on governing well those they already have. Moreover, the counsellors of Kings are so wise already that they don't need to accept or approve advice from anyone else – or at least they have that opinion of themselves. At the same time, they endorse and flatter the most absurd statements of the prince's special favourites, through whose influence they hope to stand well with the prince. It's only natural, of course, that each man should think his own inventions best: the crow loves his fledgling and the ape his cub.

'Now in a court composed of people who envy everyone else and admire only themselves, if a man should suggest something he

> has read of in other ages or seen in practice elsewhere, those who hear it act as if their whole reputation for wisdom would be endangered […].'[104]

In the further discussion, More holds on to his conviction that if Raphael could overcome his aversion to court life, his

> advice to a prince would be of the greatest advantage to the public welfare. No part of a good man's duty […] is more important than this. Your friend Plato thinks that commonwealths will be happy only when philosophers become Kings or Kings become philosophers. No wonder we are so far from happiness when philosophers do not condescend even to assist Kings with their counsels.[105]

Raphael reacts by asking More if he thinks his advice to the King of France to give up all ideas of conquering Italy or other realms would be well received when all other advisors were presenting ingenious plans for successful military campaigns to expand his Kingdom. He would argue that one King can only manage to rule a limited Kingdom ("the Kingdom of France by itself is almost too much for one man to govern well"), and that war always makes life worse for the people.[106]

More concedes that in such a setting, advices for peace and better domestic rule would not be enthusiastically received.[107]

Then Raphael continues by referring to advice to the King on various schemes on how to fill the treasury; one more manipulative of the people than the other. His councillors maintain that it will only benefit the King that his people remain destitute due to heavy taxation, since "his own safety depends on keeping them from getting too frisky with wealth and freedom. For riches and liberty make people less patient to endure harsh and unjust commands, whereas poverty and want blunt their spirits, make them docile, and grind out of the oppressed the lofty spirit of rebellion".[108]

When Raphael again argues that his views, refuting the premises of such advice, and maintaining that a King can only succeed when genuinely caring for the people, More again concedes that such views will indeed be met by deaf ears. Raphael should therefore refrain from giving advice that he "knows for certain will not be listened to".[109]

[104] More, 1516, pp. 14–15, see *supra* note 3.
[105] *Ibid.*, pp. 28–29.
[106] *Ibid.*, p. 31
[107] *Ibid.*, p. 32.
[108] *Ibid.*, p. 33.
[109] *Ibid.*, p. 36

In the councils of Kings, there is no room for lofty academic philosophy, ill adapted to the situation, continues More.

> But there is another philosophy, better suited for the role of a citizen, that takes its cue, adapts itself to the drama in hand and acts its part neatly and appropriately. This is the philosophy for you to use. [...] If you cannot pluck up bad ideas by the root, or cure longstanding evils to your heart's content, you must not therefore abandon the commonwealth. Don't give up the ship in a storm because you cannot hold back the winds. [...] Instead, by an indirect approach, you must strive and struggle as best you can to handle everything tactfully – and thus what you cannot turn to good, you may at least make as little bad as possible. For it is impossible to make everything good unless all men are good, and that I don't expect to see for quite a few years yet.[110]

In reply, Raphael explains that he cannot give up his convictions and lie. He is not sure what More means by 'indirect approach' either. Besides, in a council,

> there is no way to dissemble or look the other way. You must openly approve the worst proposals and endorse the most vicious policies. A man who praised wicked counsels only half-heartedly would be suspected as a spy, perhaps a traitor. And there is no way for you to do any good when you are thrown among colleagues who would more readily corrupt the best of men than be reformed themselves. Either they will seduce you by their evil ways, or, if you remain honest and innocent, you will be made a screen for the knavery and folly of others. You wouldn't stand a chance of changing anything for the better by that "indirect approach".
>
> This is why Plato in a very fine comparison declares that wise men are right in keeping away from public business. They see the people swarming through the streets and getting soaked with rain; they cannot persuade them to go indoors and get out of the wet. If they go out themselves, they know they will do no good, but only get drenched with the others. So they stay indoors and are content to keep at least themselves dry, since they cannot remedy the folly of others.[111]

Where does this intriguing discussion leave us? Undoubtedly, More was receptive to see the strong points of both views. His preference of using dialogues in his writings was not only a tool he used to create interesting texts but reflected a fundamental feature of his mind. He strove to understand and

[110] *Ibid.*, pp. 36–37.

[111] *Ibid.*, p. 39.

measure the strength of opposing views and arguments. Settling the issue of whether to enter the King's service was not easy for him.

There was a fundamental integrity issue at stake: would he be able to sustain his principles as a leading citizen, putting the well-being of the people first, contribute to just outcomes of trials, and turn ruthless decisions to be "as little bad as possible"?[112] Or would he be corrupted himself, unable to withstand the pressure inherent in a position where lack of explicit consent could be seen as proof of betrayal?

Such reflections pave the way for a third formulation of the fundamental question of integrity: *How can a person enter service of a ruler guided by spirited desires being convinced that he or she will be able to remain guided by reason*?

4.4. More as Statesman

This was a fundamental question for More when considering entering the King's service. He realized early one that Henry VIII was at least a potential tyrant. When he on 25 October 1529 succeeded Thomas Wolsey (1473–1530) as lord chancellor, the King was already at war against the Catholic Church and against ancient principles of English and European civilization.

At the beginning of his public life, More could not have predicted that Martin Luther (1483–1546) and other religious reformers would split the Church and reshape Europe, that Ottoman military forces would advance as far as Vienna, and that Henry VIII would desire both an annulment of his marriage to Catherine of Aragon (1485–1536) and to establish England as an independent realm of Rome.[113]

He had however, as I have shown above, long before he left his post as under-sheriff of London and became a member of the King's Council in 1518, reflected extensively on the costs and dangers for a wise and just man in serving the King.[114] In accepting to do so, he kept to the main principles he had formulated in his writings on how to civilize politics; by applying an 'indirect approach' and practical wisdom, always adapt to the situation at hand, refraining from radical and sweeping actions. During his conflict with the King he never conspired against him, plotted against him or even denounced him publicly. Nevertheless, both while in office and after stepping down, he continued to work for what he thought was the best for the commonwealth and its people.

[112] *Ibid.*, p. 35

[113] Curtis, 2011, p. 70, see *supra* note 84.

[114] More was appointed under-sheriff in 1510. As such, he was a permanent official who advised the sheriffs and sat as judge in the sheriff's court. He received a generous stipend and had a lucrative right to represent the City in the royal courts at Westminster.

More's background as both lawyer, humanist scholar and a devout Christian with inclinations for a life of contemplation and religious studies seems to have prepared him well for the kind of uncorrupted office he became known for. There are, however, considerable debate among scholars about the reasons for him to enter the King's council in 1518, and later climb to ever higher positions. Initially, he expressed reservations about the inconveniences and threats to reputation entailed in such service.[115]

The simplest explanation may be that he felt obliged to contribute to making things as little bad as possible, along the lines of the discussion in *Utopia* rendered above.[116] Entering the King's service would increase his influence in reforming the English legal and political order in a way that benefitted the people.

There might, however, also have been more specific reasons. Pope Leo X hade proposed in a bull of 6 March 1518 a truce among European powers, which would enable a united front against the Turks in response to Ottoman successes in Egypt and Syria. More may have thought that by entering royal service at this point, he could ensure that England supported such a collective security initiative to European peace-making. England's role in entering the October 1518 Universal Peace Treaty (proclaimed in London), created needs for additional skilled public servants to bring it to fruition. The treaty represented an early and important attempt to address European international relations by peaceful agreements, and it must have been attractive for More to assist in its adoption and implementation.[117]

A further explanation could be that More already successfully had taken part in extensive trade negotiations on behalf of the King before he decided to enter the King's council. When he was offered a permanent position by the King, he may have seen the advancement as a natural development in serving the country.

He had also recently shown his ability to intervene to restore public order, acting in his undersheriff capacity to quell riots in London by a group of young English apprentices. They had looted the houses, shops and warehouses of immigrant communities on a May day in 1517. More had called the rioters to order. His eloquence alone, according to the chroniclers, stemmed the worst of the violence.[118]

[115] Curtis, 2011, p. 73, see *supra* note 84.

[116] More, 1516, p. 35, see *supra* note 3.

[117] For further explanation, see Curtis, 2011, pp. 75–76, see *supra* note 84. The treaty did not succeed in securing long-term peace in Europe.

[118] Guy, 2017, Chapter 3, "The King's servant", see *supra* note 71.

When More took his oath as a councillor, Henry VIII gave him some advice, urging him to "first look unto God and after God unto him".[119] This could be interpreted as an assurance by the King that More could stay true to his principles; an assurance the King later would depart from.[120]

4.4.1. Uncorrupted Fairness

During his career as a lawyer, judge, speaker in Parliament, ambassador, and in the King's service, More was highly respected for being uncorrupted and fair. In summing up his achievements, he underlined though that he had been "a source of trouble to thieves, murderers, and heretics".[121] As a judge, he would avoid any conflict of interests, for example by not hearing cases concerning related persons.

As lord chancellor he would continue reforms of his predecessor, Thomas Wolsey, simplifying procedures and increasing access to equity courts. More regarded law as applying equally to all, and its proper application was fundamental to a healthy secular and ecclesiastical society. The administration of the laws required the greatest prudence, courage and moderation.

More's training as a lawyer was by intense oral instruction and exercises of solving cases. From 1496, he had studied at Lincoln's Inn, being constantly challenged together with his fellow students by senior barristers to solve difficult legal questions. The instruction was also organized as trials, where the students had to act as opposing counsel. In addition, there were periods of lectures given by skilled lawyers on a statute or branch of law. Legal education at the time has been characterized as "rigorous and detailed, and fostered exceptional skills in memory, forensic analysis and argumentation that would serve More well throughout his legal and political life".[122]

He was portrayed by his first biographer and son-in-law, William Roper (1496–1578), as "patient, moderate, affable and as a master of his passions through the exercise of reason, years of study and religious reflection", in contrast to the King who could move swiftly from "personal intimacy to mortal threat if policy or passion required, indicating his […] lack of capacity for constant friendship".[123]

---

[119] *Ibid.*

[120] *Ibid.*

[121] From More's epitaph for the Tomb in Chelsea Old Church, which he wrote himself in 1532. T.E. Bridgett, "Sir Thomas More's Epitaph", in *Life and Writings of Sir Thomas More*, Burns & Oates, London, 1892, pp. 250–252.

[122] Curtis, 2011, p. 71, see *supra* note 84.

[123] *Ibid.*, p. 79.

More underlined that his pre-occupation with humanist studies, poetry, literature and rhetoric had served him immensely in his public role. The study of poets, orators, and histories is of unrivalled value in the acquisition of the "practical skill" of "prudence in human affairs".[124]

4.4.2. Why Did More Hunt Heretics?

I have portrayed More as an eminent lawyer, highly respected by his fellow citizens in London, a statesman holding the highest positions in the emerging English state and a renowned humanist throughout Europe. He was a man of faith and reason, a man for all seasons, one who solved conflicts rather than exaggerating them.[125]

Some would argue, however, that this is to give him too much praise. He should rather be portrayed as a fanatic, responsible for the burning of heretics, lacking in pragmatism and willingness to compromise. Such criticism was mounted already during his lifetime and in the aftermath of his conflict with Henry VIII. It has also found expression in contemporary popular culture and scholarship.[126]

To reconcile the dissonance between the tolerance demonstrated in his humanist writings and his intolerance of Protestantism may not be easy in our time, where freedom of religion is solidly anchored in international law as well as in most national jurisdictions.[127] In *Utopia*, there is freedom of religion (except for atheism), but More was strongly against such freedom in his native England.

He treated Luther and Protestantism very harshly. During his last 10 years of service for the King, he devoted considerable energy and time to enforce

[124] *Ibid.*, p. 72.

[125] More was called a 'man for all seasons' during his lifetime. Robert Bolt's play "A Man for All Seasons" (1954) about More's life and conflict with Henry VIII, made the phrase famous. The play was subsequently made into a multi-Academy Award-winning 1966 feature film and a 1988 television movie, see Fred Zinnemann (Producer and Director), "A Man for All Seasons", motion picture, 1966, United Kingdom, Highland Films; and Robert Bolt (Producer) and Charlton Heston (Director), "A Man for All Seasons", motion picture, 1988, United States, Turner Network Television.

[126] The most important early example is John Foxe's (1516–1587) famous *Book of Martyrs* (1563), a graphic and polemic account of those who suffered for the cause of Protestantism, including in the hands of Thomas More: John Fox, *Book of Martyrs*, John Day, London, 1563. In 2009 a novelist won the Man Booker Prize for Fiction with a story in which she has More admit in conversation the allegations of torture he denied in print: Hilary Mantel, *Wolf Hall*, Fourth Estate, London, 2009, pp. 628–629. *Wolf Hall* is also the title of a widely seen TV series by the BBC2, based on the book.

[127] Although far from being practiced everywhere, as documented by among others, the Pew Research Centre.

England's heresy laws. This was not an incidental part of his life and work. It was central to his understanding of his professional duties.[128]

He, however, denied any involvement in torture, although he was not against the death penalty for heresy, which was part of the legislation and culture of the time he lived in. Historians believe that six heretics were condemned to be burned during More's tenure as lord chancellor.[129]

Heretic dissent from the dominant catholic Christianity was known in England from the late fourteenth century, when John Wycliff (1330–1384) preached a theology anticipating Protestantism. The movement became known as *Lollardy*, and ecclesiastical and royal authorities co-operated in repressing it. A statute was adopted in 1401 that provided for the burning of heretics. Another result was a profound suspicion of English translations of the Bible, which were produced by members of the Lollardy movements.[130] Finally, a concern grew among authorities that heresy led to sedition, due to the outbreak of the Peasants' Revolt (1381) at the same time when Wycliffe's teachings were attracting popular support.[131]

Under Henry VII and Henry VIII, persecution of perceived heretics intensified. More became actively involved in proceedings against followers of Luther in 1521. Henry VIII decided to write against Luther's attack on the Catholic church in his pamphlet, *Babylonian Captivity of the Church* (1520). More was called in to help with Henry's *Assertion of the Seven Sacraments* (1521).[132]

The impact of the new ideas was found by English authorities to be a threat that had to be defeated from around the mid-1520s. This was at the same time as the bloody Peasants War took place in Germany. In particular, measures to hinder the spread of a new translation of the New Testament by William Tyndale (1494–1536) was seen as important. The book was smuggled into England from 1526 on, despite efforts by the English bishops to stop it. By the end of the 1520s, networks of Lutherans and Lollards were exposed, further alarming the authorities.

---

[128] Richard Rex, "Thomas More and the heretics: statesman or fanatic?", in Logan (ed.), 2011, p. 94, see *supra* note 71. The modern tradition of portraying More as an unbalanced inquisitor derives chiefly from Marius, 1984, see *supra* note 71; and from Geoffrey Elton, *Studies in Tudor and Stuart Politics and Government*, 4 vols., Cambridge University Press, 1974–1992.

[129] *Ibid.*

[130] More was, nevertheless, in favour of the church producing an English translation of the Bible. It should, however, be without all the mistakes that the reformers' translations contained. A true English translation should be undertaken as soon as possible. Guy, 2017, Chapter 3: "The King's servant", see *supra* note 71.

[131] *Ibid.*

[132] Rex, 2011, p. 95, see *supra* note 128.

In the 1530s, the religious situation became more complicated, due to Henry VIII's 'Great Matter'. He needed to divorce from his first wife in order to re-marry (see Section 4.5.). Evangelicals tended to support divorce, while conservative Catholics were against it. When separating the English church from the papacy, Henry started a process that eventually (after his death) led to a Protestant settlement.

More ended up being the most well-known victim of Henry's Reformation despite having acted together with the King against Luther and other reformers during the 1520s.

More defined heretics as persons who held "self-defined opinions contrary to the doctrine that the commonly known Catholic church teach and hold necessary for salvation".[133] The main problem was that heretics placed their own personal opinion above the consensus of the church, which was guaranteed by the Holy Spirit. He was not willing to accept the arguments by Protestants that they based their theological views on their own reading of the Bible, as in his view it was only the Church that could determine the true meaning of Biblical texts.

For More, religion was crucial not only for salvation, but for the order of society. Heresy resulted in conflict, wars and misery. But there were more at stake: heretics also destroyed people's prospects of eternal salvation and their immortal soul. It represented treason against God and was the worst of all crimes. He thought Christian Kings to be "sacral figures", who were responsible even for their subjects' spiritual affairs. But only within the boundaries of a united church.[134]

In 1529, More was commissioned by the bishop of London, Cuthbert Tunstall (1474–1559), to possess and read forbidden books for the purpose of refuting them in English. The result was, among others, *Dialogue Concerning Heresies* (1529)[135] and *Confutation of Tyndale's Answer* (1532/1533).[136] In 1533 he published *Apology*, a pamphlet where he defended and clarified his actions as lord chancellor concerning heretics.[137]

More has been criticized for being unpolite and rude in his polemic against the Protestants. However, the reformers used very harsh language themselves, for example by coining the pope as Antichrist and featuring Catholic clergy as

[133] *The Complete Works of St. Thomas More*, vol. 10, p. 30, see *supra* note 82.

[134] Rex, 2011, p. 98, see *supra* note 128.

[135] Thomas More, *Dialogue Concerning Heresies*, in *The Complete Works of St. Thomas More*, vol. 6, see *supra* note 82.

[136] Thomas More, *Confutation of Tyndale's Answer*, in *ibid.*, vol 8.

[137] Thomas More, *Apology*, in *ibid.*, vol. 9.

obscene. More reasoned that he had to fight in a similar language, applying his considerable rhetoric skills.

On the argument that by burning heretics there was a risk of convicting innocent persons, he replied that there was the same risk in other criminal cases. Besides, a first offence could be atoned for by abjuration and penance. The obstinate or relapsed, on the other hand, were "well and worthily burned".[138]

During his last 10 years of service, both before and during his period as lord chancellor, "heresy was the single most time-consuming issue Thomas More dealt with".[139] He was very concerned, however, that actions against heretics should be in compliance with the laws. When accused of transgressing legal bonds in heresy cases, he refuted that strongly.

The policies More implemented were also in line with what the bishops of the Catholic church wanted of him. At the time, it was highly unusual that a layman played such an important role as theological polemist, demonstrating the church leaders' unusual confidence in him.

His role in confronting heresy in the service of the King was more conventional. It was first and foremost a function of his public position. "Since the time of Henry V, the oath sworn by every man who took office under the crown had included an undertaking to assist the Church in the struggle against heresy". As lord chancellor, being the head of the judiciary, he was under an obligation to repress heresy.[140]

However, More's motivation to write extensively against Protestantism was also based on personal conviction. He perceived that Protestantism represented a serious threat to the existing order in England and Europe. It rapidly attracted support from learned men such as himself. The Reformation introduced a new version of Christianity, which would lead to violent social and political revolutions in Europe.

Regardless of how convincing such justifications may appear, difficult questions remain. Could such beliefs justify that he acted against heretics in the way he did? Should he rather have made efforts to temper the bishops' and the King's wishes for repressive measures? Did More stay governed by reason in his actions against heretics or did he let spirited desires rule?

In answering such questions, one must take into account the context of More's thinking and actions. One's judgment should not be based on solely modern prepositions. By taking a contextual stand, I believe the conclusion must

[138] Rex, 2011, p. 105, see *supra* note 128.

[139] *Ibid.*, p. 107.

[140] *Ibid.*, p. 108.

be that More remained governed by reason. He acted like a first citizen and not as a fanatic.

This conclusion does not imply that his reasons should not be criticized. We should not endorse his intolerance, even if we can understand his reasoning. It does, however, mean that we can still learn about integrity from More. He stayed a man of reason, even if his reasons were wrong.

His mistake entails important lessons. Even if you preserve integrity in the More-sense by letting your reason and faith rule, following your conscience, you may be wrong. Infallible religious or philosophical truths are unattainable, even though, at a personal level, you may choose to base your life on them. At the state level, however, you should not operate according to such convictions. You should refrain from appealing to the consensus of any institution, such as the church, as something that cannot be criticized. States that present themselves as built on infallible truths lead to tyranny and oppression, even if they treat all but the heretics nice.

The full meaning of religious tolerance in the affairs of the state may not have been explicitly taught by More at any time, although his humanist writings pointed in that direction. In *Utopia*, at least, he showed that a society could function well even if it practised a lot more tolerance than England and himself as a state official.

4.5. More's Conflict with Henry VIII

The main controversy with Henry VIII was about the independence of the English Church. The King wanted The English Church to depart from the Catholic Church because of the Pope's unwillingness to accept his divorce from his first wife, Catherine of Aragon, who did not give him a son. The King wanted to marry Anne Boleyn and did so secretly on 25 January 1532, when she was already pregnant with his child. Because of the pregnancy, divorce with Catherine to avoid bigamy and his child to be born outside wedlock became urgent. An independent English Church, under the King's own leadership, would help formalize divorce and re-marriage.

To accomplish the break with Rome and destroy the power of the medieval church, the so-called Reformation Parliament played a vital role. It first met in November 1529 and lasted seven years, enacting 137 statutes of which 32 were of vital importance. In addition, the King also pressured the church Convocation to accept his demands.

Some of the most important acts and submissions that ensured that Henry VIII became head of the English Church and separated England from the Pope's influence were:

- The Annates Statute of 1532, which empowered the King to abolish payment to Rome of the first year's income of all newly installed bishops;[141]
- The Submission of the Clergy of 15 May 1532, in which the clergy promised not to legislate without royal consent;[142]
- The Act of Restraint of Appeals of April 1533,[143] which decreed that "this realm of England is an empire", cutting the constitutional cords holding England to the papacy. A month later an archbishop annulled the King's first marriage, and on 1 June Anne was crowned rightful queen of England;
- The Act of Succession of March 1534 ordered subjects to accept the King's marriage to Anne as "undoubted, true, sincere and perfect";[144]
- A second Statute "in Restraint of Annates" severed most of the financial ties with Rome while in November 1534, the Act of Supremacy announced that Henry was and always had been "Supreme Head of the Church of England;[145]
- The Act of Treason of December 1534, which made it punishable by death, to disavow the Act of Supremacy.[146] It was designed to root out and liquidate dissent, extending the meaning of treason to include all those who did "maliciously wish, will or desire by words or writing or by craft imagine"

[141] Parliament of England, Act in Conditional Restraint of Annates (23 Hen. VIII c. 20), 1532 (Annates Statute).

[142] The document was adopted in Convocation on 15 May 1532 under intense pressure from Henry VIII and handed to the King on the following day. It contained a submission to the King's demands, promising,

> *in verbo sacerdotii*, here unto your highness, submitting ourselves most humbly to the same, that we will never from henceforth [enact], put in use, promulge, or execute, any [new canons or constitutions provincial, or any other new ordinance, provincial or synodal], in our Convocation [or synod] in time coming, which Convocation is, always has been, and must be, assembled only by your highness' commandment of writ, unless your highness by your royal assent shall license us to [assemble our Convocation, and] to make, promulge, and execute [such constitutions and ordinances as shall be made in] the same; and thereto give your royal assent and authority.

Henry VIII, *Submission of the Clergy*, 1532.

[143] Parliament of England, An Acte that the Appeles in suche Cases as have ben used to be pursued to the See of Rome shall not be from hensforth had ne used but within this Realme (24 Hen. VIII c. 12), April 1533 (Act of Restraint of Appeals).

[144] Parliament of England, Act of Succession (25 Hen. VIII c. 22), March 1534.

[145] Parliament of England, Act in Absolute Restraint of Annates (25 Hen. VIII c. 20), November 1534.

[146] Parliament of England, Act of Treason (26 Hen. VIII c. 13), December 1534.

the King's death or slandered this marriage. It was eventually used against More.[147]

By these acts, the medieval order that church and state were separate entities with divine law standing higher than human law had been legislated out of existence. The English church had become a department of the Tudor state, monasteries were dissolved, and at least 13 per cent of the land of England and Wales were nationalized, making the King much wealthier and able to finance wars.[148]

Although More referred to health issues and his need for devoting more time to spiritual matters when stepping down as lord chancellor on 16 May 1532, the real reason was his unwillingness to accept that the King now possessed veto power over ecclesiastical legislation as put in place by the Submission of the Clergy. In effect, the submission meant that the leaders of the church had given up defending its institutional integrity. In his explanation to the King, he said that he would "bestow the residue of my life in mine age now to come, about the provision for my soul in the service of God, and to be your Grace's beadsman and pray for you".[149]

The remaining three years of his life would rather be characterized by both intensive activity and dramatic incidents. He would not give up his fight against the King's efforts to subdue the church, while at the same time presenting himself as the Kings good servant.[150]

More refused to attend the coronation of Anne Boleyn in June 1533, despite being officially invited and approached by bishops who wanted him to attend together with them. The refusal surely contributed to determining the fatal outcome of his struggle, putting a "sword in his enemies' hands", as one scholar put it.[151] Charges were brought against him, including for complicity with Elizabeth Barton (1506–1534), a nun who had uttered prophecies against Henry's divorce. More was, however, able to prove his innocence.

In April 1533, More refused the Oath of Succession because it transgressed on the freedom of the English Church. He was imprisoned on 17 April 1534 and tried on 1 July 1535, for denying the King's title as supreme head of the Church

147 The overview is based on Patrick Joyce, Ralph Charles Atkins and Others, "United Kingdom: The Break with Rome", in *Encyclopedia Britannica*, 12 October 2025.

148 *Ibid.*

149 Peter Marshall, "The last years", in Logan (ed.), 2011, p. 116, see *supra* note 71; Curtis, 2011, p. 69, see *supra* note 84.

150 Travis Curtright, "Sir Thomas More and his Opposition to Henry VIII in 1533", in Curtright (ed.), 2015, pp. 111, see *supra* note 7.

151 *Ibid.*, p. 112.

of England. In the trial, he was found guilty of treason despite his denial of what he considered perjured evidence. He was beheaded five days later.

4.5.1. The Ultimate Test of Integrity

What More endured after his arrest may be termed as his ultimate test of integrity. Pressure mounted against him because of his unwillingness to state his acceptance of the King's new power over the Church – from representatives of the King in the forms of threats, interrogations, and traps; from friends and former colleagues in the form of appeals of giving in; and from family members who suffered because of his imprisonment and his loss of income and estate.

The indictment comprised of four counts:[152]

1. More had maliciously refused on 7 May 1535, to accept the King's supremacy over the Church of England;
2. He had conspired against the King by writing treasonous letters to bishop John Fisher;
3. He had stirred up sedition by describing the Act of Supremacy as a two-edged sword, that is, a law that if disobeyed would mean bodily death, and if obeyed would mean spiritual death;
4. He had "maliciously, traitorously, and diabolically" denied Parliament's power to declare the King to be head of the Church.[153]

In his defence, which he had to present himself without written notes, More underlined that he had remained silent on whether the King could be the head of the English Church. His argument was based on a legal norm established by English precedent, that "silence is not a crime; in fact, silence means consent".[154]

Furthermore, none of his letters to bishop Fisher had touched upon matters of state, and they did not exist any longer. He had only expressed himself hypothetically about the Act of Supremacy (Oath of Succession): "if it was like a two-edged sword forcing a person to make a choice between physical and spiritual life, then the statute might at a later time be considered illegitimate".[155]

Refuting the fourth count, he underlined that he had never denied Parliament's power to make the King Head of the Church.

At the trial, More faced 15 judges and 12 jurors. The judges included Chancellor Thomas Audley (1488–1544), Royal Secretary Thomas Cromwell (1485–1540), and Thomas Howard third Duke of Norfolk (1473–1554), as well as an

[152] This section is based on Wegemer, 1995, see *supra* note 64.

[153] *Ibid.*, p. 210.

[154] *Ibid.*, p. 211.

[155] *Ibid.*

uncle, a brother, and the father of Anne Boleyn, the King's new wife. They all had strong interests in convicting More.

The jury of twelve was also partial, being put together to ensure the result wanted by the King. More did not have counsel or was not permitted a written account of his defence or the indictment.

The court seems to have accepted More's first three arguments, but not the fourth; that he had not denied Parliament's right to make the King head of the Church. The rest of the trial focused on this count.

The prosecution witness, Solicitor General Richard Rich (1496/1497–1567), stated that More had told him on 12 June 1535 in his cell that Parliament did not have authority to make the King head of the Church. More denied having said anything of the kind, stating that Rich was committing perjury. He then demonstrated Rich's lack of credibility as a witness. He would never have trusted him with secrets "of my conscience touching the King's Supremacy".[156]

The jury of the court still found him guilty.

More's defence was of high legal quality. He was able to demonstrate that he had done none of the illegal acts he was charged for. He referred to over 20 years of trusted positions in the state and an untainted reputation showed the credibility of his character. He demonstrated that the Act of Parliament, which the indictment against him was grounded on, was in conflict both with the laws of God and with many other "laws and statutes of our own land", including the Magna Carta (1215), which states that "the English Church shall be free, and shall have its rights undiminished and its liberties unimpaired".[157]

He knew, however, that even if there were no evidence against him, this would not be enough to save him. His real opponent was the King, and the King could not accept anything but surrender.

He did not surrender. Nor did he try to escape. He referred to his conscience, which was bound by faith and reason to defend the unity of the church. He stood the test of integrity as a lawyer, providing a solid defence for himself in line with ethical and professional standards.

He also stood the test of integrity as a person, not making concessions conflicting his personal views, while caring for his family and friends, expressing gratitude to those who supported him, and forbearance to those who facilitated the injustice that caused his death.

Few persons could have done so well in terms of upholding their own integrity – being ruled by reason and faithful to their professional and personal

[156] *Ibid.*, p. 213.

[157] England, Magna Carta Libertatum, 15 June 1215, clause 1.

convictions – under such pressure, knowing that death was a certain outcome. It is a remarkable story about skill and courage.

However, in my view, the main lesson to take from More is not that we shall never give in to pressure when confronted with lethal threats. We should rather follow More's own reasoning in his humanistic writings and learn how courage and other spirited desires should always be governed by reason. A well-trained and -educated reason.

What we should learn from him is how he did what he thought reasonable to avert the King's measures that would undermine justice and peace in England and in Christian states in Europe.

According to his view of the world, this could be summarized as being more faithful to God than to the King. He ended his life by stating that "I die the King's faithful servant, but God's first".[158]

4.6. More's Integrity Lessons

When confronted with the fact that almost all bishops and universities had agreed to the new legislation, More responded that even if that was so, throughout Christendom many more would support his view. His conscience was bound to conform to a General Council of Christendom, rather than to the council of one realm only. In this way he was denying the legal justification by Parliament of placing the King above the law, epitomized in Cromwell's statement: "You're absolutely right. It must be done by law. It's just a matter of finding the right law. Or making one".[159]

More was referring to the conscience as the bedrock of personhood, and moral and professional integrity. A conscience bound by Christian principles and by law; not by personal opinion.

In defending the church against interference from the state, he also defended individual freedom *vis-à-vis* political power, as Pope John Paul II has put it. The state should not interfere with the freedom of conscience.[160]

---

[158] Quoted from Marshall, 2011, p. 133, see *supra* note 149. Some scholars doubt the authenticity of the quote, which was reported first by the Paris News Letter, 4 August, 1535. It is, however, little doubt that it reflects More's understanding of his relation to the King; an understanding he had believed the King shared. Cf. the Center for Thomas More Studies, "About Famous Quotes" (available on its web site).

[159] Wegemer, 1995, see *supra* note 64.

[160] This is a prevailing view in Peter Berglar, *Thomas More: A Lonely Voice Against the Power of the State*, Scepter Publishers, Cleveland, 2009 (First Published in German, 1999), summarized in the foreword as follows:

> More generally, what was involved was the breaking away of society and the state from the medieval political order and the birth of the modern concept of independent nationhood. But something else also was implicated in these events, namely, the state's ambition

In his so-called 'tower works', More elaborated on the concepts of conscience, courage, and grace.[161] It is necessary to gather comfort and courage, and let it sink into the heart, even though belief in God and grace also plays a strong role. By right imagining, the abstract argument is transformed into a habitual, fast, and deep-rooted purpose. There is a form of internalized rhetoric involved, based on study and training.

More stood almost alone against immense political pressure, including from colleagues, friends and family. He frequently referred to his conscience in scrutinizing the soundness of his own motives, which were criticized of being over-scrupulous. He navigated a course between the scrupulous conscience and the over-large or elastic conscience.

He also referred to an 'informed conscience'; shaped by years of study and reflection. From early one, in his humanist writings More had raised the fundamental integrity question: *How to serve with integrity in a brutal political environment, full of intrigues, flattering, and dishonesty?* The notion of an 'informed' conscience may be interpreted to summarize that this inner voice of truth is not based on spirited desires for honour or fame, but rather on faith and reason's efforts to do as good as possible in every difficult circumstance.

He was loyal to the Catholic Church and to a settled consensus within that church. He appealed to the views throughout Christendom, that would support his view on the unity of the church. At the same time, he acted on his own conscience: "I never intend [...] to pin my soul to another man's back, not even the best man that I know this day living: for I know not where he may lead it".[162] The responsibility must be his alone.

He is very clear that he will not criticize others or condemn their conscience, but for his own part, he is content "to lose goods, land, and life too,

to impose not just de facto obedience but also active assent. Now, for the first time in history, simply tolerating the unilateral decisions of an establishment was not enough; explicit approval was demanded, and not only defiance but personal opinion was subject to persecution, with nonconformity treated as the equivalent of rebellion. In the cradle of modern Europe, then, we witness a power struggle to preserve the freedom of the individual in the face of organized power, something not always or necessarily identified with the state.

[161] The tower works include: Thomas More, *A Dialogue of Comfort Against Tribulation*, in *The Complete Works of St. Thomas More*, vol. 12, 1534, see *supra* note 82; *Treatise Upon the Passion*, 1534, in *ibid.*, vol. 13; *Treatise on the Blessed Body*, 1535, in *ibid.*, vol. 13; Thomas More, *De Tristitia Christi*, 1535, in *ibid.*, vol. 14.

[162] Thomas More to his daughter, in prison, August 1534. Quoted from Curtright (ed.), 2015, beginning of book, before pagination, see *supra* note 7.

rather than swear against my conscience".[163] Many of those who took the decisions that would end his life were former friends and colleagues. To them he stated that he looked forward to seeing them again, in another world.

In conclusion, More exemplified great personal integrity. When he was pressed for why he would not give up his convictions, when his friends and colleagues did, he referred to his conscience. But he also defended his views and rights with legal, theological and philosophical reasoning. He linked his conscience to religious beliefs and values, and underlined that conscience has to be trained and developed through study and reflection.

He did not perceive his courage as entirely a gift of grace. It also had to be nurtured through imagination, internalization of words and preparations, and to be controlled by reason.

More exemplified integrity as self-integration and consistency throughout his career. He stood for something, not giving in to pressure, at the same time always willing to reason and provide his arguments.

More is not an example of 'civil disobedience' based on personal convictions, I would argue. His reasoning and practice during the ultimate integrity test are instead closer to modern conceptions of professional integrity. As outlined above, professional integrity is characterized by a mode of reasoning that calls for the role holder to engage critically and creatively with the varied and sometimes conflicting demands of professional practice. More as a 'first citizen' was a professional, applying legal and theological arguments in line with professional standards and practice of his time.

His defence of the unity of the church and church doctrine may be seen as a reference to authoritative theological practice. In his conflict with Henry VIII, he makes efforts to give his best reading of that practice.

The same goes for his acting as a lawyer, throughout his career, and certainly in his own final case. In his defence, he provides what he believes is the best reading of English jurisprudence in a treason case like his.

It may seem paradoxical, but because More is not modern in the sense that he linked his conscience to private opinion, he becomes interesting in terms of professional integrity, which primarily refers to institutional practice and not to personal opinion.

More favoured reforms, that is, improving the standards and practice of church, law and politics gradually. Concerning church doctrine and practice, he referred to the General Council of Christendom as the final arbiter.

---

[163] Gerard B. Wegemer and Stephen W. Smith, *A Thomas More Source Book*, The Catholic University of America Press, Washington, D.C., 2004, p. 334.

He argued that new legislation should be adopted by Parliament, while judges should have discretion to apply written and unwritten law according to circumstances and their own interpretation.

4.7. Integrity in Justice

There are thus several ways in which More is relevant for discussions on how to strengthen integrity in justice.

For individuals considering the fundamental integrity question – whether to enter the world of justice professionals – there is great inspiration to take from him. He would tell them that there is a fundamental question anyone who considers working for justice institutions have to ask themselves: *Will I be able to honour the promises of my profession, despite all the pressure, cynicism and temptations I will be exposed to? Will I be able to hold my spirited desires and appetite (for money, sex, luxury) governed by reason?*

From More's writings, we know that he believed that an initial determination to live up to integrity standards is not enough. His method was to continuously train himself in integrity by binding his conscience to the standards and promises of his profession, and by reflecting on how to moderate the effects of wickedness and evil.

Safeguarding the integrity of the church, justice institutions and Parliament was a central part of More's efforts as a statesman and lawyer. He knew well that institutions could be corrupted and manipulated, and how important leadership were in setting and practising high standards. Well-functioning institutions could improve societies and human affairs vastly. They should be protected.

The catalogue of integrity failures listed in Section 4.2.2.1. above would not be unknown to More. I suspect he would respond that to let undue pressure, material temptations, personal relationships, or lack of professional and moral convictions lead you away from professional duties would be the result of the lower parts of your soul being too dominant. The antidote would be to rebalance your soul and let reason rule. He would know well that this is easier said than done. To succeed may require hard work over a long time.

However, if you are going to make advances in confronting tyranny and injustices that is what is necessary. This is also what an institution such as a court promises. Maintaining professional integrity as a leader or staff member of such institutions requires conforming your conscience to the promises and aims of justice – and following it.

That seems to me to be the essence of Thomas More's thoughts and practice of integrity.

5

Past Wrongdoing Against Romani and Sámi in Norway and the Prism of Modern International Criminal Law and Human Rights*

5.1. Introduction

From the 1850s until the 1980s, Norwegian authorities implemented policies that aimed at assimilation of the Romani ('*Tater*') people, the Sámi people, and minorities of Finnish origin (the '*Kven*' or Norwegian-Finnish people). The assimilation policies were gradually abolished during the period 1960–1990.

Before 1850, policies and negative attitudes towards the groups among authorities and the majority population sometimes resulted in worsening conditions for their way of life. In some cases, serious crimes were committed against minority persons, including murder, without the culprit being punished.[1] From the 1850s, however, policies and their implementation became more systematic, aiming at assimilating the peoples into the majority Norwegian population.

The policies were motivated by racist, religious and social motives, security considerations regarding Norwegian control of its northernmost territory, as well as by views which maintained that the groups' traditional economic, cultural or religious practices could not find a place in a modernized and steadily more industrialized Norwegian society.

From 1814 to 1905, Norway was the junior partner in a personal union with Sweden. Previously, it had been ruled by Danish kings for more than 400 years, first as part of the Kalmar Union (1397–1523), and then as the junior partner of the polity of Denmark-Norway. The harsh assimilation policies during the latter part of the 1800s and the 1900s may thus be seen in the context of belated nation-building processes, which led to intolerance towards groups that were seen by political elites and the majority population as alien to and even threatening for Norwegian culture, unity and security.

---

* This chapter was first published as Chapter 17 of Morten Bergsmo, Wolfgang Kaleck and Kyaw Yin Hlaing (eds.), *Colonial Wrongs and Access to International Law*, Torkel Opsahl Academic EPublisher, Brussels, 2020 (https://www.toaep.org/ps-pdf/40-bergsmo-kaleck-kyaw/). The author extends his gratitude to Zekeriyya Yahya Karapinar and Anne Hushagen for very useful research assistance and comments.

1 Thor Gotaas, *Taterne: Livskampen og eventyret* [*The Taters: Life Struggle and the Adventure*], Andresen & Butenschøn, Oslo, 2007, p. 92.

While it is not common in Norwegian scholarly debate to discuss the expansion of the Norwegian state into Sápmi – the traditional Sámi territory comprising northern parts of present-day Finland, Sweden, Norway and the Kola Peninsula of Russia – in the context of European colonialism, there are important arguments in favour of doing so. In the case of Norway, colonialism may be relevant in two ways: the Norwegian state was formed through quasi-colonial domination by Denmark and Sweden, and Sápmi was "claimed and settled by non-Sámi people while Sámi were assimilated into Norwegian society".[2] Norway was involved in wider colonial endeavours by Denmark-Norway, and ideologies underpinning colonialism were used to legitimize colonizing Sápmi and assimilation of the Sámi.

The aim of the assimilation policies was to make the minorities as similar as possible to the majority population. When applied to the Sámi people and the Kven, they were often named 'Norwegianization' ('fornorsking'), clearly indicating their goal. Assimilation in this context "means that individuals or groups are accepted in mainstream society on the majority's terms. It is a one-way process, where those who are assimilated must change their fundamental cultural values and lifestyles, while the majority makes no adjustments". Assimilation is different from integration processes in that the latter involves a two-way process, both majority and minority adapting to living together.[3]

The use of the Sámi languages in public schools was long restricted, and the Sámi people became socially and economically marginalized in their own homelands due to policies of favouring ethnic Norwegian farmers and developing industrial projects in their traditional territories.

The Romani people experienced harsh policies aimed at eradicating their semi-nomadic culture, including by forced sterilization, removing children from Romani families and placing them in orphanages or ethnic Norwegian foster families, by forced placing of Romani families in a labour colony, and by forced settlement.

These policies were systematized and fully implemented during the 1900s, inflicting widespread harm and frustration among the affected groups, but also resulting in their political and cultural mobilization.

---

2 Wilfrid Greaves, "Colonialism, Statehood and the Sámi in Norden and the Norwegian High North", in Kamrul Hussain, José Miguel Roncero Martin and Anna Petrétei (eds.), *Human and Societal Security in the circumpolar Arctic: Local and Indigenous Communities*, Brill Nijhoff, Leiden, 2018, p. 100.

3 Ingvill Thorson Plesner (ed.), *Assimilering og motstand: Norsk politikk overfor taterne/romanifolket fra 1850 til i dag* [*Assimilation and Resistance: Norwegian Policies Towards Tater/Romani People from 1850 to the Present*], Norwegian Ministry of Local Government and Modernization, 2015, p. 3 ('NOU 2015:7 English Summary').

In the post-war period, critical ideas eventually prevailed that were based on human rights, scientific knowledge that refuted ideas that ethnic Norwegians were superior in intelligence and level of civilization compared with the minorities, and a wider recognition of the human suffering caused by the assimilation policies.

In 1958, the Government and the Parliament agreed that Norway should *not* ratify a convention on indigenous populations, since "such groups of people do not exist in our country".[4] A little more than 30 years later, in 1990, Norway became the first state to ratify ILO Convention 169 on indigenous and tribal peoples.[5]

A Constitutional provision had been adopted in 1988 that placed responsibility on state authorities "to create conditions enabling the Sámi people to preserve and develop its language, culture and way of life".[6] A Sámi Parliament was opened in 1989, based on the 1987 Sámi Act.[7] The Finnmark Act, pioneering legislation regulating the use of land and natural resources in Finnmark county, was adopted in 2005. A range of other laws and government regulations also have bearing on the situation of the Sámi population.[8]

Today, both national law and international conventions binding on Norway provide legal rights that protect Sámi culture and material interests, including rights to land and natural resources. These rights have also been cemented through case law.[9] Arguments have been presented that Sámi customary law should be fully recognized as law in Norway, and that competence in this law should be strengthened throughout the judiciary.[10]

---

[4] Hanne Hagtvedt Vik, "Da samene ble urfolk" ["When the Sámi became indigenous people"], in *Norgeshistorie – fra steinalder til i dag. Fortalt av fagfolk* [*Norwegian history – from the Stone Age to the Present. Told by professional experts*], 25 November 2015.

[5] Convention (No. 169) concerning indigenous and tribal peoples in independent countries, 27 June 1989 ('ILO Convention 169') (https://www.legal-tools.org/doc/699b29/), is ratified by 23 states but not by Finland, Sweden and Russia, the other states with Sámi populations.

[6] Constitution of the Kingdom of Norway, 17 May 1814, Article 108 (https://www.legal-tools.org/doc/a7803b/). The Norwegian Sámi Parliament's official web site provides information about its work and organization.

[7] An English translation of the Sámi Act, 12 June 1987, is available on the Legal Tools Database (https://www.legal-tools.org/doc/sve347a7/).

[8] Government of Norway, "Lover, forskrifter og regelverk i samepolitikken" ["Laws and regulations in Sámi politics"], 20 August 2018 (available on its web site).

[9] Cf. Øyvind Ravna, "The protection of Sámi People's language, culture and way of life in Norwegian Constitution and other legislation", in Øyvind Ravna, *Cahiers d'anthropologie du droit 2011–2012*, Karthala, Paris, 2012, pp. 265–280.

[10] *Ibid.*, p. 277.

These developments have, however, not resulted in current relations between Sámi representatives and the Government to be without conflicts. The Sámi Parliament, *inter alia*, complains that the "government are giving permits and authorization to new mines and wind-power industries that effects the use of our lands, territories and resources. This happens at an increasing pace, and in many cases without the Sámi Parliament's will, and without the free, prior and informed consent of concerned Sámi right holders".[11]

The current status of the Sámi is nevertheless considerably stronger than before the shift in policies and adoption of legal rights. Sometimes the Sámi prevail in conflicts with central authorities. Their rights are supported by international human rights bodies, which continuously challenge Norway to redefine policies to protect the Sámi against discrimination and enhance the legal framework protecting Sámi land, fishing and reindeer rights.[12] Sámi culture is widely recognized among ethnic Norwegians and Sámi self-respect is increasing.

While the Sámi are recognized as an indigenous people, and as one of the two constituent peoples of the Norwegian state,[13] the status of the Romani people remains weaker. In 1999, Norway ratified the 1994 Council of Europe's Framework Convention for the Protection of National Minorities, which together with other relevant international law provisions have become the basis for Norway's minority policies.[14] Five groups were identified as national minorities: Forrest Finns, Jews, Kven, Roma ('*Sigøynere*') and Romani ('*Tater*').

---

11 Eirik Larsen, "Pre-session Universal Periodic Review (UPR) Norway – Thursday, 4 April 2019 – statement by Political Advisor Eirik Larsen", in Sámi Parliament in Norway, 18/5274-8, 11 March 2019.

12 For recent examples of such criticism, see the Concluding observations on the sixth periodic report of Norway, UN Doc. E/C.12/NOR/CO/6, 2 April 2020, paras. 46–47 (https://www.legal-tools.org/doc/ksht2d/); Concluding observations on the combined twenty-third and twenty-fourth periodic reports of Norway, UN Doc. CERD/C/NOR/CO/23-24, 2 January 2019, paras. 21–22 (https://www.legal-tools.org/doc/4bkvmh/); and Consideration of reports submitted by States parties under article 40 of the Covenant pursuant to the optional reporting procedure – seventh periodic reports of States parties due in 2017 – Norway, UN Doc. CCPR/C/NOR/7, 7 July 2017, paras. 36–37 (https://www.legal-tools.org/doc/630blt/).

13 In his official opening speech of the Sámi Parliament in 1997, King Harald V stated that the "Norwegian state is founded on the territory of two people - Norwegians and Sami". See Idar Kintel and others, "Kongens ord betyr mye for samene", on *NRK Sápmi*, 7 October 2014.

14 Information about the Convention is available on the web site of the Council of Europe, as well as the official text of the Convention. The consequences of Norwegian ratification of the Convention are outlined in Norwegian Ministry of Foreign Affairs, "St.prp. nr. 80 (1997-98) Om samtykke til ratifikasjon av Europarådets rammekonvensjon av 1. februar 1995 om beskyttelse av nasjonale minoriteter" ["Parliament Proposition 80 (1997-98) On consent to ratification of the Council of Europe's Framework Convention of 1 February 1995 on the Protection of National Minorities"], 18 June 1995 (available on Norwegian government's web site).

The Convention specifies minimum standards for the states' policies towards national minorities, as well as goals that the states commit themselves to achieve. State authorities shall facilitate conditions for persons belonging to national minorities to be able to express, hold up and develop their own identity, their own language and their culture. Minorities shall have the right to full and effective participation in the larger community.[15]

Policies based on the Convention, at the time when this chapter was first published, have had mixed results. The Convention has not been followed up with national legislation and has neither been incorporated into national law. Romani language and culture are almost invisible in the public domain, and members of the group remain divided on whether to play a more assertive role *vis-à-vis* Norwegian authorities and the wider society. Some fear that this will lead to renewed discrimination and harassment. Others maintain that visibility is necessary to defeat prejudices and discriminatory attitudes. There have been extensive conflicts concerning government support schemes to Romani culture, including accusations that funds have been misappropriated and that government safeguards against misappropriation have been too weak.[16]

In the 2010s, the Government and the Parliament adopted measures to promote truth and reconciliation. Official truth processes were implemented from 2011 to 2015 for the Romani people,[17] and since 2018 for the Sámi.[18]

15 Ministry of Local Government and Modernisation, "Nasjonale minoritetar i Noreg - Om statleg politikk overfor jødar, kvener, rom, romanifolket og skogfinnar" ["National Minorities in Norway – On State Policies Towards Jews, Kvens, Roma, Romani, and Forest Finns"], 8 December 2000.

16 Reporting on Norwegian policies and assessments by the Council of Europe Advisory Committee on the Framework Convention for the Protection of National Minorities is available on the Council of Europe web site. See also Hans Morten Haugen, "Galt samme hva vi gjør? Staten og romanifolket/taterne" ["Wrong no matter what we do? The state and the Romani People/Taters"], in *Kritisk Juss*, 2019, vol. 45, no. 3.

17 The main findings of the 'Romani Truth Commission' (which is not its official name) are presented in Knut Vollebæk and others, *Assimilering og motstand: Norsk politikk overfor taterne/Romanifolket fra 1850 til i dag* [*Assimilation and resistance: Norwegian policy towards the Roma People from 1850 until today*], Departementenes sikkerhets – og serviceorganisasjon Informasjonsforvaltning, Oslo, 2015 ('NOU 2015:7') (https://www.legal-tools.org/doc/ca4c52/). A separate attachment includes, *inter alia*, reports of 25 research projects on different aspects of past Romani policies and their consequences, see *ibid.*, Vedlegg [Attachments].

18 The Truth and Reconciliation Commission's web site includes information about its mandate and organization.

5.2. Past Wrongdoing

5.2.1. Governmental and Private Efforts to Destroy Romani Culture in Norway

They [the Romani] will no longer be a separate group of people; they will be assimilated into normal everyday life.

1957 statement by Olav Bjørnstad,
Secretary General of the Mission among the Homeless[19]

The Romani people – also called 'tater', 'travellers', 'splint', 'vagabonds', 'vagrants' and some other terms – have lived in Norway at least since the beginning of the 1500s. Linguistic and other research indicate that the group originally migrated from North India to Europe. Estimates indicate that the number of Romani people at present may amount to 4,000–10,000.[20]

The Romani people live and are economically active in different parts of Norway. Historically, some Romani resided parts of the year in neighbouring Sweden, which also has resident Romani. There were numerous inter-marriages between Romani and persons belonging to other ethnic groups, including Norwegians.

In pre-industrial Norway, the Romani people often found work on farms, helping with horses and other animals, functioning as seasonal workers and travelling salespersons. They were active in music, storytelling and crafts, and retained strong family identities and traditions.

Authorities, and sometimes local populations, have been sceptical or had negative attitudes towards Romani people in different degrees since they arrived in Norway.[21] However, from 1850, and increasingly from 1900, they were subject to heavy-handed assimilation policies by the authorities. These policies were expressed through laws and legislative decrees that had clear discriminatory effects.

The Government and the Parliament delegated to a large extent implementation of these policies to a private organization, the Christian philanthropic

---

[19] Quoted from Per Haave, "'Omstreifer'-politikk på 1900-tallet" ["Vagrant-policies during the 1900s"], in *Norgeshistorie – fra steinalder til i dag. Fortalt av fagfolk*, 25 November 2015.

[20] Report by Nils Muiznieks, Commissioner for Human Rights of the Council of Europe, following his visit to Norway from 19 to 23 January 2015, CommDH(2015)9, 18 May 2015, p. 15 (https://www.legal-tools.org/doc/whlvgy/). Other estimates indicate that the number could be up to 30,000, see Ole K. Berge, Åsne Dahl Haugsevje and Nanna Løkka, *Kulturell berikelse – politisk besvær: Gennomgang av politikken overfor nasjonale minoriteter 2000–2019* [*Cultural enrichment – political problems: Review of policies towards national minorities 2000–2019*], TF-rapport nr. 490, Telemarksforsking, Bø, 2019, p. 23.

[21] For an overview of Norwegian policies towards Romani people in different periods, see NOU 2015:7, Chapter 4, see *supra* note 17.

association *Norwegian Mission among the Homeless* ('Mission').[22] In practice, the Mission was the most prominent organization in this field from 1907 to 1986, and state agencies and local authorities were instructed by the Government and the Parliament to co-operate with it.

These policies made substantial harm and created negative prejudice towards the minority, which has led to fear and distrust between the minority and mainstream society. This has had, and still has, major consequences for many members of the Romani people.

These policies focused on transfer of child custody, forced settlement and forced sterilization of the Romani people. Estimates indicate that about 30 per cent of children were taken from their parents within the group (about 1,500 children) during the first two generations of the 1900s.[23] Research into some of the cases points to families being in difficult situations and needing support to take care of their children. However, there are many examples that the authorities were motivated by illegitimate motives, such as removing the children from a travelling lifestyle. Removing children from their parents was part of the wider efforts of eradicating Romani culture.[24]

Svanviken labour colony was established by the Mission in 1908. From 1949 to 1970, 38 Romani families were placed in the colony, most for five years. Fifteen mothers were sterilized, constituting 40 per cent of the women. The numbers of placed families in other periods are not known.[25]

The purpose of the colony's operation was to prepare families to live in modern Norwegian society and make them "positive and constructive members of society". However, the director of the colony in the period 1955–1969 maintained that many of the 'colonists' were not fit to be parents. Therefore, they should not be permitted to have children.[26]

---

[22] The organization was founded in 1897 by a priest, Mr. Jakob Walnum. It had several names until 1935, when it got the name it retained throughout the period it had the role as the main implementer of Norwegian policies towards the Romani people, 'Norsk misjon blant hjemløse' ['Norwegian Mission Among the Homeless']. This period lasted until 1986, when the organization changed name to 'The Church's Social Service' ('Kirkens Sosialtjeneste'). See Hallgeir Elstad, "Norsk Misjon blant Hjemløse", in *Store norske leksikon*, 5 September 2019.

[23] Gunnar M. Ekeløve-Slydal, *Norsk romani-/taterpolitikk: fortid, nåtid, fremtid* [*Norwegian Romani/Tater policies: Past, present, future*], Norwegian Helsinki Committee, Oslo, 2009, p. 21.

[24] NOU 2015:7, p. 75, see *supra* note 17.

[25] The Mission also established a labour colony for unemployed men, Bergfløtt Labour Colony, as well as six orphanages. *Ibid.*

[26] For more information about Svanviken labour colony, see *ibid.*, pp. 16–18.

Picture 1: Svanviken labour colony.

Forced sterilization to reduce the number of children in the group also took place in other contexts, based on a 1934 law on sterilization. Some cases of forced sterilization took place without evaluations based on the law and sometimes conducted illegally, without the women being informed.[27]

The Mission originally considered sterilization a violation of Christian social work. However, it soon changed opinion and came up with a Christian justification for 'racial hygiene', arguing for sterilization of 'defective Romani'. The Mission estimated that these made up a third of the group, which in 1927 reportedly consisted of about 2,100 people.

During World War II, from the turn of the year 1942–1943, the pro-Nazi regime in Norway introduced a new law which provided even greater access to forced sterilization. In the spring of 1945, a supplement was drawn up with provisions on the '*vagrants*'. This supplement was, however, not adopted before the end of the war. From 8 May 1945, the Sterilization Act of 1934 was again in force and remained so until 1977.

---

[27] Per Haave, "Sterilisering av omstreifere" ["Sterilization of vagrants"], in *Norgeshistorie – fra steinalder til i dag. Fortalt av fagfolk*, 25 November 2015. The following sections are based on Mr. Haave's research, which has been published in NOU 2015:7, Attachment no. 18, see *supra* note 17, and in Per Haave, "Sterilisering av tatere – kirurgi på 'rasemessig grunnlag'" ["Sterilization of taters – surgery based on 'racial' foundations"], in Bjørn Hvinden (ed.), *Romanifolket og det norske samfunnet* [*The Romani people and Norwegian society*], Fagbokforlaget, Vigmostad og Bjørke AS, Bergen, 2000, pp. 32–73.

In the period 1934–1977, a total of 44,233 persons were sterilized based on the law. It has been documented that 125 of these were Romani. Of these, 109 were sterilized under various provisions of the 1934 Act:

- 50 women and 7 men at their own request (Section 3, first paragraph);
- 18 women and 4 men at their own application with the consent of the guardian or the auxiliary guardian (Section 3, second paragraph);
- 26 women and 4 men at the request of the guardian or the auxiliary guardian, or from others with the consent of the guardian or the auxiliary guardian (Section 4);
- the other 16, including one man, were sterilized under the 1942 Act.

Of women that the Mission and authorities believed to be Romani, more than 3.5 per cent were sterilized in the period 1934–1977. The total number of sterilized women was just under 2 per cent of the female population in Norway. Especially from the late 1930s to the late 1940s, Romani women were more subject to forced sterilization than women in general.

More than 230 Romani women may have been sterilized outside the law. Such sterilization was only permitted if pregnancy and childbirth would jeopardize the woman's life and health (so-called medical sterilization). However, many such sterilizations had no medical justification. This also applies to several of the sterilizations performed on women at the Svanviken labour colony.

Norwegian sterilization legislation exemplifies a general trend that legislation was not specifically targeting Romani but was nevertheless designed to facilitate measures against the group.[28] People belonging to the group were over-represented among those affected.

A range of legislative acts and official policies were the basis for the assimilation measures against the Romani. The most important are presented below.[29]

In 1851, the Parliament gave funding to a programme of Mr. Eilert Sundt (1817–1875, a famous priest and sociologist) providing housing to Romani families.[30] The programme failed, and funding was eventually withdrawn. It had, however, a lasting effect and marked the start of practices that entailed forced settlement of Romani families by the Mission in co-operation with local authorities.

---

28 NOU 2015:7, p. 49, see *supra* note 17.

29 The overview is based on *ibid.*, Chapter 4.

30 Eilert Lund Sundt was a Norwegian theologian, social and cultural scientist. He devoted his life to the study of ordinary people's lives and history. He is regarded as the founder of sociology in Norway.

In 1896, the first childcare act (‘*vergerådsloven*’) was adopted in Norway, creating committees to evaluate the situation of children and organize transfer of custody from their family to orphanages or foster families if deemed necessary for the well-being of the child. The law was succeeded in 1953 by a new Child Care Law, but the practice of removing children from Romani families continued. In some cases, children were taken from families before official authorization.

In the same year, the Parliament delegated authority to Mr. Jakob Walnum, a priest, to implement a plan to reduce the number of Romani people and to initiate other measures to support implementation of the childcare act.

The Vagrant Act (‘*løsgjengerloven*’) was adopted in 1900 and entered into force in 1907. It prohibited ‘vagrant practices’, which were considered to constitute threats to society, such as extensive traveling without having permanent residence and occupation and use of alcohol. The law was repealed only in 2006, but many of its provisions had been repealed earlier. The measure of forced labour was repealed in 1970. The law was the legal basis of the programme of forced settlement of Romani families that was run by the Mission.

In 1907, the government delegated the responsibility for forced settlement of Romani people to the Mission. The main instrument used by the Mission to facilitate settlement was a five-year stay for Romani families at the Svanviken labour colony, where the parents had to learn to live in a settled way, become financially responsible, speak Norwegian, and to break with their Romani relatives. Women were trained in housework, while men were trained in farming and crafts.

In 1908, the Parliament adopted restrictions on the practices of traveling salespersons, also targeting traveling Romani who were selling tools, art crafts and services (‘*omførselshandel*’).

In 1927, 1935 and 1948, there were official campaigns to register ‘vagrants’ and report them to the Mission. The Mission also received copies of criminal police registration of criminal offences, likely with the purpose of completing its own registration of Romani people.[31]

A 1934 parliamentary law on sterilization was subsequently applied to authorize forced sterilization of Romani women and a few Romani men. In 1937, regulations were put in place by the Government that obliged the police to help transfer custody of Romani children to the Mission.

A 1951 law prohibited Romani to use horses to transport goods or people. The law was repealed only in 1974.

[31] NOU 2015:7, p. 61, see *supra* note 17.

Although the Mission was a driving force in defining the target group and formulating policies, its actions were carried out on behalf of the state, which largely funded its operations. There was close co-operation between the Mission and local authorities on transfer of child custody and forced settlement.

Summing up, both during the first part of the 1900s, when Norway was ruled by the Liberal Party, and after World War II, when the social-democratic Labour Party formed the Government, assimilation policies were in place that aimed at destroying Romani culture and way of life. These policies had their origin in 'social reforms' during the late 1800s, which were designed to address negative aspects of travelling lifestyles, abuse of alcohol and child poverty.

The policies were backed up by legislation that seldom specifically targeted Romani people, but in effect led to discrimination and confirmed popular prejudice that they belonged to a sub-standard group of human beings.

The policies were framed by an alliance of the Protestant state church, the emerging bourgeoisie and the political elite. They were implemented by a missionary organization that was running six orphanages, two labour colonies, and was well-connected and influential *vis-à-vis* other public institutions that had any impact on the implementation of Romani policies.

The aim of the policies was to remove children from the Romani culture of their families or to change the culture and lifestyle of their parents into mainstream Norwegian culture.

During the 1930s, views were presented by influential members of Norwegian society that assimilation of Romani was impossible due to their inferior biological characteristics.[32] During World War II, when Norway was occupied by Germany, plans for the complete sterilization of Romani people were made, but not implemented.

During the post-war period, the assimilation policies lasted for four decades before a gradual shift took place in policies, which recognized that Romani rights and culture should be protected. As late as in the preparatory works for the 1964 Law on Social Protection, a passage is included stating that the "goal is eventually to liquidate the entire vagrant system and adapt both children and adults to orderly social conditions. Most important is to take care of the children while they are still quite small and before they have gotten used to vagrancy".[33]

5.2.2. Stigmatization of Sámi Culture

Sámi (previously often referred to as Lapps or Finns) are descendants of nomadic peoples who inhabited northern Scandinavia for thousands of years. Their

[32] Haave, 2015, see *supra* note 27.

[33] Quoted from NOU 2015:7, p. 75, see *supra* note 17.

traditional occupations were hunting, trapping, fishing and reindeer herding. They have been present in the northernmost Norwegian county, Finnmark, for at least 2,000 years.[34]

When the Finns entered Finland, starting about 100 AD, Sámi settlements were probably dispersed over the whole country; today they are confined to its northern extremity. In Sweden and Norway, the Sámi have similarly been pushed north, although today many Sámi also live in the bigger cities in the south of the countries. In the late 1900s, there were from 30,000 to 40,000 Sámi in Norway and about 20,000 in Sweden, 6,000 in Finland, and 2,000 in Russia.[35]

During early Norwegian statehood, the main issue with the Sámi was their religion (animism, polytheism, shamanism). The 1025 Christian Law obliged all people on the territory to adhere to Christian doctrines. After the 1536 Reformation, only Protestant Christianity was accepted, excluding also Catholic monastic orders.[36]

The Reformation brought sharper attention to the Sámi in the Nordic countries. The ancient Sámi religion was still strong in Finnmark and other parts of Sápmi. Several of the witchcraft cases in Finnmark during the 1600s were against mainly male Sámi.[37] The Sámi was, however, not targeted more than ethnic Norwegians in these cases. They constituted an estimated 37.5 per cent of the population in Finnmark (1,200 of 3,200 residents), while their share of witchcraft cases was only 21 per cent. However, there was an additional motivation to take over their land in some of the cases.[38]

The government's acquisition of land within the fjords and in rural areas in the north resulted in stronger integration of Sámi settlement areas into the Danish-Norwegian Kingdom at the time. The Sámi people's use of former common areas was increasingly restricted.

In broad terms, Sámi and non-Sámi people had interacted in the northern regions of today's Norway and Sweden for centuries. From the 1500s, however, these mutual interactions gave gradually way to a system of control of Sámi lands and lives by Denmark-Norway and Sweden. These states "gradually established and enforced a social hierarchy in which they enjoyed cultural

[34] Key facts on Sámi history and culture are taken from "Sami People", in *Encyclopedia Britannica*, 13 September 2025.

[35] *Ibid.*

[36] Erling Sandmo, "Det flerkulturelle Norge mellom 1500 og 1800" ["The multicultural Norway between 1500 and 1800"], in *Norgeshistorie – fra steinalder til i dag. Fortalt av fagfolk*, 25 November 2015.

[37] Rune Blix Hagen, "Trolldomsforfølgelse av samer" ["Whitchcraft persecution of Sámi people"], in *Norgeshistorie – fra steinalder til i dag. Fortalt av fagfolk*, 24 August 2016.

[38] *Ibid.*

superiority and political dominance over Sámi, and in which Sámi were no longer allowed to make decisions governing the course of their collective society or, in many cases, their individual lives. This relationship resembles those between Indigenous peoples and colonizing powers elsewhere in the world".[39]

The consolidation of state power in northern Scandinavia and the Kola Peninsula, including by border agreements between Denmark-Norway and Sweden in 1751, and with Russia in 1826, gradually undermined Sámi systems of self-rule in their traditional areas of economic activities.

The old Sámi social order was based on the '*siida* system', in which different hunting teams together formed the basis for larger community units, a Sámi village or a rural unit. The '*siidas*' had a well-established democratic system of governance, where settlement in an area was based on ecological adaptation and relocation according to resources.[40]

Most of the '*siidas*' operated with several seasonal settlements, utilizing the natural resources of different areas. The '*siida*' system may have been one of the reasons that Sámi were able to avoid confrontations with Norwegians at the time of colonization. They simply withdrew to one of their other settlements to avoid conflict, but at the same time their radius of action and access to prey were reduced.

The gradual colonizing of Sámi land thus replaced a flexible system of using the land by different units of Sámi, to a system with state or private ownership of land. Legislation favoured Norwegians acquiring such ownership, in particular the 1902 Land Sale Act, which stated that *only* Norwegian citizens who could speak, read and write Norwegian, and who used Norwegian daily, could buy land. The land property had to be given a Norwegian name. The law was repealed only in 1965, but it was rarely enforced after World War II.[41]

These developments were complemented by measures that stigmatized Sámi culture, religion and language. Such measures facilitated the goal of absorbing "Sámi into the Norwegian nation".[42] Sámi were made to believe that

39 Greaves, 2018, p. 107, see *supra* note 2.

40 Neil Kent, *The Sámi Peoples of the North*, C. Hurst & Co., London, 2018, pp. 21, 37–38; Harald Gaski, "Samenes historie" ["The history of the Sámi"], in *Store Norske Leksikon*, 8 June 2020.

41 Steinar Pedersen, "Jordloven for Finnmark – samer måtte ofre språket for å få kjøpe jord" ["The land law for Finnmark – Sámi had to give up their language to be allowed to buy land"], in *Samiske veivisere*, 21 May 2019.

42 Statement by Norwegian Prime Minister Johan Sverdrup (1884–1889). Quoted from Laila Susanne Vars, "Samene i Norge: Fra fornorsking til forsoning?" ["Sámi in Norway: From Norwegianization to Reconciliation?"], in Nik. Brandal, Cora Alexa Døving and Ingvill Thorson Plesner (eds.), *Nasjonale minoriteter og urfolk i norsk politikk fra 1900 til 2016* [*National*

their own culture was of little worth and that the only way they could be included in the emerging modern state was to give it up and "become Norwegian".

The processes of colonization and assimilation did not take place without conflicts, although these conflicts almost never escalated into violent clashes (the exception being the 1852 Kautokeino Rebellion, which involved religious revivalists and was directed against local government officials).[43]

The conflicts between representatives of Danish-Norwegian authorities who asserted the king's right in Sámi core areas, and Sámi people defending their unwritten customary rights, developed into more severe confrontations during the end of the 1600s than in later times. This was a period when, in addition to Norwegian settlements in Sámi areas close to the coast, mining industry started. Climate was colder during the second half of the 1600s, leading to pressure on limited resources and high mortality rates among the Sámi.

After the witchcraft processes ceased, and especially in the wake of strong Christian Pietist movements in the Nordic countries from about 1700, extensive Christian missionary activities were conducted in the northernmost regions of the kingdom, in Greenland and in Finnmark.

Although many priests and bishops supported teaching religion in native Sámi languages, with some of them learning to speak and write in these languages, the missionary activities may nevertheless have contributed significantly to changing attitudes among local Norwegian authorities and subsequently among central authorities towards Sámi culture.

Many representatives of the Church viewed Sámi as savages, "possessed by the devil", who could only become "viable Norwegians" with the help of the Christian faith. This view formed a formidable motivation for the systematic Norwegianization project, which began in the 1850s. It provided Norwegianization with a strong rationale for why and how the Sámi people should be Norwegianized.[44]

Early views on Sámi often underlined their competence as fishermen, boat builders, hunters, navigators in the snowy wilderness of the Arctic, as well as their hospitality and peaceful ways of organizing society. The Italian diplomat and traveller Mr. Giuseppe Acerbi (1773–1846) captured these views well: "I have seen very few places where the people live in so easy and happy a

Minorities and Indigenous Peoples in Norwegian Politics from 1900-2016], Cappelen Damm Akademisk, Oslo, 2017, p. 177.

[43] Kent, 2018, p. 111, see *supra* note 40.

[44] Bente Persen, "«At bringe dem frem til mands modenhed» – En studie av fornorskingen av samene i Porsanger 1880–1980" ["«To bring them forth to man's maturity» – A study of Norwegianization of the Sámi in Porsanger 1880–1980"], Master Thesis, University of Oslo, 2008.

simplicity as in the maritime districts of Lapland".[45] Sámi were perceived as uncorrupted by civilization, as 'noble savages'.

In Medieval times and up to the gradual colonization of their lands from the 1500s, Sámi products such as fur, reindeer skins and martin pelts were attractive items in European trade. The Sámi were respected taxpayers; some of them at times had to pay tax both to Russia, Denmark-Norway, and Sweden due to unclear borders and influence of several states over the same territory.[46]

Shaping views that were underpinning the later Norwegianization project, the church missionaries either demonized Sámi culture or described Sámi as childish. As Rector Mr. Andreas Gjølme in Sør-Varanger in Finnmark wrote in 1886:

> The Lapp people are childlike people in more than one respect. As people, they have the child's impulsive, naïve, undeveloped point of view, and it is the goal of Norwegianization that they are brought to the maturity of man, if this is at all possible. This is an immense and lasting goal to work towards.[47]

While some Norwegian practices regarding Sámi language and culture were relatively liberal until the 1850s, policies from that time became increasingly strict. Norwegianization of Sámi and Kven became the ultimate goal of Norway's minority policies in the north during the following 130 years. The period may be divided into four main phases.

The first phase started in 1851, when the Parliament allocated money to the so-called Finn or Lapp Fund. This was an item in the national budget to finance measures to change the language and culture of the Sámi. The main focus was on language, and the school became the main 'battlefield' with the teachers as 'frontline soldiers' in the state's assimilation campaign.[48] As in other states at the time, the school was the cornerstone in nation building.[49] The full range of the assimilation policies came, however, to influence almost all spheres

[45] Kent, 2018, p. 5, see *supra* note 40.

[46] *Ibid.*, p. 39.

[47] Quoted from Lorenz Khazaleh, "Norwegianization of the Sami was religiously motivated. Interview with Bente Persen", University of Oslo, 25 May 2011.

[48] Einar Niemi, "Kulturmøte, etnisitet og statlig intervensjon på Nordkalotten" ["Cultural Encounter, Ethnicity and State Intervention in the Northern Hemisphere"], in Rut Boström Andersson (ed.), *Den nordiska mosaiken: språk og kulturmöten i gammal tid och i våra dager* [*The Nordic Mosaic: Language and Cultural Encounters in Old Times and in Our Days*], Uppsala University, 1997, p. 268.

[49] Henry Minde, "Assimilation of the Sami – Implementation and Consequences", in *Journal of Indigenous Peoples Rights*, 2005, vol. 3, p. 7.

of society and public institutions, including by outlawing or marginalizing Sámi musical instruments, clothing and other cultural items.

This phase, which lasted until the late 1860s, represented a brake with previous policies, which accepted Sámi and Kven languages almost on an equal footing with Norwegian. In line with humanistic and romantic ideas of the first part of the 1800s, to speak one's native tongue had been seen as a right for all peoples. However, this liberal view was opposed by the Norwegian upper class of Finnmark, and in the Norwegian Parliament from 1848.[50]

The measures applied in the first phase focused on the Sámi in so-called 'transitional districts', that is, areas that were ethnically mixed with a substantial proportion of Norwegian speakers such as in the coastal areas of Finnmark. The Lapp Fund financed teaching of Norwegian language and culture in these districts.

During the second phase, starting in the late 1860s and lasting until 1905, when Norway became independent from Sweden, the Parliament was concerned by Finnish immigration to East Finnmark. A prevailing view was that assimilation policies so far had not given the desired results. A shift in motivations took place, from 'civilizing' Sámi and Kven so that they could become part of the emerging modern Norwegian society, to security concerns. The Parliament decided in 1868 that the Lapp Fund should be increased, and finance assimilation measures aimed at the Kven population in addition to the Sámi.[51]

The school instruction for the mixed language districts in Finnmark and Troms (the second northernmost county of Norway) was further sharpened. Up to the 1880s, it was permissible to use Sámi and Kven as the language of instruction in Christianity teaching and otherwise as a language of assistance to facilitate the learning of Norwegian. In practice, this led to pupils also receiving training in their mother tongue.

In 1880, the authorities launched a document entitled "Instructions for teachers in Lappian [Sámi] and Kven transitional districts", introducing a new system for teachers' salaries, differentiating them by how many Sámi and Kven children they could convert to speaking Norwegian, and removing all mother tongue education. The instruction marked "the final breakthrough for the strict Norwegianization policy".[52]

---

[50] *Ibid.*, p. 11.

[51] Knut Einar Eriksen and Einar Niemi, *Den finske fare: Sikkerhetsproblemer og minoritetpolitikk i nord 1860–1940* [*The Finnish menace: Boundary problems and minority policy in the North 1860–1940*], Universitetsforlaget, Oslo, 1981, pp. 30–47.

[52] Minde, 2005, p. 13, see *supra* note 49.

From 1889, the language requirements were further tightened, with intervention in the private sphere as teachers now also had to ensure that children only spoke Norwegian during their breaks.

The school's Norwegianization policy took its final form with the school instruction of 1898, the so-called Wexelsen Decree ('*Wexelsenplakaten*'). Although there was no prohibition against the use of auxiliary language in the school, in reality only Norwegian was used as language of instruction in mixed-language school districts. The exception was in Karasjok and Kautokeino, where it was allowed to use Sámi in Christianity teaching. In other places, Sámi and Kven languages should be limited to what was strictly necessary, "as an aid to explain what is incomprehensible to the children".[53]

There was also increased scepticism against employing Sámi or Kven teachers, as they were "not suited to promote Norwegianization among their fellow countrymen with the desired success", as stated by Director General Mr. Nils Herzberg of the Ministry of Church and Education during discussions in the Parliament in 1877. The Wexelsen Decree gave a green light to the proposal, which instituted work prohibition on ethnic grounds.[54]

In order to co-ordinate and control the Norwegianization campaign, Finnmark was the first county in Norway to have its own school director. Mr. Bernt Thomassen, school director from 1902 to 1920, was pushing Norwegianization policies with great vigour. He was at the forefront of the development of the boarding school system in Finnmark and contributed actively to the assimilation policies embracing most aspects of social life. Boarding schools became an important institution for promoting Norwegian language and culture and thus reach the goals of the policies. Up to World War II, 50 boarding schools had been built in Finnmark. Some 2,800 of 7,900 schoolchildren had to leave their families and live at the schools. It was not easy for the children whether they were Sámi, Kven or Norwegian, but it was undoubtedly tougher for those who had to learn a new language as quickly as possible (having no previous knowledge of Norwegian).

The third phase lasted from approximately 1905 to 1950. Measures launched during the second phase were continued, while the political situation changed due to developments after World War I. The 1919 Versailles Treaty of peace resulted in Norway having a common border with both Russia and Finland. The fear of both Finnish intrusion on Norwegian territory and for Sámi mobilization against the education policies led to more secrecy concerning the

[53] *Ibid.*, p. 14.

[54] *Ibid.*, pp. 14–15.

policies. A secret body, the Finnmark Board, was established in 1931 to strengthen implementation of the policies.

The Lapp Fund was substantially increased during the first part of the 1900s to finance the building of boarding schools, which started as 'border fortifications' in Kven-dominated areas. Later also other parts of Finnmark were included in the programme.

A new school director for Finnmark, Mr. Christian Brygfjeld, took over in 1923. He rejected demands made by the Sámi to soften Norwegianization measures, expressing clearly racist views:

> The Lapps have had neither the ability nor the will to use their language as written language. [...] The few individuals who are left of the original Lappish tribe are now so degenerated that there is little hope of any change for the better for them. They are hopeless and belong to Finnmark's most backward and wretched population and provide the biggest contingent from these areas to our lunatic asylums and schools for the mentally retarded.[55]

Mr. Brygfjeld ranked the Sámi well under the Kven, the latter being a cultured, "industrious and competent" people. While Norwegianization of the Sámi was an effort to 'civilize' sub-standard people, the Kven needed to be Norwegianized due to security considerations because of their Finnish origin and a fear that they would sympathize with Finland if conflict broke out.

In 1935, a new Labour Party government took over, but no changes were made in the assimilation policies of the previous non-socialist governments.

The Elementary School Act of 1936 took away the possibility of even using Finnish as an auxiliary language, which was still the case with Sámi. The assimilation regime was thus tightened concerning the Kven, based on security concerns.

The fourth and final phase, the termination or settlement phase, lasted from 1950 to about 1980. During this period, Norwegianization continued in the schools as late as in the 1960s, even after the Parliament had repealed the Wexelsen Decree.

However, due to Sámi political mobilization and international influence, new Sámi policies were developed. In the Parliament, many supported proposals that Sámi languages should be taught in schools. In Finnmark, however, such proposals were still met by strong resistance. Some support to Sámi culture and institutions started to be provided by the state during the 1970s. During the same

[55] Quotation from Eriksen and Niemi, 1981, p. 258, see *supra* note 51. The English translation is published in Minde, 2005, p. 17, see *supra* note 49.

time, Sámi organizations started to be active in the international movement of indigenous peoples.[56]

A decisive issue mobilizing Sámi resistance to Norway's disregard for Sámi interests and rights, was the so-called Alta controversy of 1979–1981. This was a series of protests concerning the construction of a hydro-electric power plant in the Alta river in Finnmark. Many Norwegians supported Sámi rights to reindeer husbandry as well as ecological considerations that the plant should not be constructed.

The controversy became a symbol of the wider fight for Sámi rights, *against* cultural discrimination and *for* political autonomy and material rights,[57] and led to important legislative and policy changes.

Summing up, based on ideas that stigmatized Sámi culture, as well as security considerations that implied that the Norwegian state could not expect loyalty from in particular the Kven but sometimes also Sámi people living in border areas in Finnmark, the Norwegian state implemented policies that aimed at eradicating Sámi culture, religion and language. The ideas that stigmatized Sámi culture was based on religion, national, Social Darwinist and racist motives.

These policies had profound consequences for Sámi self-esteem and cultural identity. The state efforts may have been made easier by already existing racism against the Sámi, but the efforts in themselves contributed to "a massive downgrading of those who were subjected to the policy".[58] Research indicate that between 1930 and 1950, the proportion of people who identified as Sámi in Kvænangen Municipality was reduced from 44 per cent to 0 per cent. This was not, however, because all Sámi left and never returned. Many of them did return after the war but would not identify themselves as Sámi anymore.[59]

Similar policies of assimilation were conducted in other states, indicated by terms such as 'Russification', 'Germanification' and 'Americanization'. Assimilation policies in Norway were, however, more "determined, continuous and long-lasting" than in most other countries.[60]

---

56 Einar Niemi, "Fornorskingspolitikken overfor samene og kvenene" ["Norwegianization policies towards the Sámi and the Kven"], in Nik Brandal, Cora Alexa Døving and Ingvill Thorson Plesner (eds.), *Nasjonale minoriteter og urfolk i norsk politikk fra 1900 til 2016* [National Minorities and Indigenous Peoples in Norwegian Politics from 1900 to 2016], Cappelen Damm Akademisk, Oslo, 2017, p. 147.

57 Minde, 2005, p. 6, see *supra* note 49.

58 *Ibid.*, p. 20.

59 *Ibid.*, p. 9.

60 *Ibid.*, p. 8.

5.2.3. Colonization of Sápmi

As has been indicated, an important wider framework for the assimilation policies was the overtaking and securing of Norwegian territorial control over parts of Sápmi, which eventually became the northernmost county of Norway, Finnmark.

There are traces of ethnic Norwegians settling in Norway's arctic regions from before the thirteenth century, with not only churches being established earlier (such as Trondenes Church outside Harstad, which is considered the world's northernmost surviving medieval building), but with sources on Viking chieftains based along the coast of Northern-Norway several centuries earlier (such as Tore or Thorir Hund, whose early eleventh century base was on Bjarkøy, and whose brother was a chief in Trondenes). The Norwegians mainly settled and created coastal villages to develop fisheries, which became increasingly important for Norway's exports. Gradually, the influx of Norwegians and other non-Sámi people put more pressure on the Sámi. There was also pressure on them from Sweden, Finland and Russia. The border agreements between Denmark-Norway and Sweden in 1751, with Finland in 1809, and with Russia in 1826 were pivotal in securing the states' interests in Sápmi and in undermining Sámi interests. The so-called 'Lappkodicil', an attachment to the 1751 border agreement, obviously helped by providing free access to the reindeer herding Sámi to cross the border. However, it did not help in all respects.

Picture 2: The Sápmi area.

Until the border agreement in 1751, Norwegian authorities relied on alliances with the Sámi to strengthen their influence in the area. Before the agreement, Finnmark in reality "belonged to no nation and remained contested grounds. All three powers [Denmark-Norway, Russia and Sweden] made opposing demands on the area and used the taxation of the Saamis as grounds for claiming sovereignty".[61]

After the agreement, however, such tactics gave way to restrictive policies that could be implemented without concerns to the need for Sámi support. The Sámi had lost their most effective tool *vis-à-vis* the expanding and competing kingdoms of Denmark-Norway and Sweden.[62] Now the most important goal became to secure loyalty from the Sámi towards the Danish-Norwegian state, as well as to strengthen presence of ethnic Norwegians in the territory.

Immigration from Finland during the eighteenth and nineteenth centuries led to intensified pressure on the Sámi. Norwegianization intensified to strengthen national security and to avoid losing territory to Russia or Finland, which from 1809 became a Russian grand duchy. After Finnish independence in 1917, the so-called 'Finnish menace' remained an important factor. It was considered essential for the territorial integrity of the Norwegian state that Norwegian became the dominant language in all parts of the country.[63]

In understanding the power dynamics of the region and its consequences for the Sámi, one has to look at Sweden's role as a leading Scandinavian state with colonial ambitions. Swedish territory covers the fertile reindeer herding areas across the north-central plateau of Sápmi. Swedish authorities made efforts to colonize Sápmi from the 1600s, by exploiting the natural resources of Sápmi and by populating an area that several states laid claim on.[64]

This process became increasingly strong during the later parts of the 1700s. The 1749 Lapland Regulations resulted in a growing amount of land being granted to Swedish farmers. Sámi efforts to convince "Swedish authorities that their livelihoods would be endangered" failed. At the same time, the territory of Sápmi was "measured, surveyed and mapped, divided into provinces, parishes and tax lands". And this domestication of the land went hand in hand with "domestication of its dwellers. Civilizing efforts of Lutheran missionaries and school masters aimed at reforming the minds and bodies of the students and creating obedient subjects".[65]

[61] Grunlög Fur, *Colonialism in the Margins: Cultural Encounters in New Sweden and Lapland*, Brill, Leiden, 2006, p. 53.

[62] Greaves, 2018, p. 109, see *supra* note 2.

[63] The security motives of Norwegianization has been thoroughly documented by Eriksen and Niemi, 1981, see *supra* note 51.

[64] David Lindmark, "Colonial Encounter in Early Modern Sápmi", in Magdalena Naum and Jonas M. Nordin (eds.), *Scandinavian Colonialism and the Rise of Modernity: Small Agents in a Global Arena*, Springer-Verlag, New York, 2013, p. 131.

[65] *Ibid.*, pp. 132–133.

Terms to describe this intrusion into Sápmi such as 'agricultural expansion', 'settlement of non-Sámi' or 'internal colonization' do not capture the asymmetrical character of the power relationships entailed in the processes. Neither do they recognize that Sámi society and economy were well-organized and well-governed despite the lack of a Sámi nation-state and military defence.

Another important indicator of colonial relationship is the educational system, which offers a restricted curriculum for the colonial subjects "to inculcate knowledge, values and attitudes deemed necessary to controlling the colonized".[66] Lessons were limited to reading, writing and arithmetic, and sometimes vocational skills. "In this manner, the colonized were prepared to enter the labor market equipped with the norms and values essential to creating a loyal, diligent and conscientious working class".[67]

By creating obedient and efficient students, colonial education contributed "to laying the groundwork for political dominance, and economic exploitation". Virtues instilled included "order, precision, punctuality and obedience", preparing the colonized students to fulfil the demands of colonial society. In addition, the students were subject to extensive Christianity lessons, buttressing these norms further.[68]

The root of colonial education of the Sámi in Sweden was a school founded in Lycksele in 1632, through a private donation. However, it was about 100 years later that a public education program for Sápmi was established. In these early years, there were selective enrolment of students and a study period of only two years. The basic tenets of the education model, however, became influential for both Swedish and later, Norwegian Sámi education. Sámi children were isolated from their families and environment and were under constant surveillance of their teacher at the boarding schools. In a Swedish instruction to the headmaster from 1735, the headmaster's surveillance is put in a direct analogy to the omnipresence of God, who "sees into their souls and hearts and knows how often they transgress his commandments even in the slightest degree".[69]

The aim of the education at the time was thus to reform the students, reshape their will and transform their spirituality, and to achieve a complete "internalisation of Christian philosophy and religiosity". In other words, in addition to facilitating the settling of non-Sámi in Sápmi, taking over and transforming to private ownership the land Sámi had used for centuries, the Scandinavian

[66] *Ibid.*, p. 133.

[67] *Ibid.*

[68] *Ibid.*

[69] *Ibid.*, p. 134.

states also aimed at an 'invasion within'. The educated Sámi should become a tool for the ruling elites to gradually master and govern the uneducated Sámi.[70]

For the Sámi, the influx of Scandinavian settlers, who were granted tax exemption and other benefits when they moved to Sápmi and farmed its land, as well as the assertion of centralized political authority without taking into account their views and interests "looked suspiciously like an invasion".[71] True, colonization of Sápmi was less violent and more gradual than European colonialism elsewhere. In other aspects, however, the Scandinavian expansion and assertion of power were similar to European colonialism. The purpose was to displace and deny independence to the Sámi, and to 'invade' their minds by educational measures.

Sweden could be seen as the driving force in the colonization of Sápmi, influencing the lives of Sámi but also the policies of its Scandinavian neighbours.

> Swedish expansion into Sápmi thus influenced the political and demographic shape of northern Europe, since it expanded the zone of sovereign control and led to extended boundary disputes between Sweden, Denmark-Norway, and Russia. The borders that resulted brought Sápmi under the control of centralized Christian, European sovereigns.[72]

This taking over of territory and competition between Scandinavian states and Russia to dominate Sápmi played an important role in motivating efforts at eradicating Sámi culture and language. As has been shown, these processes may be seen through the lens of Western colonialism, "a political-economic phenomenon whereby various European nations explored, conquered, settled, and exploited large areas of the world".[73]

Other factors, however, also played a role. Research indicate that while assimilation policies intensified in Norway during the first part of the 1900s, they became more relaxed in Sweden. In Norway, the policies became increasingly a state issue based on security concerns, where the role of the northern Norwegian authorities was reduced. The increasingly harsh policies should probably be understood in the context of society becoming increasingly nationalistic around the establishment of the Norwegian state as independent of Sweden in 1905. 'Internal alien people' were deemed to be a threat for the Norwegian statehood. In Sweden, policies seem to have become more relaxed because

---

70 *Ibid.*, p. 135.

71 Fur, 2006, p. 17, see *supra* note 51.

72 Greaves, 2018, p. 103, see *supra* note 2.

73 Charles E. Nowell, Richard A. Webster and Harry Magdoff, "Western Colonialism", in *Encyclopedia Britannica*, 3 October 2025.

the state was stronger. It held that the Sámi did not pose a threat and could be accepted as they were.[74]

During World War II, the whole of Norway was occupied by Germany, but the most severe fighting took place in Finnmark, affecting at times the whole civilian population. Pressured to retreat by Soviet troops in the autumn of 1944, German military authorities issued orders that the entire population of 70,000 should be evacuated. Some 23,000 refused and went into hiding in caves and other forms of shelter. Almost all houses and buildings were destroyed by the retreating German army. Many Sámi decided to stay behind.[75]

Nazi Germany's views of the Sámi were complex. Ideologues like Mr. Heinrich Himmler (1900–1945) viewed the Sámi as belonging to non-Germanic peoples who had kept their blood clean. He therefore wanted to create an apartheid state in Finnmark so that the Sámi people would retain their characteristics. The Germans also needed knowledge on how to survive in the harsh climate. Few managed this better than the reindeer-herding Sámi who had a unique knowledge of the conditions in the north. The occupying authorities therefore left the reindeer-herding Sámi industry largely untouched.[76]

After the war, Finnmark was rebuilt according to Norwegian design with little, if any, consultation with the Sámi. There was, however, a gradual shift in policies as border conflicts with Finland lapsed. In 1948, a breakthrough for more sympathetic views towards the Sámi occurred. Sámi political mobilization became more forceful and state policies started to accept Sámi language and culture in education and society.[77]

However, this was just the beginning of a long process, which has not yet ended, to define the role and rights of the Sámi people on Norwegian territory and in Norwegian politics and society.

5.2.4. The Racist Elements in Past Romani and Sámi Policies

In recognizing that the taking over of Sápmi by the Scandinavian states may be seen through the lens of colonialism, there is an implicit acceptance of the role played by racist elements in its ideological underpinnings. Colonialism represents instrumentalization of territory and human beings, based on assumptions that the people originally living in the colonized territory have less civilization,

[74] Eriksen and Niemi, 1981, p. 348, see *supra* note 51.

[75] Fredrik Fagertun (ed.), *Krig og frigjøring i nord* [*War and liberation in the North*], Orkana akademisk, Oslo, p. 215.

[76] Bjørg Evjen, "Møter og holdninger mellom samer, norske nazimyndigheter og representanter for okkupasjonsmakten" ["Encounters and attitudes between Sámi, Norwegian Nazi-authorities and representatives of the occupying power"], in *ibid.*, pp. 85–98.

[77] Eriksen and Niemi, 1981, p. 349, see *supra* note 51.

less rights, or belong to an 'inferior race' compared to the people of the colonizing state.

In general, 'racism' signifies actions, practices or beliefs that in some way reflect the view that humans may be divided into separate and exclusive biological entities. The view holds that there is a causal link between inherited physical traits and traits of personality, intellect, morality and other cultural and behavioural features. In this way, some races are seen as innately superior to others.

Such racist ideas were clearly present in the most prevalent ideological efforts to legitimize assimilation policies towards Norway's minorities, in particular the Romani and the Sámi. The background of these policies was a combination of educational policy ambitions, nation-building ideology, as well as a desire for stronger border security in the north. In the early 1900s, Social Darwinism and racial-biology thoughts became important. These were ideas that most people accepted at the time, and served both as a defence and a basis for Norwegian policy. According to these ideas, the Sámi and the Romani were 'helped' by getting rid of their languages, religions, dress styles or other cultural features that signalled minority identity. Instead, they were given access to a thriving Norwegian culture. At different times, ideas shifted on whether it was feasible to assimilate the minorities. Some held that the groups were not intellectually or morally able to adhere to practices of the culture because of their alleged 'inferior biological characteristics'.

During the first part of the 1900s, the Mission thought it possible to 'save' Romani if they were educated. During the period between World Wars I and II, however, more radical proposals were presented by influential 'experts' and politicians to forcibly sterilize all members of the group. These proposals were clearly motivated by racist ideas about the inferior biological nature of the people. Social Darwinism and racial biology became influential among political and scientific elites in Norway, as in several other European states at the time.

Romani people were often portrayed as socially and intellectually inferior; at times, such characterization was also applied to the Sámi. At other times, it was their pagan religion and 'uncivilized' lifestyle that was pointed to as the basis for the policies.

5.2.5. Other Motives

The concentration of Kvens in villages and small towns close to the Finnish border were seen as a security issue from the 1800s and until World War II. The loyalty of the Kvens, and to a certain degree of the Sámi, to the Norwegian state was in doubt. In this context, Norwegianization was seen as a tool to defend Norwegian territory.

Norway chose mainly to defend its territorial integrity by cultural and religious means, such as erecting churches and symbols of Norwegian culture to increase visibility and presence in the area. Since some of the Sámi followed their reindeer across borders, they were not seen as contributing to nation-building and securing the territory of Norway's northernmost province.

During the 1900s, Finnmark's natural resources increasingly drew investments and modernization of its economy. The building of large hydro-electric power plants, mines and other economic developments increased pressure on traditional territories for reindeer herding during the post-war period. Current examples are development of windmill farms, which may intrude on Sámi reindeer areas. Such conflicts between Sámi and majority-Norwegian economic interests in the area has a long history and may also have contributed to efforts to assimilate them.

There were also motives that were not related to security or economy. From the late 1800s, there were strong movements in Norway to increase protection of socially disadvantaged children, including by ensuring their education to become morally upright and hardworking. Norway was among the first states in the world to have a public child welfare system. However, ideas of protecting children, for their own and for the society's good, merged with derogatory beliefs concerning minorities. Like in Australia, Canada and New Zealand, measures targeting children and families became part of policies to facilitate assimilation of minorities.[78]

A view prevailed among elites and large parts of the population that the demography of the nascent state should be as uniform as possible. This conformity ideology aimed at imposing the Protestant faith, Norwegian culture, and strong loyalty towards the Norwegian state. As opposed to the Sámi and the Kven living in the north, the Romani was never seen as a security problem. However, they were seen as a threat towards reaching the goal of conformity.[79]

In this way, taking care of Romani children became a means to repress Romani culture and facilitating assimilation. Similarly, the somewhat less intrusive boarding school system in Finnmark aimed at weakening the bonds between the children and their Sámi family and culture, and transferring them into Norwegian language and culture.

[78] Karen-Sofie Pettersen, "For barnas skyld? Ideologi og praksis i tiltakene rettet mot taternes barn" ["For the sake of the children? Ideology and practice in measures towards Romani children"], in Hvinden (ed.), 2000, pp. 74–75, see *supra* note 27.

[79] *Ibid.*, p. 76.

5.3. Norwegian Public Discourse on the Past Wrongdoing

The Norwegian King and several governments have, since the late 1990s, apologized to the Sámi and the Romani for the harm inflicted by the past wrongdoing. As an example, in his official speech at the opening of the Sámi Parliament in 1997, the King stated that the "Norwegian state is founded on the territory of two people – Norwegians and Sámi. Sámi history is closely intertwined with Norwegian history. Today, we must apologize the injustice the Norwegian state has previously inflicted on the Sámi people through a harsh Norwegianization policy".[80]

The wording of the King in describing past wrongdoing is telling of the way Norwegian authorities speak. The prevailing political discourse adheres to rather unspecific terms such as "injustices", "failed policies", "assimilation policies" and "Norwegianization". Human rights language and a recognition that the policies represented infringement of core values protected by human rights and international criminal law remain largely absent. This may change in the future due to the influence of the truth commissions.

When the head of the Romani Truth Commission, Mr. Knut Vollebæk (1946–), former Minister of Foreign Affairs and former Organization for Security and Co-operation in Europe Commissioner on National Minorities, presented the Commission's report on 1 June 2015, he said that he was shocked by the way Romani had been treated in Norway:

> State policy has been unsuccessful and disruptive. It has created a fear of authorities that have been inherited. […] At the Svanviken labour colony, serious interference with the privacy of residents has been revealed. The situation there was characterized by control and directives. Little was up to the individual, and people were often placed there unwillingly.
>
> Studies show that around 40 per cent of women at Svanviken were sterilized. Previous research has shown that Romani have been sterilized in Norway until the 1970s. Many formally voluntary sterilizations were done under duress, with threats of losing the children you had if you were not sterilized.[81]

The extensive research conducted by the Commission confirmed past wrongdoing against the Romani. It also concluded that parts of the wrongdoing represented violations of human rights as understood today and violations of ethical norms and values that were present in Norwegian society at the time, and

---

80 The speech is available in Norwegian language on the web site of the Norwegian Royal House.

81 Quotation translated from Norwegian by the author, based on the author's notes. Facts presented in the quotation are rendered in the official report by the Commission. For an overview of official apologies to the Romani, see NOU 2015:7, pp. 81–88, see *supra* note 17.

which today are protected by human rights.[82] In this way, the Commission introduced more specific ways of describing the past abuses.

In particular, the Commission concluded that practices at Svanviken labour colony until the 1970s violated the European Convention on Human Rights Article 8 (right to respect for private and family life) as it is understood today. This also holds for the extensive practice of transferring Romani children to orphanages and to Norwegian foster families.

> The Committee believes that at that time it should have been understood that the practice was contrary to the fundamental considerations which the right to privacy and family life was intended to protect, and which Norway from 1953 was legally obliged to respect. In addition, the Committee finds that several laws and regulations were designed or applied in such a way that they contributed to discrimination or did not provide adequate protection against such behaviour, which today would be a violation of human rights.[83]

The Commission also stated that many cases of sterilization of Romani women represented breaches of national laws. In such cases, women were pressured to accept sterilization, or they were sterilized without fulfilling the legal criteria for forced sterilization. If such sterilization had been conducted today, "it would have constituted a gross violation of integrity which fundamentally breaks with the European Convention on Human Rights [Article 3]". However, the European Court of Human Rights found only in 2011 that "illegitimate forced sterilization constituted a violation of Article 3" of the Convention.

The Commission therefore could not conclude that the practice of forced sterilization of Romani people during the post-war period represented violations of the right to privacy or the right not to be subjected to inhuman or degrading treatment as international human rights were interpreted at the time. According to current interpretations, however, such practices represent "serious violations of human rights".[84]

The Commission did not discuss past practices under international criminal law provisions. Nevertheless, it advanced considerably the way of talking about past abuses by introducing human rights language. Whether the Sámi, Kven and Forrest Finns Truth Commission will introduce similar language remained, at the time when this chapter was first published, to be seen. According to its mandate, it shall map former abusive policies, investigate their consequences for individuals and the groups, and propose measures to facilitate reconciliation.

[82] *Ibid.*, p. 74.

[83] *Ibid.* (author's translation).

[84] *Ibid.*, p. 78.

The mandate does not specifically refer to human rights as a point of reference, but in a meeting with the leader of the Commission, Former Head of the Christian Democrat Party in Norway, Mr. Dagfinn Høybråten (1957–), the author was told that the Commission nevertheless would make such assessments.[85]

The only example of considerations known to the author concerning application of international criminal law norms to the past wrongdoing in Norway, is a report published by the Norwegian Helsinki Committee in 2009, drafted by the author. Chapter VI of the report discusses statements by a representative of a Romani organization and by Professor Mr. Knut Aukrust (1953–), a former Head of the Board of the Norwegian Holocaust Centre, that the Romani people in Norway had suffered genocide.[86]

The report concluded that neither legal criteria for crimes against humanity nor for genocide as defined by the Rome Statute of the International Criminal Court was fulfilled. There was not an intent to physically destroy the Romani people or parts of it. Rather, the intention was to assimilate the group and destroy its culture. Proposals were made in the mid-war period for a systematic campaign of sterilizing Romani people, but they were not followed up. Research indicate that the percentage of Romani women being subject to forced sterilization may have been twice the average, but there was not a practice that constituted a "widespread or systematic attack" directed against a civilian population.

The report concluded that,

> there is a great difference between the Norwegian persecution and situations that have so far led to convictions of genocide and crimes against humanity. But it is still frightening that Norwegian policies contained actions that are elements of such crimes. Prevailing views in Norway was akin to thinking that in other contexts has led to the destruction of a population (genocide) or the execution of widespread and brutal attacks on a group of people (crimes against humanity).
>
> In particular, in the 1930s and 1940s, it was argued that the Romani people […] were an inferior race or an inferior mixed race and that one therefore had to prevent childbirth. Fortunately, this

---

85 Meeting with Mr. Dagfinn Høybråten, Chair of the Commission, and Ms. Liss-Ellen Ramstad, Head of the Secretariat of the Commission, 4 December 2019. The Truth and Reconciliation Commission's web site provides further information.

86 Ekeløve-Slydal, 2009, see *supra* note 23, Chapter 6. The report played an important role in convincing Norwegian authorities to establish the 'Romani Truth Commission', see NOU 2015:7, p. 11, see *supra* note 17.

line of thinking did not prevail, and the Mission abandoned it in the late 1940s.[87]

5.4. Past Wrongdoing as Violations of Core Values Protected by Current International Criminal Law and Human Rights

There are several reasons why it is important to describe and evaluate past wrongs as infringements of core values or generic legal goods protected by current international criminal law and human rights norms.[88]

First, by doing so, the seriousness of the past wrongdoing is underlined. Human rights and international criminal law may be the closest we ever get to a global consensus about norms that can protect individuals and groups against the most harmful practices by states or powerful private organizations. Even if wrongdoing took place before a prohibition of its specific actions was established as an international legal norm, the protected legal good or value may have been present and at least accepted by some segments of the population at the time.

Norwegian assimilation policies breached ethical norms, which were based on values that later came to be protected by international human rights norms. Values protecting private and family life, for instance, have old roots in Norwegian Christian traditions, but were set aside in dealing with minority families. There were also voices at the time which specifically referred to humanistic values in criticizing parts of the policies. The goal of assimilating the minorities was nevertheless given preference over the adherence to fundamental societal values; values that later were consolidated and confirmed by international laws after World War II.

Referring to such values and demonstrating how they are protected by modern international criminal and human rights law can be seen as a belated way of providing access to international law. This is not done by a detailed legal analysis, but by defining protected values and then describing how past wrongdoing infringed these values. This is what I mean by *the prism of modern international criminal law and human rights*, referred to in the title of this chapter.

---

87 NOU 2015:7, p. 41, see *supra* note 17.

88 For the approach developed in this chapter, I am in debt to Morten Bergsmo, *Myanmar, Colonial Aftermath, and Access to International Law*, Occasional Paper Series No. 9 (2019), Torkel Opsahl Academic EPublisher, Brussels, 2019 (https://www.toaep.org/ops-pdf/9-bergsmo/). In particular, I took note of Section 2 (pp. 5–14), discussing whether Burma under British rule was subject to colonial practices falling "squarely within the generic legal good or value protected by the prohibition against population transfer into occupied territory? If the answer is in the affirmative, is this not important to recognise if we want to understand the recent situation in Rakhine and the excessive polarisation around accountability?" (p. 11).

It is a way of applying modern law to shed light on past wrongdoing without resorting to technical legal analysis.

Second, even if there were no large-scale military conflicts or violent attacks involved in Norway's colonizing of Sápmi or the implementation of harsh assimilation policies towards its minorities, the underlying ideas and justifications of these actions and policies were often similar to justifications that motivate atrocious crimes, that is, racist and de-humanizing ideas that belittled dignity and worth of the minority groups, their way of life, their language and their culture.

Subsuming past wrongdoing as infringements of specific values protected by modern international law points to the need to look beyond the somewhat undramatic and 'peaceful' context of the actions, to the brutal and detrimental aims behind the conduct.

The small size of the minorities in Norway may have been an important factor in reducing the risk of escalation of armed conflict between government and minority-based forces. Confronted with a powerful state, both the Sámi and the Romani chose to avoid confrontations, developing tactics of escaping rather than fighting back.

It is hard to forget a statement by the Swedish Lutheran priest and missionary Samuel Rheen (1615–1680), who arrived in Jokkmokk in Swedish Sápmi to preach to the Sámi (he served from 1666 to 1671), complaining that the "Lapps are a people who, for the major part, are thoroughly unsuited to waging war, for they lack manly courage".[89] However, it was not lack of manly courage, rather a well-thought out survival strategy in the Arctic climate and conditions that led the Sámi to avoid fighting.[90]

In the following, the author argues that some of the measures implemented by Norwegian authorities to assimilate the Sámi and the Romani clearly represented violations of some of the core values protected by modern international criminal and human rights law, such as territorial and bodily integrity, equal access to the law, and protection of religion, language and culture.

Third, in discussions with members of the groups, the author was often asked what international norms may offer in terms of remedy for past wrongdoing. Not much, the author had to concede, but a determination of the past wrongs as violations of international criminal law and/or human rights may at least point

[89] Kent, 2018, p. 31, see *supra* note 40.

[90] As an ironic note, sometimes the Sámi took part in warfare between Russia, Denmark-Norway and Sweden. They were seen as formidable fighters, moving swiftly on skis while shooting their arrows. See *ibid.*, p. 14.

to the state as the responsible party, the violator, and they and their ancestors as the victims.

The next question was often how Norway can be seen by many (both within Norway and internationally) as a champion of human rights and international criminal law when it has not properly dealt with its own past wrongdoing against its small minorities. There were two parts to the author's answer. First, Norway's past wrongs are not so well-known, and second, Norway is now trying to remedy its past wrongdoing with a range of measures, including by establishing compensation schemes, establishing schemes to support minority language and culture, and having truth and reconciliation processes.

In this way, Norway has started processes to confront and deal with its past wrongs, and thereby also making genuine efforts to deal with double standard perceptions when it supports accountability mechanisms for contemporary international crimes and human rights violations elsewhere.

The Romani Truth Commission concluded that there is little evidence that Norwegian practices represented clear violations of international legal norms as they were interpreted at the time. They did, however, clearly violate the core values protected by current interpretations of contemporary international norms. "In light of today's values, the objectives and measures of the 20th century assimilation policies towards the Romani appear discriminatory and oppressive".[91] Statements like this by a government appointed Commission clearly represent a step in the right direction.

5.4.1. Territorial Integrity of Sámi Land

Norway was, over a protracted period, giving benefits to ethnic Norwegians if they settled in Sápmi, and laws were introduced that discriminated against the Sámi, for example, by requiring Norwegian language skills and citizenship to buy land. There was no military conquest; the territory was not forcedly taken from another state, although there were at times competition between the neighbouring states to dominate, tax and include parts of the territory.

Nevertheless, Norway intruded into an area traditionally used by the Sámi and dominated it. Sápmi was not an empty wilderness but populated by people who had organized themselves and were able to live well from the available resources in this arctic region and trade with other peoples. It is true that the area is "among the most sparsely populated in Europe, and its vast, often snow-covered landscape has long served to attract those enamoured by its natural, unspoiled beauty. Yet such sweeping assertions hardly do justice to the vitality of

[91] NOU 2015:7, p. 78, see *supra* note 17.

the Sámi homeland and the rich culture and history of the Sámi people, who have inhabited the region for thousands of years".[92]

The question here is whether Norway's practices represent a violation of values protected by the international criminal law norm that prohibits the "transfer, directly or indirectly, by the Occupying Power of parts of its own civilian population into the territory it occupies". To answer that question, one has to decide on whether the Norwegian part of Sápmi can be seen as "territory under forms of domination similar to occupation" such as "colonial rule".[93]

This constitutes a complex issue, including whether Norway's 'facilitation' of Norwegian settlement in Sápmi amounted to "transfer, directly or indirectly" of its population. It goes beyond the scope of this chapter to deal with this. It is considerably easier to determine whether Norwegian policies infringed *values* protected by the legal norm. Such values include to avoid undermining the economic survival of the native population or to endanger its separate existence as a distinct ethnic group.[94]

In the case of Sápmi, the criterion could be re-formulated as *preserving the integrity of the land so that the Sámi way of life could be sustained.* Without keeping the vast territory intact, open to reindeer herding or other use which required the territory to be kept without borders or barriers created by private property, vital parts of Sámi economy and culture would suffer. Seen in this perspective, Norwegian settlement practices clearly constituted infringements of such values, as did border regulations with the neighbouring states of Sweden, Finland and Russia. In addition, assimilation policies intended and in practice led to further weakening of Sámi culture and economy.

Some similarities and differences can be observed between what the European colonial powers did in overseas colonies and what the Norwegian state did in Sápmi. I take the British Empire's transfer of Indian citizens to Arakan (now Rakhine State) in colonial Burma as a case of comparison.[95]

---

92 Kent, 2018, p. 1, see *supra* note 40.

93 See Bergsmo, 2019, p. 9, *supra* note 88. General Assembly Resolution 1541 (XV), UN Doc. A/RES/1541(XV), 15 December 1960, Principle IV (https://www.legal-tools.org/doc/hqlf9y/), puts as a precondition for a colonial situation to exist, that the territory in question must be "geographically separate" and that it is "distinct ethnically and/or culturally from the country administering it". This pre-condition is known as the 'salt-water test' of colonialism and excludes integral or adjacent territories that are or may be colonized by a parent state. Norway's colonizing of Sápmi is clearly not an example of 'salt-water colonization', but nevertheless adheres to other criteria of colonialism.

94 See Bergsmo, 2019, p. 11, see *supra* note 88.

95 As outlined in *ibid.*

The most important similarity between the two cases is the consequences. As a result of the transfer or facilitated immigration of foreigners, the native population faced demographic shifts in their territories detrimental to their economy and culture. The existence of the native populations as distinct groups was undermined.

Although the facilitated immigration of Indian people into Burma under British administration and Norwegian people into Sápmi took place prior to the adoption of the international criminal law norm in question (which was first introduced in the 1949 Geneva Convention IV, Article 49(6)), the value protected by the norm was violated in both cases by changing the demographic structure of the respective regions and threatening the existence of the native populations as separate peoples.

When established, the norm was "intended to prevent a practice adopted during the World War II by certain Powers, which transferred portions of their own population to occupied territory for political and racial reasons or in order, as they claimed, to colonize those territories".[96] On this background, the Norwegian facilitation of immigration into Sápmi arguably falls more squarely within the concerns behind the norm than the British case because of its seemingly 'political' and 'racial' nature.

The transfer of civilians into Arakan under British administration did not include British people. This was different from Sápmi, where Norwegian authorities facilitated settlement of Norwegians with an aim of ascertaining control and annexing the area into Norwegian jurisdiction. In this respect, the Norwegian practice is arguably more similar to what Turkey has been doing after its 1974 invasion of the northern part of Cyprus.

As mentioned, the Sámi did not defend their land by force. They, however, put up defence in the form of cultural resistance from the early 1900s. That strategy paid off from the 1970s onward, and they have gradually gained respect for their status as an indigenous people with land rights. An important reinforcement of that defence has been Sámi representatives gaining competence in and making use of international law provisions to strengthen their legal position.

5.4.2. Bodily Integrity

Torture and other forms of mistreatment were not part of the assimilation policies.[97] However, bodily integrity as a value was violated through practices of

[96] Jean S. Pictet (ed.), *Commentary on IV Geneva Convention*, International Committee of the Red Cross, Geneva, 1958, p. 283 (https://www.legal-tools.org/doc/7d971f/).

[97] Torture or inhuman or degrading treatment is prohibited in a range of international human rights treaties. It is a war crime and can also, as part of a systematic or widespread attack on a civilian population, be a crime against humanity.

forced sterilization against Romani people, and by placing Romani children in orphanages and Sámi children in boarding schools with little control of adult abuse. The extent of such abuse – in the form of cruel punishment or sexual abuse – is unknown, but it is well-established that it took place.

International criminal law explicitly prohibits "enforced sterilization" as a crime against humanity.[98] The crime of genocide may consist of preventing childbirth in a group, if the intention is to physically destroy the group.[99] In the *Akayesu* case, a Trial Chamber of the International Criminal Tribunal for Rwanda clarified that forced sterilization may be an example of such measures.[100] It also follows from international human rights norms that such practices should be abolished.

Human rights concerns have played an important role in opposing programmes and legislation permitting or promoting forced sterilization of particular groups of the population. Hitler-Germany's programmes of sterilization contributed to a human rights-based resistance, but even before this time, opponents in the United States and Britain argued on the basis of human rights.[101]

After World War II, the Declaration of the World Conference on Human Rights in Teheran in 1968 was important in adapting human rights to reproductive issues. Principle 16 of the Declaration reads:

> The protection of the family and of the child remains the concern of the international community. Parents have a basic human right to determine freely and responsibly the number and the spacing of their children.[102]

Based on this provision, a collective term for a bundle of rights related to conception, pregnancy and childbirth was developed: 'reproductive rights'.[103]

---

98 Rome Statute of the International Criminal Court, 17 July 1998, Article 7(1)(g) ('ICC Statute') (https://www.legal-tools.org/doc/7b9af9/).

99 *Ibid.*, Article 6(d).

100 International Criminal Tribunal for Rwanda, *Prosecutor v. Jean-Paul Akayesu*, Trial Chamber, Judgment, 2 September 1998, ICTR-96-4-T, para. 507 (https://www.legal-tools.org/doc/b8d7bd/).

101 Daniel J. Kevles, "Eugenics and Human Rights", in *British Medical Journal*, 1999, vol. 319, pp. 435–438.

102 Final Act of the International Conference on Human Rights, UN Doc. A/CONF.32/41, 13 May 1968, p. 4, Principle 16 (https://www.legal-tools.org/doc/46bde6/).

103 The World Health Organization's definition of reproductive rights is: "Reproductive rights rest on the recognition of the basic right of all couples and individuals to decide freely and responsibly the number, spacing and timing of their children and to have the information and means to do so, and the right to attain the highest standard of sexual and reproductive health. They also include the right of all to make decisions concerning reproduction free of discrimination,

Especially the World Health Organization has promoted these rights, arguing that authorities must have a rights-based approach to population issues. A central provision in this context is prohibition of forced sterilization.

There can be little doubt that values inherent in international criminal law prohibitions and human rights norms were infringed upon by practices of forced sterilization that targeted in particular Romani women in Norway. The protected value is that *every woman should be left in control of her fertility, regardless of her ethnicity*.

Research interviews with Romani persons who were placed in the Mission's orphanages during childhood indicate that punishment included "cuff on the ears, pulling by the hair, blows with various implements, such as whip or cane, and confinement over shorter or longer periods of time in small and often dark rooms". The children experienced the use of punishment as unpredictable, disproportionately severe, and often unnecessary and unfair. Some of the interviewees told that they were subject to sexual abuse by adult persons working at the orphanages or connected to it in some way.[104]

Such punishment and abuse clearly represent infringement of values protected by international criminal law and human rights norms that prohibit integrity violations, such as torture and inhuman treatment. Many of the interviewees reported that the abuse they suffered as children had negative consequences for their health and self-respect for the rest of their lives.

5.4.3. Equal Access to the Law[105]

Legislation that did not specifically target Romani but had adverse effects on members of the group due to their way of living, was an important part of the

coercion and violence". See "Reproductive Rights", United Nations Department of Economic and Social Affairs (available on its web site).

104 Anne-Berit Sandvik, "Å være tater i barne- og skolehjem" ["To be Tater (Romani) in orphanages or boarding schools"], in Hvinden (ed.), 2000, pp. 109–113, see *supra* note 27.

105 This right is guaranteed in several core international human rights instruments, such as: (1) Article 7 of the Universal Declaration of Human Rights, 10 December 1948 ('UDHR') (https://www.legal-tools.org/doc/de5d83/), which states: "All are equal before the law and are entitled without any discrimination to equal protection of the law"; (2) Article 1 of the International Convention on the Elimination of All Forms of Racial Discrimination, 21 December 1965 (https://www.legal-tools.org/doc/43a925/), which defines racial discrimination as "any distinction, exclusion, restriction or preference based on race, colour, descent, or national or ethnic origin which has the purpose or effect of nullifying or impairing the recognition, enjoyment or exercise, on an equal footing, of human rights and fundamental freedoms in the political, economic, social, cultural or any other field of public life"; and (3) Article 26 of the International Covenant on Civil and Political Rights, 16 December 1966 ('ICCPR') (https://www.legal-tools.org/doc/2838f3/), which states that "[a]ll persons are equal before the law and are entitled without any discrimination to the equal protection of the law. In this respect,

assimilation policies. The laws listed in Section 5.2.1. above, such as the vagrant law, the child welfare law, as well as laws dealing with trade and animal welfare, were applied in different degrees to target Romani practices.

Legislation and legal practices also played an important role in assimilation policies towards the Sámi, as well as in efforts to take over their land. In particular, legislation that restricted the use of Sámi languages in education and laws that benefited ethnic Norwegians in buying land were instrumental for the Norwegian state to reach its assimilation goals.

Discriminatory attitudes by police was an important effect of the policies. However, the limited research available indicates that police attitudes and actions against minorities varied substantially between police districts. In some districts, the main approach was to hinder 'vagrants' or Romani people from coming and to find ways to expel them as soon as possible. In other districts, the chief of police had more neutral or even accommodating attitudes. In conflicts with non-Romani people, however, the police would often discriminate against the Romani and give the other party (a Norwegian or a person belonging to another nationality) the benefit of the doubt.[106]

In general, constitutional norms of equality before the law and equal access to the law often failed to influence the handling of individual cases. While the police did not systematically persecute Romani, "personal and discretionary application of the law by the police contributed to weakening legal protection of the Romani people at the individual level".[107] Often, police intervention in cases involving Romani people depended on available resources in the police district. If a 'vagrant' left the district, many chiefs of police were eager to close any cases related to that person.[108]

While the police often treated Romani people with discrimination, courts seem in general to have taken a more neutral stance, although examples of stigmatizing attitudes influencing the outcome of criminal cases do exist.[109]

---

the law shall prohibit any discrimination and guarantee to all persons equal and effective protection against discrimination on any ground such as race, colour, sex, language, religion, political or other opinion, national or social origin, property, birth or other status".

[106] For an overview of some of the issues related to police and courts dealing with cases involving Romani people, see Chalak Kaveh, "Taterne/romanifolket i det norske politi- og rettsvesenet 1900–1980: En studie av politiets og domstolenes praktisering av lovverket" ["Romani people in the Norwegian police and courts: A study of police and court application of the legislation"], in NOU 2015:7, pp. 240–308, see *supra* note 17.

[107] *Ibid.*, pp. 305–306.

[108] *Ibid.*

[109] *Ibid.*

There are many individual accounts by Sámi and Romani that people were misled, discriminated or otherwise badly treated by the police. Mistrust towards Norwegian authorities remain widespread among Romani people, and for many it remains illusory that the police or courts could provide justice. According to recent research, Sámi women report less frequently than ethnic Norwegian women cases of domestic violence to the police. One of the reasons may be that many Sámi still lack confidence in the larger Norwegian community as a result of the assimilation and Norwegianization policy of the past. This particularly affects meetings between those affected by violence with a Sámi background and non-Sámi employees in health and social services and police.[110]

The lack of trust in police and other public institutions among Sámi and Romani is in stark contrast to average perceptions among Norwegian citizens about these institutions, characterized by high levels of trust.[111]

In conclusion, it is well-documented that Romani and Sámi suffered from legislation that was discriminatory or applied in discriminatory ways, from prejudices among police, and to some degree (but less) from similar negative attitudes in courts. There is, however, also evidence that legislation, courts and even police at times moderated the effects of the assimilation policies.

In general, the groups still have little trust in judicial institutions and legal protection of their rights, confirming that values protected by human rights provisions ensuring equal access to the law and non-discrimination in legal matters were violated during the long period of assimilation policies.

Equality before the laws is a deeply ingrained Norwegian value, with roots in pre-Christian societies. However, this value was not applied to Norway's minorities during a protracted period of assimilation.

5.4.4. Protection of Privacy and Family

Both the Sámi and the Romani experienced widespread disrespect for private and family life as these rights are currently understood.[112]

---

[110] Norwegian Centre for Violence and Traumatic Stress Studies, *Om du tør å spørre, tør folk å svare: Hjelpeapparatets og politiets erfaringer med vold i nære relasjoner i samiske samfunn* [*If you dare to ask, people dare to answer: The experiences of the health services and police with violence in close relationships in Sámi communities*], Norwegian Centre for Violence and Traumatic Stress Studies, Oslo, 2017, p. 8.

[111] According to annual surveys, around 80 per cent of the population in Norway has high or very high thrust in the police. See Politidirektoratet [Police Directorate], "Innbyggerundersøkelsen" ["Inhabitant survey"], Norwegian Police, 2014–2019.

[112] The right to privacy and family life is stated in Article 12 of UDHR, see *supra* note 105: "No one shall be subjected to arbitrary interference with his privacy, family, home or correspondence, nor to attacks upon his honour and reputation. Everyone has the right to the protection of the law against such interference or attacks". Similar wording can be found in Article 17 of

Sámi children were sent away from their family to boarding schools where only Norwegian was spoken. Many of them only knew a Sámi language when they entered school, and for many of them it took years to fully adapt to a foreign learning environment.

Romani children were taken from their parents and placed in orphanages or Norwegian foster families. In many cases, contact with their biological parents were prohibited and no information about their background were given when they asked.

According to the Romani Truth Commission, taking children away from their parents was among the key measures of the assimilation policy:[113]

> Measures against children were a key instrument in the assimilation of the Tater/Romani people. Children were taken away from their parents and placed in orphanages and foster care, and custody was transferred to the Mission. From 1900, in the course of two generations, almost one third of the children born in Tater/Romani families were taken away by the Child Welfare Services. This had dramatic consequences for the minority as a whole.
>
> The usual justification for separating the children from their parents was that the parents' lifestyle was harmful to the children. The Mission also deliberately severed ties between parents and children. The situation for the children who were taken away, varied. Many children suffered neglect, maltreatment and/or abuse. The consequences for many of the children were unstable, unpredictable and insecure childhoods. The Committee concludes that the widespread practice of separating the children from their families was clearly incompatible with the right to privacy, as this is understood today.
>
> The same applies to several aspects of the treatment at Svanviken labour colony up to the 1970s. At Svanviken, restrictive control was exerted on the residents' daily life. This included for instance controlling the residents' correspondence. In the period 1950-1970, 40% of the women who were placed in Svanviken were sterilised while they were there. The Committee is not aware of any other institution in Norway that has such a high degree of sterilisation.

ICCPR, see *supra* note 105. Moreover, Article 10(1) of International Covenant on Economic, Social and Cultural Rights, 16 December 1966 (https://www.legal-tools.org/doc/06b87e/), states that the "widest possible protection and assistance should be accorded to the family, which is the natural and fundamental group unit of society, particularly for its establishment and while it is responsible for the care and education of dependent children".

113 NOU 2015:7 English Summary, p. 3, see *supra* note 3.

Fundamental values ingrained in Norwegian traditions, and protected by modern human rights, were disregarded in the context of Norway's assimilation policies during a large part of the twentieth century. The main value places the responsibility for the upbringing and education of the child on its biological parents. Only in exceptional cases can this responsibility be shifted to others, when it is necessary in order to protect the well-being of the child.

In the Norwegian context, the most relevant international human rights provision is to be found in the European Convention on Human Rights, Article 8, which states that "[e]veryone has the right to respect for his private and family life, his home and his correspondence". These rights can only be restricted "in accordance with the law" and if the restriction "is necessary in a democratic society for the sake of national security, public security or the country's economic well-being, to prevent disorder or crime, to protect health or morality, or to protect the rights and freedoms of others". Typically, one will assess whether forced transfer of custody is taken in accordance with a statutory procedure, whether one has adequately taken into account the best interests of the child, whether the parents have been involved in the process, whether their right to meet with the child is being respected, and whether their right to correspondence with the child has been respected.

No cases against Norway for transferring Romani children and breaking all contacts with their biological parents were submitted to the European Court of Human Rights. In a few other Norwegian cases, the first from 1996 (*Adele Johansen v. Norway*), the Court found that even if the transfer of custody was justified, given the facts of the case, breaking all contacts between the child and its biological parents was not.

Estimates indicate that about 400 transfers of custody of Romani children took place in Norway after the European Convention on Human Rights entered into force and became binding on Norway.[114] How many of these cases would have been found to be in violation of the right to private and family life today is not possible to say. There can be little doubt, however, that many of the cases amounted to violations of values protected by the right to privacy and family.

5.4.5. Protection of Religion, Language and Culture

Both Sámi and Romani peoples were denied freedom of religion or belief.[115] Their traditional believes were repressed, stigmatized and sometimes used to

---

[114] Ekeløve-Slydal, 2009, p. 18, see *supra* note 23.

[115] Freedom of religion or belief is protected by several international human rights instruments, such as UDHR Article 18, see *supra* note 105; ICCPR, Article 18, see *supra* note 105; European Convention on Human Rights, 4 November 1950, Article 9 ('ECHR') (https://www.legal-tools.org/doc/8267cb/). ECHR Article 9(1) states that "[e]veryone has the right to freedom of

justify assimilation policies and actions. An irony is that for both groups, versions of Christianity later became a mobilizing force against state repression and in building more self-esteem. Some of the priests involved in missionary activities in Sápmi also contributed significantly to documenting Sámi languages, since they believed that the gospel and the Bible should be available for the Sámi in their mother tongues.

Such positive contributions can, nevertheless, never justify the systematic infringements of values inherent in human rights norms that any individual should be free to choose his own religious or philosophical beliefs. Disregard for such values was at the core of the assimilation policies.

For both groups, Norwegianization meant that they were *pressured* to give up their own language.[116] It was not prohibited to use the languages, but they were marginalized in education and in contact with official institutions. Many Sámi refused to give up their language, while the Romani kept parts of their language as a hidden tool to communicate without Norwegian authorities and society being able to understand it. The status and survival chances of the

---

thought, conscience and religion; this right includes freedom to change his religion or belief and freedom, either alone or in community with others and in public or private, to manifest his religion or belief, in worship, teaching, practice and observance".

On the other hand, ICCPR Article 18(2) states that "[n]o one shall be subject to coercion which would impair his freedom to have or to adopt a religion or belief of his choice". The European Court of Human Rights recognized that religious freedom includes efforts to "convince" others, but this "does not extend to abusive behaviour such as applying unacceptable pressure, or actual harassment". See European Court of Human Rights, Research Division, "Overview of the Court's case-law on freedom of religion", 31 October 2013, para. 18. Also ILO Convention 169, Article 5 (a), see *supra* note 5, states that "[i]n applying the provisions of this Convention: the social, cultural, religious and spiritual values and practices of these peoples shall be recognised and protected, and due account shall be taken of the nature of the problems which face them both as groups and as individuals".

[116] A main international human rights reference point is ICCPR, Article 27, see *supra* note 105, which states that "[i]n those States in which ethnic, religious or linguistic minorities exist, persons belonging to such minorities shall not be denied the right, in community with the other members of their group, to enjoy their own culture, to profess and practise their own religion, or to use their own language". Aside from this provision, UDHR, ICCPR and ECHR do not refer to the protection of language and culture as separate rights like the right to privacy and family life or freedom of religion. However, there are provisions that prohibit discrimination based on, *inter alia*, language or culture. The ILO Convention 169, Article 28(1), see *supra* note 5, states that "[c]hildren belonging to the peoples concerned shall, wherever practicable, be taught to read and write in their own indigenous language or in the language most commonly used by the group to which they belong", and Article 28(3) states that "[m]easures shall be taken to preserve and promote the development and practice of the indigenous languages of the peoples concerned". In a European context, the Framework Convention for the Protection of National Minorities and the European Charter for Regional or Minority Languages, 1 February 1998, firmly establishes the right to minority language and culture.

languages were nevertheless considerably weakened, and while Sámi languages today may have gained a stronger position, it remains an open question whether the Romani language will survive in Norway.[117]

Both Sámi and Romani ways of life were portrayed as uncivilized and repressed by the Norwegian state and the Church.[118] Both cultures survived to a degree, however, and have influenced Norwegian mainstream culture heavily without many Norwegians being aware of or appreciating it. Recently, Sámi music, crafts and other cultural products have gained more appreciation. Romani culture, however, is still largely invisible in Norwegian society.

5.5. Measures Initiated to Repair Harm Caused by Past Wrongdoing

In the second half of the twentieth century, Norwegian policies started to change. Attention was drawn by media and public discourse to the problems endured by people belonging to the minorities due to the previous policies. In particular, the Sámi people became more assertive in efforts to maintain its culture through the use of Sámi languages in schools and media and by protecting their reindeer pastures.

Norwegian authorities have initiated a range of measures to repair damage caused by past wrongdoing and promote reconciliation, such as compensation schemes and support to Sámi, Kven and Romani cultures and languages. Some 95 per cent of the territory of Norway's northernmost county Finnmark has been transferred to a specialized agency ('*Finnmarkseiendommen*') which takes decisions on natural resources and territorial issues. Three of six members of the board of the agency are appointed by the Sámi Parliament.

Legislation that facilitated the assimilation policies has been repealed, and laws, regulations or ratification of international conventions that protect minority language and culture have been put in place. Norway has strong constitutional and legislative protection of all categories of human rights and has

[117] For reporting on and assessment of Norway's minority language policies and the situation of the languages, see Council of Europe, "Reports and Recommendations", on *Council of Europe, Norway* (available on its web site). Norwegian authorities have supported several projects to document Romani language and to write books in Romani. The University of Oslo has created an online Norwegian-Romani dictionary.

[118] ICCPR, Article 27, see *supra* note 105, forms the basis for human rights norms protecting minority cultures. ICESCR also contains provisions that safeguard cultural rights, such as Article 6 and Article 15. ILO Convention 169, see *supra* note 5, includes many provisions on cultural rights such as Articles 4 and 13. Article 4(1) of ILO Convention 169, see *supra* note 5, states that "special measures shall be adopted as appropriate for safeguarding the persons, institutions, property, labour, cultures and environment of the peoples concerned". For Norway's policies regarding minority culture, the European Framework Convention for the Protection of National Minorities plays a particularly important role.

established several national Ombud institutions and a National Human Rights Institution to protect them.[119]

While a few commentators have argued that justice mechanisms should become part of the restorative process, this has not happened. Some also argue that, while Norway has been a strong supporter internationally of justice mechanisms, it has been reluctant to apply such measures domestically. Instead, the government established an official truth and reconciliation process for the Romani people (2011–2015) and in 2018, Parliament established a similar process for the Sámi, the Kvens and the Forest Finns. The latter process is ongoing at the time of writing, with consultations and interviews with individuals belonging to the minorities, historical research, and other measures. At the time when this chapter was first published, the Commission was scheduled to end its work on 1 September 2022, with the submission to Parliament of a report with its findings.

The Romani Truth Commission was established by Royal (that is, governmental) Decree on 3 January 2011.[120] The Commission was mandated to study and describe the policies and measures towards Tater or Romani people since the 1800s, with special emphasis on the objectives, implementation and instruments of these policies.

The Commission was also requested to consider the findings in light of Norwegian legislation and international human rights norms, and whether the findings form a basis to consider new measures that may contribute to justice and reconciliation. The initiative to establish the Commission came from representatives of the Romani people themselves, and was supported, among others, by the Norwegian Helsinki Committee. The mandate was updated in 2013, at the same time as the Commission and its Secretariat changed leadership and composition.[121]

---

[119] For more information, see the web pages of the Parliamentary Ombudsman, the Equality and Anti-Discrimination Ombud, and the Ombud for Children. The National Human Rights Institution has a special focus on Sámi and minority rights, with a separate office in Kaotokeino, Finnmark.

[120] The official name of the Commission was (in the author's translation) 'The Committee to investigate implementation of the policy towards the Taters/Romani people', referred to in official documents as the 'Tater/Romani Committee'. However, in interviews and private talks, its second leader, Mr. Knut Vollebæk, often referred to it as the 'Tater/Romani Truth Commission'.

[121] NOU 2015:7 English Summary, p. 6, see *supra* note 3. The first leader of the Commission was Mr. Asbjørn Eide (1933–), the former Director of the Norwegian Centre of Human Rights and a former member of the United Nations Sub-Commission on the Promotion and the Protection of Human Rights (1981–2003), where he was one of the advocates for the establishment of the Working Group on Indigenous Populations. After stepping down as the Commission's leader, Mr. Eide remained a member of the Commission.

Pursuant to the Commission's interpretation of its mandate, it should "investigate the policies towards Tater/Romani people with emphasis on how these policies have worked, the present situation, and what can build trust and good relations between the minority and the society at large".[122]

The Commission consisted of 10 members with backgrounds in politics, academic research and law, as well as two representatives of the Romani people. A secretariat was established with three full-time staff, and a resource group with representatives of four Romani organizations and one representative of the Norwegian Helsinki Committee.

The main methods of the Commission were to conduct public meetings with members of the Romani people, individual interviews, undertake or commission archival research, and internal discussions and consultations with the resource group.

In the author's assessment, the Commission presented ground-breaking research and a balanced and well-written report containing topical recommendations for further improvements of Norwegian policies. During its time of functioning, the Commission received some media attention and its leaders (first Mr. Eide and then Mr. Vollebæk) and some of its members published topical articles in some of the most read Norwegian newspapers.

The Ministry responsible for minority policies followed up the report after it was presented on 1 June 2015, with a series of open meetings to further introduce its findings and recommendations to members of the group. It soon became clear, however, that Romani people were in strong disagreement with the content and the wisdom of its recommendations. Some argued that the Commission had failed to reach out to important parts of the Romani people, namely those who were not members of Romani organizations. These were people who preferred to live 'discretely' with their Romani identity, and they did not want to be exposed by the Commission or by Romani organizations funded by the state. There was a fear among some that their children would suffer renewed bullying in schools if their Romani identity became known.

Minorities are seldom monolithic in views and approaches to state authorities and, given the complex composition of the Romani people in Norway, it was to be expected that there would be different views on the truth process in their ranks. The Commission and the ongoing debates about its conclusions nevertheless managed to engage people in discussions on their priorities and visions for how to develop Romani identity while being fully integrated in modern Norwegian society.

122 *Ibid.*

The Sámi, Kven and Forest Finn Truth and Reconciliation Commission also faces similar challenges, tackling differing viewpoints from sub-groups and individuals belonging to the minorities. The fact that the Sámi has official status as Norway's indigenous people, while Kven and Forest Finns have status as national minorities may add to these challenges.

There are, however, well-founded hopes that such challenges can be dealt with. The Commission's work represents a unique opportunity to come to terms with some of the darkest chapters of Norwegian history, giving harmed people a chance to speak about their grievances, and to discuss remedies for a better future.

5.6. Conclusions

Norwegian assimilation policies inflicted pain and suffering on large numbers of persons belonging to the Sámi and the Romani peoples. The policies included violations of values protected by modern international criminal law as well as human rights norms.

Norway's intrusion into and efforts to dominate Sápmi may be seen through the lens of European colonialism, even though Norway itself, until independence in 1905, was dominated by its Scandinavian neighbouring states. The colonial logic of instrumentalization of natural resources and humans, designing education with the aim of producing obedient and hard-working subjects, may be detected in Norway's earlier relationship with Sápmi and the Sámi, further underlining the importance of coming to terms with past abuses.

In later years, Norwegian authorities have shown genuine will to address some of the harms caused by past wrongdoing. Much remains to be done in order to achieve reconciliation and to rebuild minority cultures in Norway. The past assimilation policies were effective in destroying culture, language – and self-esteem. Repairing this harm is easier said than done. Norwegian authorities should nevertheless be given credit for at least trying to do the right thing.

6

ICTY Shifts Have Made Its Credibility Quake*

6.1. Changing Direction at the Expense of Victims and Accountability

For many victims of core international crimes in the 1990s in the former Yugoslavia, the International Criminal Tribunal for the Former Yugoslavia ('ICTY') served as the hope for justice. Victims and civil society actors sought accountability from the ICTY for those bearing the greatest responsibility for the crimes. Acquittals in 2012–2013 of high-ranking Croat and Serb officials – Ante Gotovina, Mladen Markač, Momčilo Perišić, Jovica Stanišić, and Franko Simatović – shook this aspiration and generated concerns about the quality of the legacy of the ICTY.

Carl Bildt, former Swedish foreign minister, expressed a feeling shared by many: "It is becoming increasingly difficult to see the consistency or logic in the different judgments".[1] Some went further, claiming that the acquittals "might eventually emasculate the capacity of the institutions of international justice to bring to justice the highest-ranking persons responsible for heinous war crimes. Only the actual killers will be punished, not the mass murderers".[2]

Criticism of the acquittals was supplemented by irrefutable evidence of deep disunity among ICTY judges. Frederik Harhoff, then ICTY Judge, sent an e-mail on 6 June 2013 to 56 friends, questioning the Tribunal's credibility, in an expression of grave personal concern. International media reported extensively.[3] Much of the subsequent criticism focused on the role of the then ICTY President Theodor Meron (later President of the International Residual Mechanism for

* This chapter was first published as Gunnar M. Ekeløve-Slydal, "ICTY Shifts Have Made Its Credibility Quake", FICHL Policy Brief Series No. 49 (2016), Torkel Opsahl Academic EPublisher, Brussels, 2016 (https://www.toaep.org/pbs-pdf/49-slydal/), on 8 April 2016, and does not consider subsequent case law.

1 Chuck Sudetic, "War crimes in the former Yugoslavia: Two puzzling judgments in The Hague", *The Economist*, 1 June 2013 (https:/www.legal-tools.org/doc/04d6c8/).

2 See *ibid.*, comment by Chuck Sudetic. Sudetic is a respected war crimes journalist and co-author with Carla Del Ponte of *Madame Prosecutor: Confrontations with Humanity's Worst Criminals and the Culture of Impunity. A Memoir*, The Other Press, 2009 (https://www.legal-tools.org/doc/a33e23/).

3 See, *inter alia*, "U.N. Court Acquits 2 Serbs of War Crimes", *The New York Times*, 30 May 2013, and "Hague Judge Faults Acquittals of Serb and Croat Commanders", *The New York Times*, 14 June 2013. An English translation of Judge Harhoff's letter is available at https://www.legal-tools.org/doc/e3d89c/.

Criminal Tribunals ('MICT')), alleging that he sought to unduly influence other Tribunal judges. The criticism extended to the International Criminal Tribunal for Rwanda ('ICTR') which shares its Appeals Chamber with the ICTY.[4]

Changes in judicial interpretation at a late stage in the life of the ICTY affecting the ability of the Tribunal to hold leaders accountable, combined with an apparent power struggle between an American Tribunal president and a Danish judge, leading to the exclusion of the latter, has not only revealed serious disunity, but has reduced trust in the Tribunal in ways which disorients victims, their families, and the wider struggle against impunity. The situation far exceeds normal doctrinal controversy. Regrettably, there remains a strong, unanswered need for President Meron to take responsibility for this unfortunate situation. My organization, the Norwegian Helsinki Committee, has presented this view in a letter to President Meron.

6.2. ICTY Judges Pioneered Joint Criminal Enterprise in Contemporary International Criminal Law

Finding suitable modes of liability for persons in senior positions was one of the ICTY's challenges from the start of its substantive work in July 1994. Such persons are rarely involved in the actual physical commission of crimes, but may bear responsibility through their leadership role. According to the ICTY Statute, military commanders and political leaders can be responsible for crimes committed by their subordinates on the grounds of, *inter alia*, "aiding and abetting"[5] and "superior responsibility".[6] In addition, the ICTY has applied the so-called joint criminal enterprise ('JCE') doctrine, which has its origin in trials before national courts and international tribunals in the aftermath of the World War II.[7] It considers a participant in an organized criminal group with a common plan or purpose liable for crimes committed by the group, provided the requisite *actus reus* and *mens rea* are satisfied.

The ICTY Statute does not explicitly refer to JCE, but ICTY jurisprudence introduced it in the *Tadić* case in 1999. Duško Tadić, a former local leader of the Serbian Democratic Party ('SDS') and a member of Bosnian Serb paramilitary forces, was found guilty by the Appeals Chamber because of his active participation in a group that killed five men. He shared a common plan, design or

4 Among contested judgments, the Appeals Chamber acquitted Justin Mugenzi (Minister of Trade during the 1994 genocide) and Prosper Mugiraneza (Minister of Public Service) on 4 February 2013. They had been convicted at trial to 30 years of imprisonment.

5 Statute of the International Criminal Tribunal for the Former Yugoslavia, 25 May 1993, Article 7(1) (https://www.legal-tools.org/doc/b4f63b/).

6 *Ibid.*, Article 7(3).

7 See ICTY, *Prosecutor v. Tadić*, Appeals Chamber, Judgment, 15 July 1999, IT-94-1-A, paras. 189, 191 and 195 ('*Tadić* Appeal Judgement') (https://www.legal-tools.org/doc/8efc3a/).

purpose with the group.[8] When formulating the JCE doctrine, the Appeals Chamber held that it is part of customary international law.[9] It also said that it is dictated by the object and purpose of the Statute,[10] and that it is in line with the collective nature of many international crimes.[11] Over the years, although sometimes criticized, JCE has been an important concept of attributing criminal responsibility for crimes to persons in leading positions.

6.3. ICTY Judges Started to Acquit

The criticism of the acquittals points to a resulting failure to hold political or military leaders accountable and lack of judicial consistency.[12] Such consistency is important to determine the content of law and establish predictability, as the ICTY has itself emphasized.[13] Three of the acquittals stand out.

Case 1: The ICTY Prosecutor had charged Ante Gotovina, Mladen Markač, and Ivan Čermak with war crimes and crimes against humanity committed during 'Operation Storm'. According to the indictment, they ordered unlawful artillery attacks and created a climate of impunity through a failure to prevent, investigate or punish crimes committed by members of the Special Police against Serb civilians.[14] The Trial Chamber found Gotovina and Markač guilty for their participation in a JCE, with the common plan to expel the Serb civilian population from the Krajina.[15] Gotovina was sentenced to 24 years of imprisonment, Markač to 18 years, while Čermak was acquitted. The Appeals Chamber contested the evidence of the existence of a JCE. The Trial Chamber had based its conclusion on an overall assessment of several "mutually-reinforcing findings", but primarily on the unlawfulness of artillery attacks against four cities.

8 *Ibid.*, para. 231.

9 *Ibid.*, para. 220.

10 See Article 18 of the Vienna Convention on the Law of Treaties, 23 May 1969 (https://www.legal-tools.org/doc/6bfcd4/).

11 On JCE, see *Tadić* Appeal Judgement, paras. 189–204, see *supra* note 7.

12 See, for instance, Janine Natalya Clark: "Courting Controversy: The ICTY's Acquittal of Croatian Generals Gotovina and Markač", in *Journal of International Criminal Justice*, 2013, vol. 11, no. 2, pp. 399–423, and Bridget Conley, "Acquittals at the ICTY and the Limitations of a Legal Approach to Conflict", in *Reinventing Peace*, 14 June 2013 (https://www.legal-tools.org/doc/1b4b22/).

13 See, for example, ICTY, *Prosecutor v. Stakić*, Appeals Chamber, Judgment, 22 March 2006, IT-97-24-A (https://www.legal-tools.org/doc/09f75f/), where *consistency* is given as reason for employing the JCE doctrine rather than a different mode of co-perpetration that the Trial Chamber had applied.

14 'Operation Storm' was a Croat military action conducted in July–September 1995 in order to take control of territory in Krajina in Croatia, an area traditionally populated by Serbs.

15 ICTY, *Prosecutor v. Gotovina et al.*, Trial Chamber, Judgment (Volume II), 15 April 2011, IT-06-90-T, paras. 2314, 2368–75, 2578–87 (https://www.legal-tools.org/doc/86922c/).

The Appeals Chamber found, however, that the artillery attacks were lawful.[16] It therefore acquitted Gotovina and Markač on 16 November 2012 (in a 3–2 decision).

Case 2: Momčilo Perišić, former Chief of the Yugoslav Army General Staff, was charged with murder, extermination, inhumane acts, attacks on civilians, and persecution as crimes against humanity and/or violations of the laws or customs of war. The crimes took place in the territory of Bosnia-Herzegovina and Croatia between August 1993 and November 1995.[17] Perišić was charged, *inter alia*, with aiding and abetting crimes against Bosnian Muslims and Bosnian Croats in the Bosnian towns of Sarajevo and Srebrenica due to his role in facilitating military and logistical assistance to the Army of 'Republika Srpska'.[18] The Trial Chamber found Perišić guilty and sentenced him to 27 years of imprisonment. The Appeals Chamber, however, stated that aiding and abetting requires a close link between the assistance provided and the particular criminal activities. The assistance must be "specifically" – rather than "in some way" – directed towards the crimes.[19] The 28 February 2013 *Perišić* Appeal Judgment held that the evidence in the case was not enough to establish the specific direction of the assistance towards the crimes, and acquitted him. In a further development, the ICTY Prosecutor, on 3 February 2014, filed a motion for reconsideration of the *Perišić* Appeal Judgment. The Judgment based itself on flawed requirements and could not stand, the Prosecutor argued.[20] On 20 March 2014, the Appeals Chamber denied the motion.[21]

Case 3: The Prosecutor charged Serbian General and former chief of the Serbian Intelligence Service Jovica Stanišić and his subordinate Franko Simatović with persecution, murder, deportation, and forcible transfer from 1 April 1991 to 31 December 1995 against Croats, Bosnian Muslims, Bosnian Croats, and other non-Serb civilians in large areas of Croatia and Bosnia-Herzegovina. The primary mode of liability was participation in a JCE. The 13 May 2013 Trial Judgment found both men not guilty for lack of conclusive evidence of

16 ICTY, *Prosecutor v. Gotovina and Markač*, Appeals Chamber, Judgment, 16 November 2012, IT-06-90-A, paras. 91–96 (https://www.legal-tools.org/doc/03b685/).

17 ICTY, *Prosecutor v. Perišić*, Appeals Chamber, Judgment, 28 February 2013, IT-04-81-A (https://www.legal-tools.org/doc/f006ba/).

18 *Ibid.*, para. 3.

19 *Ibid.*, paras. 25–36.

20 ICTY, Office of the Prosecutor, "Statement of the ICTY Prosecutor Serge Brammertz in Relation to the Motion for Reconsideration Submitted by the Prosecution in the Perisic Case", 3 February 2014 (https://www.legal-tools.org/doc/195e1f/).

21 ICTY, *Prosecutor v. Perišić*, Appeals Chamber, Decision on Motion for Reconsideration, 20 March 2014, IT-04-81-A (https://www.legal-tools.org/doc/6cdbd5/).

participation in the JCE. It further applied the specific direction requirement to clear them of aiding and abetting the crimes.[22]

The contested judgments in the *Perišić* case, and partly in the *Stanišić and Simatović* case, concern legal doctrine; namely, whether specific direction is a requisite element of aiding and abetting. On 23 January 2014, the *Šainović et al.* Appeal Judgment unequivocally overturned the *Perišić* view. According to the ruling, aiding and abetting "consists of practical assistance, encouragement, or moral support which has a substantial effect on the perpetration of the crime".[23] Specific direction of crimes is *not* a requirement, it held.[24] This view has been upheld in subsequent appeals.[25]

The conclusion of the *Gotovina and Markač* Appeal Judgment is far-reaching. War crimes were extensively discussed after 'Operation Storm', and there have been a number of cases before Croatian courts. However, according to the ICTY's conclusion there is not enough evidence to say that the Croat leadership at the time had a plan to empty the Krajina of Serbs.

The outcome of these cases is consequential for the wider understanding of the 1992–1995 wars in Bosnia-Herzegovina. It means that the ICTY to date has not convicted any officials of the Serbian government for involvement in atrocities in Bosnia-Herzegovina. There is a prevailing and very well-documented view that Bosnian Serb military and paramilitary units attacking the civilian population in Bosnia were heavily dependent on support from Belgrade.[26]

[22] ICTY, *Prosecutor v. Stanišić and Simatović*, Trial Chamber, Judgment, 30 May 2013, IT-03-69-T, Volume I (https://www.legal-tools.org/doc/066e67/) and Volume II (https://www.legal-tools.org/doc/698c43/).

[23] ICTY, *Prosecutor v. Šainović et al.*, Appeals Chamber, Judgment, 23 January 2014, IT-05-87-A (https://www.legal-tools.org/doc/81ac8c/). The "specific direction" requirement is discussed at pp. 1643 *et seq*. The quotation is from para. 1649.

[24] On this point, the *Šainović et al.* Appeal Judgment is also in line with the *Taylor* Appeal Judgment of the Special Court for Sierra Leone, see *Prosecutor v. Taylor*, Appeals Chamber, Judgment, 26 September 2013, SCSL-03-01-A, paras. 471–481 (https://www.legal-tools.org/doc/3e7be5/).

[25] See ICTY, *Prosecutor v. Popović et al.*, Appeals Chamber, Judgment, 30 January 2015, IT-05-88-A (https://www.legal-tools.org/doc/4c28fb/), *Prosecutor v. Stanišić and Simatović*, Appeals Chamber, Judgment, 9 December 2015, IT-03-69-A (https://www.legal-tools.org/doc/198c16/), and *Prosecutor v. Nyiramasuhuko et al.*, Appeals Chamber, Judgment, 14 December 2015, ICTR-98-42-A (https://www.legal-tools.org/doc/b3584e/).

[26] See ICTY, *Prosecutor v. Tadić*, Appeals Chamber, Judgment, 15 July 1999, IT-94-1-A, paras. 83–162 (https://www.legal-tools.org/doc/8efc3a/). In a far-reaching conclusion, the Appeals Chamber found that "the armed forces of the Republika Srpska were to be regarded as acting under the overall control of and on behalf of the FRY [the Federal Republic of Yugoslavia (Serbia and Montenegro)]".

Such an outcome of the lengthy processes in The Hague will certainly remain contested.

6.4. Perceived Impartiality as a Binding Legal Requirement

A major point of contention in Judge Harhoff's well-known e-mail was the suggestion that the Tribunal's doctrinal shift came about as a result of pressure exerted by President Meron on colleagues. Such a suspicion would be serious for any court, in particular the ICTY which from its inception has been accused of bias by actors in the territorial states under its jurisdiction. Judge Harhoff contended that President Meron put "tenacious pressure on his colleagues" in the *Gotovina and Markač* and *Perišić* cases to achieve acquittals, and raised the question whether the President himself had been under pressure from American and Israeli military circles.

Further to a motion filed by Vojislav Šešelj, a special Chamber appointed by the then ICTY Vice President Carmel Agius – now ICTY President – decided that, as a consequence of his e-mail, Judge Harhoff was disqualified to be a judge in the *Šešelj* case. According to the decision, the letter showed bias in favour of conviction of Serb military commanders without evidentiary basis.[27] Interestingly, dissenting Judge Liu Daqun concluded that the letter seen in its context did not indicate such bias. On 7 October 2013, the special Chamber – by majority, Judge Liu dissenting – rejected a request filed by the Prosecution to reconsider its previous decision.[28]

There has been considerable academic discussion whether the disqualification of Judge Harhoff was justified or not. There still exists a pervasive view that he was forced to leave the ICTY, not because his criticism of the acquittals was unfounded, but rather because he breached unwritten rules of collegial loyalty.

Given the precarious situation at the ICTY, the question of bias on the part of President Meron has also been raised. Indeed, if the test applied so swiftly to Judge Harhoff – whether a reasonable, informed outside observer, with knowledge of all the relevant circumstances would apprehend bias – is applied to President Meron in cases where the mode of liability is JCE or aiding and

[27] ICTY, *Prosecutor v. Šešelj*, Trial Chamber, Decision on Defence Motion for Disqualification of Judge Frederik Harhoff and Report to the Vice-President, 28 August 2013, IT-03-67-T, para. 13 (https://www.legal-tools.org/doc/5b4aa1/).

[28] ICTY, *Prosecutor v. Šešelj*, Trial Chamber, Decision on Prosecution Motion for Reconsideration of Decision on Disqualification, Requests for Clarification, and Motion on Behalf of Stanišić and Župljanin, 7 October 2013, IT-03-67-T (https://www.legal-tools.org/doc/20a960/).

abetting, it is regrettably not clear that he would pass.[29] There exists a troublesome picture of a president who has gone beyond his powers and role.[30]

6.5. Institutional Responsibility and External Expectations

We may well argue that wrongful convictions are a far greater scandal than incorrect acquittals. *In dubio pro reo* is the right approach of any criminal court. However, the problem we are facing at the ICTY differs: it concerns a shift in the evaluation of evidence and the quality of legal analysis. In fact, it represents ways of undermining trust in the independence of judges that President Meron has described well, stating that when "judges are independent and act in accordance with the law, their decisions have a certain predictability, because they are based on existing law, judicial precedent, and the unbiased application of that law to the facts at issue".[31]

Victims and human rights organizations have looked to The Hague for justice and for a reliable historic record after the extremely abusive armed conflicts of the 1990s in the former Yugoslavia. No other institution represented such a degree of quality of documentation, evidence and legal argument, they believed.

The 2012–2013 acquittals and the split among the judges on key points of legal analysis have put the ICTY's ability to fulfil its mandate at risk. Even though the latest Appeals Chamber decisions, at the time when this chapter was first published, seem to have 'corrected' some mistakes, concerns remain whether President Meron enjoys the perception of independence and impartiality required by both the Tribunal and MICT to properly fulfil their mandates.

My organization – as well as many other actors who we have consulted – has come to the painful conclusion that there is persistent reason to doubt the impartiality of President Meron. Regrettably, this doubt has a cancerous staying power. We are so-called 'informed observers', a part of the community of actors

---

29 This bias test is based on Rule 15 of the ICTY Rules of Procedure and Evidence, 6 October 1995 (https://www.legal-tools.org/doc/rkps3b/), as applied in ICTY, *Prosecutor v. Furundžija*, Appeals Chamber, Judgment, 21 July 2000, IT-95-17/1-A, para. 189 (https://www.legal-tools.org/doc/660d3f/). The Appeals Chamber held that there is an unacceptable appearance of bias if "the circumstances would lead a reasonable observer, properly informed, to reasonable apprehend bias".

30 See the thorough report by the Danish newspaper, "Fellow judges support ousted colleague's criticism of Hague tribunal", *Information*, 5 December 2013. The report concludes that new information "reinforce doubts as to whether the procedure against the Danish judge was truly impartial and based on factual evidence. Or whether political and disciplinary considerations were really behind his removal from office. Furthermore, *Information* learned that there is growing dissatisfaction among the 22 judges at the ICTY with President Theodor Meron's brusque management style and controversial handling of appeals cases" (p. 2).

31 Theodor Meron, "Judicial Independence and Impartiality in International Criminal Tribunals", in *American Journal of International Law*, 2005, vol. 99, p. 359.

that has helped make and protect the ICTY for more than 20 years. If such 'informed observers' perceive bias on the part of an ICTY Judge and MICT President, and have the courage to say so publicly, that has immediate relevancy under the ICTY's law. Losing trust among the informed part of the public is detrimental for a judge of an institution whose authority depends on being – and being perceived as – impartial.

INDEX

G

H

I

J

K

L

M

N

O

P

R

S

T

U

V

W

TOAEP TEAM

VOLUMES IN TOAEP'S *PUBLICATION SERIES*

Morten Bergsmo, Mads Harlem and Nobuo Hayashi (editors):
Importing Core International Crimes into National Law
Torkel Opsahl Academic EPublisher
Oslo, 2010
FICHL Publication Series No. 1 (Second Edition, 2010)
ISBN: 978-82-93081-00-5

Nobuo Hayashi (editor):
National Military Manuals on the Law of Armed Conflict
Torkel Opsahl Academic EPublisher
Brussels, 2023
Publication Series No. 2 (Third Edition, 2023)
ISBN print: 978-82-8348-226-3
ISBN e-book: 978-82-8348-225-6

林 伸生 (主编):
国家武装冲突法军事手册研究
Torkel Opsahl Academic EPublisher
Brussels, 2023
Publication Series No. 2 (Chinese Edition, 2023)
ISBN print: 978-82-8348-119-8
ISBN e-book: 978-82-8348-120-4

Morten Bergsmo, Kjetil Helvig, Ilia Utmelidze and Gorana Žagovec:
The Backlog of Core International Crimes Case Files in Bosnia and Herzegovina
Torkel Opsahl Academic EPublisher
Oslo, 2010
FICHL Publication Series No. 3 (Second Edition, 2010)
ISBN: 978-82-93081-04-3

Morten Bergsmo (editor):
Criteria for Prioritizing and Selecting Core International Crimes Cases
Torkel Opsahl Academic EPublisher
Brussels, 2024
Publication Series No. 4 (Third Edition, 2024)
ISBN print: 978-82-8348-238-6
ISBN e-book: 978-82-8348-239-3

Morten Bergsmo and Pablo Kalmanovitz (editors):
Law in Peace Negotiations
Torkel Opsahl Academic EPublisher
Oslo, 2010
FICHL Publication Series No. 5 (Second Edition, 2010)
ISBN: 978-82-93081-08-1

Morten Bergsmo, César Rodríguez Garavito, Pablo Kalmanovitz and María Paula Saffon (editors):
Distributive Justice in Transitions
Torkel Opsahl Academic EPublisher
Oslo, 2010
FICHL Publication Series No. 6 (2010)
ISBN: 978-82-93081-12-8

Morten Bergsmo, César Rodriguez-Garavito, Pablo Kalmanovitz and María Paula Saffon (editors):
Justicia Distributiva en Sociedades en Transición
Torkel Opsahl Academic EPublisher
Oslo, 2012
FICHL Publication Series No. 6 (2012)
ISBN: 978-82-93081-10-4

Morten Bergsmo (editor):
Complementarity and the Exercise of Universal Jurisdiction for Core International Crimes
Torkel Opsahl Academic EPublisher
Oslo, 2010
FICHL Publication Series No. 7 (2010)
ISBN: 978-82-93081-14-2

Morten Bergsmo (editor):
Active Complementarity: Legal Information Transfer
Torkel Opsahl Academic EPublisher
Oslo, 2011
FICHL Publication Series No. 8 (2011)
ISBN print: 978-82-93081-56-2
ISBN e-book: 978-82-93081-55-5

Morten Bergsmo (editor):
Abbreviated Criminal Procedures for Core International Crimes
Torkel Opsahl Academic EPublisher
Brussels, 2017
FICHL Publication Series No. 9 (2017)
ISBN print: 978-82-93081-20-3
ISBN e-book: 978-82-8348-104-4

Sam Muller, Stavros Zouridis, Morly Frishman and Laura Kistemaker (editors):
The Law of the Future and the Future of Law
Torkel Opsahl Academic EPublisher
Oslo, 2010
FICHL Publication Series No. 11 (2011)
ISBN: 978-82-93081-27-2

Morten Bergsmo, Alf Butenschøn Skre and Elisabeth J. Wood (editors):
Understanding and Proving International Sex Crimes
Torkel Opsahl Academic EPublisher
Beijing, 2012
FICHL Publication Series No. 12 (2012)
ISBN: 978-82-93081-29-6

Morten Bergsmo (editor):
Thematic Prosecution of International Sex Crimes
Torkel Opsahl Academic EPublisher
Brussels, 2018
Publication Series No. 13 (Second Edition, 2018)
ISBN print: 978-82-8348-025-2
ISBN e-book: 978-82-8348-024-5

Terje Einarsen:
The Concept of Universal Crimes in International Law
Torkel Opsahl Academic EPublisher
Oslo, 2012
FICHL Publication Series No. 14 (2012)
ISBN: 978-82-93081-33-3

ترجِ آینارسن
مفهوم جرایم جهانی در حقوق بین الملل
ترجمه دکتر فریدون جعفری
Torkel Opsahl Academic EPublisher
Brussels, 2023
Publication Series No. 14 (Persian Edition, 2023)
ISBN print: 978-82-8348-202-7
ISBN e-book: 978-82-8348-203-4

莫滕·伯格斯默 凌岩(主编):
国家主权与国际刑法
Torkel Opsahl Academic EPublisher
Beijing, 2012
FICHL Publication Series No. 15 (2012)
ISBN: 978-82-93081-58-6

Morten Bergsmo and Ling Yan (editors):
State Sovereignty and International Criminal Law
Torkel Opsahl Academic EPublisher
Beijing, 2012
FICHL Publication Series No. 15 (2012)
ISBN: 978-82-93081-35-7

Morten Bergsmo, Cheah Wui Ling and Antonio Angotti (editors):
Old Evidence and Core International Crimes
Torkel Opsahl Academic EPublisher
Brussels, 2024
Publication Series No. 16 (Second Edition, 2024)
ISBN print: 978-82-8348-228-7
ISBN e-book: 978-82-8348-229-4

Yi Ping:
戦争と平和の間——発足期日本国際法学における「正しい戦争」の観念とその帰結
Torkel Opsahl Academic EPublisher
Beijing, 2013
FICHL Publication Series No. 17 (2013)
ISBN: 978-82-93081-66-1

Morten Bergsmo and Song Tianying (editors):
On the Proposed Crimes Against Humanity Convention
Torkel Opsahl Academic EPublisher
Brussels, 2014
FICHL Publication Series No. 18 (2014)
ISBN: 978-82-93081-96-8

Morten Bergsmo and Carsten Stahn (editors):
Quality Control in Fact-Finding
Torkel Opsahl Academic EPublisher
Brussels, 2020
Publication Series No. 19 (Second Edition, 2020)
ISBN print: 978-82-8348-135-8
ISBN e-book: 978-82-8348-136-5

Morten Bergsmo, Cheah Wui Ling and Yi Ping (editors):
Historical Origins of International Criminal Law: Volume 1
Torkel Opsahl Academic EPublisher
Brussels, 2014
FICHL Publication Series No. 20 (2014)
ISBN: 978-82-93081-11-1

Morten Bergsmo, Cheah Wui Ling and Yi Ping (editors):
Historical Origins of International Criminal Law: Volume 2
Torkel Opsahl Academic EPublisher
Brussels, 2014
FICHL Publication Series No. 21 (2014)
ISBN: 978-82-93081-13-5

Morten Bergsmo, Cheah Wui Ling, Song Tianying and Yi Ping (editors):
Historical Origins of International Criminal Law: Volume 3
Torkel Opsahl Academic EPublisher
Brussels, 2015
FICHL Publication Series No. 22 (2015)
ISBN print: 978-82-8348-015-3
ISBN e-book: 978-82-8348-014-6

Morten Bergsmo, Cheah Wui Ling, Song Tianying and Yi Ping (editors):
Historical Origins of International Criminal Law: Volume 4
Torkel Opsahl Academic EPublisher
Brussels, 2015
FICHL Publication Series No. 23 (2015)
ISBN print: 978-82-8348-017-7
ISBN e-book: 978-82-8348-016-0

Morten Bergsmo, Klaus Rackwitz and Song Tianying (editors):
Historical Origins of International Criminal Law: Volume 5
Torkel Opsahl Academic EPublisher
Brussels, 2017
FICHL Publication Series No. 24 (2017)
ISBN print: 978-82-8348-106-8
ISBN e-book: 978-82-8348-107-5

Morten Bergsmo and Song Tianying (editors):
Military Self-Interest in Accountability for Core International Crimes
Torkel Opsahl Academic EPublisher
Brussels, 2015
FICHL Publication Series No. 25 (2015)
ISBN print: 978-82-93081-61-6
ISBN e-book: 978-82-93081-81-4

Wolfgang Kaleck:
Double Standards: International Criminal Law and the West
Torkel Opsahl Academic EPublisher
Brussels, 2015
FICHL Publication Series No. 26 (2015)
ISBN print: 978-82-93081-67-8
ISBN e-book: 978-82-93081-83-8

ولفگانگ کالک
معیارهای دوگانه:
حقوق کیفری بین‌المللی و غرب
Torkel Opsahl Academic EPublisher
Brussels, 2025
Publication Series No. 26 (Persian Edition, 2025)
ISBN print: 978-82-8348-259-1
ISBN e-book: 978-82-8348-260-7

Liu Daqun and Zhang Binxin (editors):
Historical War Crimes Trials in Asia
Torkel Opsahl Academic EPublisher
Brussels, 2016
FICHL Publication Series No. 27 (2015)
ISBN print: 978-82-8348-055-9
ISBN e-book: 978-82-8348-056-6

Morten Bergsmo, Mark Klamberg, Kjersti Lohne and Christopher B. Mahony (editors):
Power in International Criminal Justice
Torkel Opsahl Academic EPublisher
Brussels, 2020
Publication Series No. 28 (2020)
ISBN print: 978-82-8348-113-6
ISBN e-book: 978-82-8348-114-3

Stian Nordengen Christensen:
Counterfactual History and Bosnia-Herzegovina
Torkel Opsahl Academic EPublisher
Brussels, 2018
Publication Series No. 30 (2018)
ISBN print: 978-82-8348-102-0
ISBN e-book: 978-82-8348-103-7

Stian Nordengen Christensen:
Possibilities and Impossibilities in a Contradictory Global Order
Torkel Opsahl Academic EPublisher
Brussels, 2018
Publication Series No. 31 (2018)
ISBN print: 978-82-8348-104-4
ISBN e-book: 978-82-8348-105-1

Morten Bergsmo and Carsten Stahn (editors):
Quality Control in Preliminary Examination: Volume 1
Torkel Opsahl Academic EPublisher
Brussels, 2018
Publication Series No. 32 (2018)
ISBN print: 978-82-8348-123-5
ISBN e-book: 978-82-8348-124-2

Morten Bergsmo and Carsten Stahn (editors):
Quality Control in Preliminary Examination: Volume 2
Torkel Opsahl Academic EPublisher
Brussels, 2018
Publication Series No. 33 (2018)
ISBN print: 978-82-8348-111-2
ISBN e-book: 978-82-8348-112-9

Morten Bergsmo and Emiliano J. Buis (editors):
Philosophical Foundations of International Criminal Law: Correlating Thinkers
Torkel Opsahl Academic EPublisher
Brussels, 2018
Publication Series No. 34 (2018)
ISBN print: 978-82-8348-117-4
ISBN e-book: 978-82-8348-118-1

Morten Bergsmo and Emiliano J. Buis (editors):
Philosophical Foundations of International Criminal Law: Foundational Concepts
Torkel Opsahl Academic EPublisher
Brussels, 2019
Publication Series No. 35 (2019)
ISBN print: 978-82-8348-119-8
ISBN e-book: 978-82-8348-120-4

Morten Bergsmo, Emiliano J. Buis and Song Tianying (editors):
Philosophical Foundations of International Criminal Law: Legally-Protected Interests
Torkel Opsahl Academic EPublisher
Brussels, 2022
Publication Series No. 36 (2022)
ISBN print: 978-82-8348-121-1
ISBN e-book: 978-82-8348-122-8

Terje Einarsen and Joseph Rikhof:
A Theory of Punishable Participation in Universal Crimes
Torkel Opsahl Academic EPublisher
Brussels, 2018
Publication Series No. 37 (2018)
ISBN print: 978-82-8348-127-3
ISBN e-book: 978-82-8348-128-0

Xabier Agirre Aranburu, Morten Bergsmo, Simon De Smet and Carsten Stahn (editors):
Quality Control in Criminal Investigation
Torkel Opsahl Academic EPublisher
Brussels, 2020
Publication Series No. 38 (2020)
ISBN print: 978-82-8348-129-7
ISBN e-book: 978-82-8348-130-3

Tom Willems, Carsten Stahn, Darren Frey and Antonio Angotti (editors):
Quality Control in Fraud and Corruption Investigations
Torkel Opsahl Academic EPublisher
Brussels, 2025
Publication Series No. 39 (2025)
ISBN print: 978-82-8348-281-2
ISBN e-book: 978-82-8348-282-9

Morten Bergsmo, Wolfgang Kaleck and Kyaw Yin Hlaing (editors):
Colonial Wrongs and Access to International Law
Torkel Opsahl Academic EPublisher
Brussels, 2020
Publication Series No. 40 (2020)
ISBN print: 978-82-8348-133-4
ISBN e-book: 978-82-8348-134-1

Morten Bergsmo and Kishan Manocha (editors):
Religion, Hateful Expression and Violence
Torkel Opsahl Academic EPublisher
Brussels, 2023
Publication Series No. 41 (2023)
ISBN print: 978-82-8348-141-9
ISBN e-book: 978-82-8348-142-6

Gavin E. Oxburgh, Trond Myklebust, Mark Fallon and Maria Hartwig (editors):
Interviewing and Interrogation: A Review of Research and Practice Since World War II
Torkel Opsahl Academic EPublisher
Brussels, 2023
Publication Series No. 42 (2023)
ISBN print: 978-82-8348-200-3
ISBN e-book: 978-82-8348-201-0

Mark Klamberg, Jonas Nilsson and Antonio Angotti (editors):
Commentary on the Law of the International Criminal Court: The Statute
Volume 1
Torkel Opsahl Academic EPublisher
Brussels, 2023
Publication Series No. 43 (Second Edition, 2023)
ISBN print: 978-82-8348-204-1
ISBN e-book: 978-82-8348-205-8

Mark Klamberg, Jonas Nilsson and Antonio Angotti (editors):
Commentary on the Law of the International Criminal Court: The Statute
Volume 2
Torkel Opsahl Academic EPublisher
Brussels, 2023
Publication Series No. 44 (Second Edition, 2023)
ISBN print: 978-82-8348-206-5
ISBN e-book: 978-82-8348-207-2

Mark Klamberg, Jonas Nilsson and Antonio Angotti (editors):
Commentary on the Law of the International Criminal Court:
The Rules of Procedure and Evidence
Torkel Opsahl Academic EPublisher
Brussels, 2023
Publication Series No. 45 (2023)
ISBN print: 978-82-8348-208-9
ISBN e-book: 978-82-8348-209-6

Song Tianying:
Legal Construction of Common Humanity: Human Agency in a Cosmopolitan War Crimes Law
Torkel Opsahl Academic EPublisher
Brussels, 2025
Publication Series No. 46 (2025)
ISBN print: 978-82-8348-255-3
ISBN e-book: 978-82-8348-275-1

Gunnar M. Ekeløve-Slydal:
Norm Efficacy and Justification in International Criminal Law
Torkel Opsahl Academic EPublisher
Brussels, 2025
Publication Series No. 47 (2025)
ISBN print: 978-82-8348-288-1
ISBN e-book: 978-82-8348-289-8

All volumes are freely available online at http://www.toaep.org/ps/. For printed copies, see http://www.toaep.org/about/distribution/. For reviews of earlier books in this Series in academic journals and yearbooks, see http://www.toaep.org/reviews/.

www.ingramcontent.com/pod-product-compliance
Lightning Source LLC
Chambersburg PA
CBHW071337230926
51849CB00006B/507/J
* 9 7 8 8 2 8 3 4 8 2 8 8 1 *